Jane S. Baylor

July, 1981

MOUNTBATTEN

MOUNT

RANDOM HOUSE   NEW YORK

BATTEN

RICHARD HOUGH

Library of Congress Cataloging in Publication Data

Hough, Richard Alexander, 1922–

Mountbatten.

Includes index.

1. Mountbatten, Louis Mountbatten, Earl, 1900–1979

2. Admirals—Great Britain—Biography. 3. Great Britain. Navy—Biography. 4. Viceroys—India—Biography.

DA89.1.M59H68   941.082′092′4 [B]   80-6023

ISBN 0-394-51162-x

Manufactured in the United States of America

24689753

First Edition

TO HIS MEMORY

FOREWORD

I first met Lord Mountbatten in 1971, appropriately at sea, and for several weeks had the opportunity of discussing naval history with him from time to time, more especially eighteenth-century naval history, upon which I was then working. Later he invited me to write his family history and a dual biography of his remarkable mother (Queen Victoria's favourite granddaughter) and his naval father, Prince Louis of Battenberg, who was First Sea Lord in 1914 and worked in harness with the young Winston Churchill.

Lord Mountbatten was unstinting in his help over *Louis and Victoria* (published in the United States as *The Mountbattens*) and made available to me much manuscript material relevant to the life of his parents. For this purpose I also had access to the Royal Archives, Windsor, and enjoyed the privilege of interviews with members of his family, old shipmates and others.

Lord Mountbatten gave me equally willing and generous help over several of my more recent books. But my suggestions from time to time that I should write a one-volume informal biography of him were invariably met by the reply that he did not wish any biography to be written or any official biographer to be nominated until after his death. Given that the official biography is still several years away, I feel that there is now room for an informal study of Lord Mountbatten's life.

R. H.

July 1980

CONTENTS

CHRONOLOGICAL TABLE

Chronological Table of the Life of Admiral of the Fleet the Earl Mountbatten of Burma, KG, PC, GCB, OM, GCSI, GCIE, GCVO, DSO, FRS, Hon. DCL, Hon. LLD.

Born Frogmore House, Windsor	25 June 1900
Christened Albert Victor Nicholas Louis Francis (Prince Louis of Battenberg)	17 July 1900
Educated mainly at home but also at Macpherson's Gymnastic School, Sloane Street, London	Jan. 1905–Nov. 1909
Mr. Gladstone's Day School, Eaton Square	Nov. 1909
Lockers Park preparatory boarding school	Sept. 1910–March 1913
Osborne Naval Training College	May 1913–Nov. 1914
Royal Naval College, Dartmouth	Nov. 1914–June 1916
Appointed Midshipman, serving in Admiral Sir David Beatty's flagship H.M.S. *Lion*	July 1916–Feb. 1917
Transferred to H.M.S. *Queen Elizabeth*, Beatty's Grand Fleet flagship	Feb. 1917–June 1918
Name and title changed to Lord Louis Mountbatten	June 1917
Promoted Sub-Lieutenant, briefly visits Western Front	July 1918
Appointed H.M. submarine *K6* briefly; then second-in-command and First Lieutenant H.M.S. *P.31*	July 1918
Cambridge University as undergraduate	Oct. 1919–March 1920
World cruises with H.R.H. Prince of Wales in H.M.S. *Renown*	March–Oct. 1920 Oct. 1921–June 1922
Promoted Lieutenant	1920

CHRONOLOGICAL TABLE

Engaged Edwina Ashley	14 Feb. 1922
Married St. Margaret's, Westminster	18 July 1922
Appointed H.M.S. *Revenge*	1923
Signal School, Portsmouth, and Royal Naval College, Greenwich	1924–26
Patricia Mountbatten (now Countess Mountbatten of Burma) born	14 Feb. 1924
Reserve Fleet Wireless and Signals Officer	1926
Assistant Fleet Wireless and Signals Officer, Mediterranean Fleet	1927–28
Promoted Lieutenant-Commander	1928
Signals and Wireless Officer, 2nd Destroyer Flotilla	1928–29
Senior Wireless Instructor, Signals School, Portsmouth	1929–31
Pamela Mountbatten (now Lady Pamela Hicks) born	1929
Fleet Wireless Officer, Mediterranean Fleet	1931–33
Promoted Commander	1932
Appointed H.M.S. *Daring* in command	1934
Appointed H.M.S. *Wishart* in command	1935
Admiralty Naval Air Division	1936
Promoted Captain in command H.M.S. *Kelly* and 5th Destroyer Flotilla	1939
On active service, English Channel, Atlantic, North Sea (Norwegian campaign) and Mediterranean (Battle of Crete). *Kelly* damaged several times, and sunk	23 May 1941
Awarded D.S.O.	1940
Appointed Commodore and Chief Adviser Combined Operations Command, and subsequently Chief of Combined Operations and member of British Chiefs of Staff, with rank of Acting Vice-Admiral	1941–43
Dieppe raid	19 Aug. 1942
Quebec Conference, when appointed Supreme Allied Commander South-East Asia command with rank of Acting Admiral and courtesy ranks of General and Air Marshal	Aug. 1943–46
Battle of the "Admin. Box"	Feb. 1944
Accepts Japanese surrender at Singapore	12 Sept. 1945
Elevated to title of Viscount, and reverts to rank of Rear-Admiral	1945
Viceroy of India	March–Aug. 1947
Governor-General of India	Aug. 1947–June 1948

CHRONOLOGICAL TABLE

Created 1st Earl Mountbatten of Burma	1947
Flag Officer Commanding 1st Cruiser Squadron, Mediterranean Fleet	1948–49
Promoted Vice-Admiral	1949
Fourth Sea Lord	1950–52
C.-in-C. Mediterranean Fleet, and C.-in-C. Allied Forces Mediterranean from 1953	1952–54
Promoted Admiral	1953
Appointed Personal A.D.C. to the Queen	1953
First Sea Lord	18 April 1955
Promoted Admiral of the Fleet	1956
Chief of UK Defence Staff and Chairman of Chiefs of Staff Committee (C.D.S.)	1959–65
Appointed Colonel of Life Guards, Colonel Commandant of Royal Marines, etc.	1965
Died	27 Aug. 1979

ILLUSTRATIONS

———◆◇◆———

Dickie and Charlie after "shooting" (Reproduced with permission of *The Bodley Head*).

Edwina and Chaplin (Reproduced with permission of *The Bodley Head*).

Edwina, age twenty-seven (*Rex Features*).

Goodwood Races (*Radio Times Hulton Picture Library*).

Mountbatten, Edwina and her sister, Mary (*Radio Times Hulton Picture Library*).

Mountbatten with his first Rolls-Royce (*Popperfoto*).

Douglas Fairbanks, Patricia, Edwina and her father (*Popperfoto*).

Discussing tactics before a chukker, June 1937 (*Fox Photos*).

The Royal Navy Polo Team (*Fox Photos*).

Pranks at Balmoral Castle (*Popperfoto*).

The Penthouse, Park Lane (*H. V. Joel*).

Mountbatten and his senior officers in jovial mood (*Keystone*).

On the *Kelly*'s bridge (*Keystone*).

The *Kelly* torpedoed and listing, 1940 (*Fox Photos*).

Noël Coward in *In Which We Serve* (*National Film Archive*).

Three generations of Mountbattens (*H. V. Joel*).

Mountbatten the Chief of Staff with Brooke, Portal and Ismay (*Keystone*).

Mountbatten the orator, on quayside at Bombay (*Central Press*).

General Stilwell and Mountbatten at Kandy (*Fox Photos*).

Mountbatten, General Wheeler and the Chiang Kai-sheks, 1944 (*Keystone*).

Between pages 208 and 209

The new Viceroy and Vicereine at Delhi airport (*Keystone*).

1947: the last Viceroy and Vicereine (*Fox Photos*).

In full rig (*Popperfoto*).

With Mahatma Gandhi, 1947 (*Keystone*).

With Pandit Nehru at Delhi (*Keystone*).

Communal riots, Calcutta (*Keystone*).

Nehru, Ismay, Mountbatten and Jinnah (*Keystone*).

The christening of Mountbatten's first grandson (*Keystone*).

With Prince Philip (*Popperfoto*).

With second grandson (*Keystone*).

C.-in-C. Mediterranean Fleet, 1951 (*Keystone*).

Grand Harbour, Malta, 1954 (*Central Press*).

With Edwina, Princess Anne and Prince Charles (*Central Press*).

Mountbatten as First Sea Lord (*Camera Press*).

Edwina at her last London home, Wilton Crescent (*Popperfoto*).

Edwina's bedroom at Wilton Crescent (*H. V. Joel*).

Mountbatten's study at Wilton Crescent (*H. V. Joel*).

The Board of Admiralty, February 1959 (*Popperfoto*).

The Suez crisis, 1956 (*Fox Photos*).

Pamela's wedding (*Fox Photos*).

A wreath of lilies cast into the sea, after the burial of Edwina (*Popperfoto*).

With President Kennedy and General Lemnitzer at the White House (*Keystone*).

Mountbatten on the day of retirement as Chief of Defence Staff, 1965 (*Keystone*).

With Prince Philip and Prince Charles (*Keystone; Rex Features*).

Retirement job: Mountbatten at Wormwood Scrubs (*Popperfoto*).

With Princess Anne in Vienna (*Camera Press*).

With Noël Coward (*Noël Coward Archives*).

Last visit to the submarine *Superb* (*Royal Navy Photographs*).

At Broadlands with Jock Brown (*G. W. Gale*).

At Classiebawn with his grandchildren (*Camera Press*).

Shadow V off Mullagmore. (*Keystone*).

Classiebawn Castle and the coast of County Sligo.

Westminster Abbey funeral procession (*Keystone*).

From Prince Charles (*Frank Spooner Pictures*).

Dolly, Mountbatten's horse, before his coffin (*Frank Spooner Pictures*).

MOUNTBATTEN

THE MURDER

*C*lassiebawn Castle is a turreted, early-Victorian stone mansion built to his order by the British Prime Minister Lord Palmerston on his Irish estate in County Sligo, now the Republic of Ireland. It sits on the highest point of a promontory overlooking the sea. From the tall neo-Gothic windows you can see north and north-west across the bay to the sawtooth silhouette of the Donegal mountains, while below the Atlantic rollers break against the shore.

The wild, savage Irish country is nowhere more savage than along this coast of County Sligo, which has seen as much killing and suffering as anywhere in Ireland. Among the sand dunes to the east and west of Classiebawn (the White Hollows) are the graves of Bronze Age warriors. Countless ships have been thrown onto these shallow, shelving, carboniferous sandstone cliffs, which are themselves like the crank-tilted hulls of scattered wrecks.

In September 1585 three Spanish galleons, survivors of the Armada, were wrecked here. "I numbered in one strand above 1,100 dead corpses of men which the sea had driven upon the shore," reported Sir Geoffrey Fenton to Lord Burghley at the court of Queen Elizabeth I. Other Spanish sailors and soldiers by the hundred were stripped and clubbed to death as they staggered ashore at Donegal Bay.

Lord Palmerston was born two hundred years after these infamous killings. As a young man he travelled from Dublin across Ireland to inspect his inherited estate. "It commences at about 6 or 7 miles north from Sligo," he wrote to his sister, "and continues with scarcely any interruption for 5 or 6 miles along the coast, bounded on one side by the sea and on the other by bog and high craggy mountains."

Bursting with idealism, the young man was eager to improve the sorry state of his tenants, to build good school houses and roads, and "to put the Parish Church *in a state of repair so as to make it fit for service." The local peasants were fortunate. Unlike most absentee English landlords, Palmerston came frequently to his estate, ensured that it prospered, and planted coarse grass "to hold the land" where the sand blew and threatened the pasture. On the sheltered side of the promontory near Cliffony he built a harbour.*

"It is nearly completed," he wrote in 1826, "and will be an excellent one for my purpose, with enough depth to admit vessels of 300 tons, and as much as any harbour on the west coast of Ireland." He named it Mullaghmore (the Great Summit) for the hill above it, upon which he built his castle. It is a castle in name only. It is not even very big, merely gauntly prominent in its isolation, so that on a clear day it can be seen in all its ridiculous ostentation clear across Donegal Bay.

Classiebawn Castle and the Palmerston estate came into the property of Lord Mountbatten through the seventh Earl of Shaftesbury, stepson-in-law and private secretary to Palmerston, and thence through the Ashley family to Mountbatten's wife, Edwina.

Shortly before eleven-thirty on the morning of 27 August 1979, a Mountbatten family holiday party of six walked down the four wide front steps of this castle. Besides Lord Mountbatten, there were his elder daughter, Patricia; her husband, Lord Brabourne; his eighty-three-year-old mother, the Dowager Lady Brabourne; and the fourteen-year-old identical-twin sons of the Brabournes, Timothy and Nicholas. Patricia Brabourne and her father had agreed only a few minutes earlier that they should not waste such a lovely morning, and that it was time to lift the lobster pots they had set the previous day.

The rest of the house party, including Mountbatten's younger daughter, Lady Pamela Hicks and her husband, and Hugh Tunney, the Irish meat millionaire, had decided not to join them. Tunney, who leased Classiebawn and its 1500-acre estate from Mountbatten, with the stipulation that the family could stay there for one month every year, had already expressed anxiety about Mountbatten's annual August holiday so close to the strife-torn Ulster border. But Mountbatten shrugged off these warnings and insisted that the many-coloured family flag with the motto "In Honour Bound" should fly from the castle's mast as always.

At dinner the previous evening he had said, "I can't think of a more wonderful thanksgiving for the life I have had than that everyone should be jolly at my funeral." He had already prepared that funeral down to the last minute detail, although he had discussed it only with his private secretary, in the utmost confidence, the Queen and the closest members of his family. To pore over the invitation list and revise it from time to time, as people died or fell out of favour, was a frequent occupation. He had also completed his obituary television film for the BBC. Shortly before he left for Ireland he had told the columnist Audrey Whiting, "I can't go on forever. I'd rather snuff out in a hurry."

Earlier that evening, while it was still light, he had asked the castle's domestic staff of twenty to gather together to be photographed with him and his family. Now, before getting into the car, he said "Good morning" to Garda Kevin Henry and his fellow officer who had been on protective duty since six o'clock. They had small arms and two pairs of binoculars in their Ford, which was, appropriately, an Escort model. Mountbatten's news that the party was going out in his boat came as no surprise to the Gardai. Shadow V, a 29-foot, clinker-built motor cruiser, a converted fishing boat, lay at its mooring in the harbour of Mullaghmore village less than a mile away. Concealed beneath its decking, between the cockpit and the engine, was a plastic tube of gelignite. It weighed 5 pounds, and was 17 inches long and 2 1/2 inches in diameter.

The Dowager Lady Brabourne got into the front passenger seat of the car, John Brabourne was the driver, and the rest climbed into the back, Mountbatten last. He was wearing lightweight blue trousers, sand shoes, and a long-sleeved jersey specially knitted for him and displaying on the front the badge of H.M.S. Kelly, the wartime destroyer he had been commanding when she was blown up and sunk by a single 1,000-pound bomb. One hundred and thirty men of the ship's company had died on that occasion thirty-eight years earlier.

The car containing the Mountbatten party drove down the winding narrow drive between open pasture land, through the little spinney by the lodge gates where the emblems of Mountbatten and his wife carved upon the pillars were already covered in lichen, and onto the public road leading to the village.

Mullaghmore is now a holiday resort. The slopes of Classiebawn's promontory are scattered with chalets and trailers, and the few surviving old peasant huts are newly whitewashed, with bright curtains in the windows and children's toys scattered around the trim gardens while television aerials tower above. No one tills the soil here anymore, except to plant nasturtiums, and the children are plump, and barefoot from choice. On this beautiful Bank Holiday Monday, they were streaming up from the curved sweep of sand with their parents, many in bright swimsuits, for their midday meal.

The Gardais' Ford Escort slowed down behind the Mountbatten car. In the bay there were sailing boats, inflatable dinghies, fishing boats and motorboats. The sea was calm, with a gentle north-west breeze blowing. Lord Brabourne turned off right, leaving the Gardai behind, and onto the narrow pier which encloses two sides of the harbour. He parked the car beside Shadow V, which was moored five berths from the end of the pier. There were seven fishermen about, some working on tackle, among them young Paul Maxwell from Enniskillen, just across the border of Ulster, which is only twelve miles away. The regular boatman for Shadow V *could not come this year, but everyone had taken a fancy to the fifteen-year-old boy. He knew that the Mountbatten party was likely to visit the lobster pots they had set the previous day.*

A number of the holidaymakers and locals had already recognized Mountbatten, and many eyes followed him. The villagers liked him for his cheerfulness, friendliness and the trade he attracted. They watched him step out of the car, an impressive figure, six feet two inches tall, an aristocratic face with a long, slightly hooked and distinctive nose—the Mountbatten nose—and a well-shaped mouth that seemed as enquiring and responsive as the blue-grey eyes—seaman's eyes—that missed nothing. Ears long, too, on a big head with fine hair, white now but almost as full as a half-century ago when he was the handsomest man in London.

He walked towards the boat, feet wide-splayed, stooping a little, the twin grandsons at his side. He was talking to them and laughing. Paul Maxwell had the diesel engine turning over. The boys helped their grandmother on board, then their mother. Lord Brabourne remained on the pier to photograph the party before he joined them. Less than a quarter of an hour had passed since they left Classiebawn Castle.

Lord Brabourne sat on a swivel chair, the three boys stood in the centre of the boat, his mother sat on the starboard side, his wife on the port side. Mountbatten was at the wheel. He opened the throttle and decisively steered Shadow V *out between the mole on the north side of the harbour and the pier head, with the authority of an Admiral of the Fleet who had been handling boats since he was five years old.*

As the boat turned to port to follow the line of the coast, its new white and green paintwork glinting in the sun, the Gardais' Ford Escort joined the traffic along the narrow coast road. Garda Kevin Henry followed the progress of Shadow V *through a pair of binoculars. Until recently the boat had been guarded night and day, and an officer had always gone out with Mountbatten. But he had asked for security to be relaxed: "Whoever would want to murder an old man like me?"*

Among the steady stream of cars along the coast road was a yellow Ford Cortina containing two members of the Provisional I.R.A. One of them had a remote-control device, the kind used for controlling model planes, concealed in his lap.

Mountbatten eased back Shadow V's *throttle to bring the boat alongside the lobster pots. They were just two hundred yards from the shore and three hundred yards from the head of the pier. The boys in the boat had cast handlines, and Lord*

Brabourne was leaning over the gunwale to haul up the first pot. A number of people on shore and in boats were watching Shadow V *as she slowed, besides the two Gardai, and only a short distance from them, the two men in the yellow Cortina. Kevin Henry told his driver to halt at the roadside. In his own boat David Mulligan, a retired Irish Army officer, was taking a party of German holidaymakers for a day's fishing. A Mr. Brian Wakeley was a few hundred yards farther out to sea than the Mountbatten boat.*

The explosion, when it came a minute later (at exactly 11:45, *according to one member of the Garda) was like an ultraloud rifle shot close to the ear. The boat disintegrated in a cloud of smoke and spume, and countless fragments of timber and metal, rope and cushions, life jackets and shoes filled the air and fell in an oval pattern of splashes in the sea. The gelignite had been only a few inches from Mountbatten's feet when it was detonated. He was thrown high into the air, along with everyone on board, many of them losing everything they wore in the blast.*

A number of nearby boats, including David Mulligan's and Brian Wakeley's, converged on the area. Wakeley managed to haul one naked body into his boat. It was Paul Maxwell, horribly mutilated and already dead. The Brabournes were dragged from the water into an inflatable boat, both conscious. One by one the rest of the party were taken from the sea.

Everyone in the village had heard the explosion, and the news of its origin raced through the beach parties: "They've blown up Lord Mountbatten's boat . . . !" The barking of many dogs, shouting and screams could be heard.

The first of the injured were brought ashore and up the slipway on stretchers. Crowds pressed round, enterprising young men with cameras jostling them. Nicholas was dead, his twin was injured about the face and body, the old dowager was fatally hurt. The Brabournes' legs were broken, they were badly lacerated and had other injuries.

Mountbatten's body was found some distance away, face down, his head and body peppered with wood splinters, his left leg shattered and the ankle joint almost destroyed. Most of his clothes had been ripped off by the blast, but his rescuers could still make out the Kelly's *emblem on what was left of his jersey. According to the pathologist's report, he had been rendered unconscious and incapable of saving himself.*

As a boy, Mountbatten had dreamed of dying at sea while leading a great fleet in a great victory, like his hero Nelson. He had never commanded a fleet in battle, and in World War II his destroyer was always in trouble before it was eventually sunk by the enemy. But if Shadow V *was no more than a converted fishing launch, he had at least been killed while in command.*

Within minutes, the news of his death was known all over the world. He was apparently killed by the Provisional I.R.A. to demonstrate to the world that no target—not even a member of the British royal family—was immune from the I.R.A.'s "soldiers" in their war to destroy a separate Ulster under the British crown, and against the British army's occupation of Northern Ireland. Mountbatten was a prize target not only because of the world-wide shock his death would cause but also because he was seen as an English occupier of land stolen from the Irish people, and as a representative of the ruling English monarchy. Second only to his cousin, Queen Elizabeth II, there was no more attractive victim for the I.R.A. than this widely admired and much loved Englishman.

THE BOY SAILOR

*H*is Serene Highness, Prince Louis of Battenberg was born at Frogmore House, near Windsor Castle on 25 June 1900. His mother, Princess Victoria, was the favourite granddaughter of Queen Victoria; his father, also named Prince Louis of Battenberg, was a captain in the British navy. The baby weighed just eight pounds.

On hearing the news of his birth, Queen Victoria ordered her carriage and drove to see him. In spite of her own too numerous labors and those of her children and grandchildren, the delivery of a new child never failed to interest her. "He is a beautiful large child," she noted. He was also, as it happened, the last great-grandchild of her lifetime and her last godchild. "Will you please call him Albert?" she asked the baby's mother. The Queen's consort had been dead for thirty-nine years, but his name was still frequently on her lips.

On 17 July, an unusually hot day, the Queen was driven from Windsor for the christening. She was eighty-one years old, small and bowed. She had reigned for sixty-three years. She was infirm and almost blind, but her dignity and authority had in no way diminished.

Recounting the family story, Mountbatten used to tell how, in spite of his hefty size, the old Queen sat holding him in her arms throughout the ceremony while he was named Albert Victor Nicholas Francis— and then had her spectacles pushed off by her godson. He bellowed throughout, but his great-grandmother thought he behaved very well.

Six months later the Queen's remarkable resilience and strength of will at last began to fade. Mountbatten's parents were summoned to Osborne House on the Isle of Wight, where the Queen was lying mortally ill. She died at six-thirty on the evening of 22 January 1901, surrounded by her children and grandchildren, a silent multitude of kings and queens, princes and princesses, grand dukes and grand duchesses, and her eldest grandson, the Emperor of Germany, Kaiser Wilhelm II, whose good right arm—his left had been withered at birth—lay under her pillow in support as she passed away.

One of those closest to her in mind and spirit for so many years, and closest to her bedside as she died, was Mountbatten's mother. "Look on me as a mother," the Queen had instructed her grandchild when her own mother had died more than twenty years earlier. The Queen was "her true friend." No one around that bedside was more grief-stricken.

The consequences of the death of the old queen were profound and numerous. One of the least important results, but one with a certain subtle bearing on Mountbatten's life and on the image he presented to the world, was that the name Albert was quietly relegated to last place, now that his godmother was no longer able to take offence.

"My brother and sisters," Mountbatten used to explain to friends, "always wanted to call me Nicky, but my parents pointed out that it would lead to confusion with the Tsar. They then for some curious reason suggested Dickie, and my mother was most amused because they obviously didn't know that her private pet name for my father was 'Dickie bird.' "

Perhaps his older brother and sisters were not so naïve as their mother supposed, and the endearment that they overheard was somehow associated in their minds with this new infant brother. In any case, it turned out to be apt. As a young man Mountbatten was very close to his father, and resembled him in many ways, something that his mother recognized while he was still a small boy. "I was a great father worshipper," Mountbatten would often say, "because I did think he was wonderful." It was a statement that accounted for a great deal in his character and his performance in life.

The oldest ruling Protestant dynasty in the world is the house of Hesse, once an independent Grand Duchy on the Rhine River in Germany. Hessian roots go back to Charlemagne. The present Queen married a Hessian ("Where did they get all that talent?" she asks), and so did her great-great-aunt Alice, Queen Victoria's daughter and Lord Mountbatten's grandmother.

The Hessians, great soldiers, married into the Greek, Russian, Spanish, Danish and Swedish royal families, too. They brought with them
versatility and great misfortune: they inherited haemophilia from the
British royal family, were assassinated by the Bolsheviks, and met frequent catastrophe long before Lord Mountbatten and his grandson
were murdered in Ireland.

Mountbatten was born a Battenberg instead of a plain Hesse because
of another piece of ill fortune, or ill judgement. His grandfather, Prince
Alexander, eloped with a mere countess, no better than a commoner, so
he was stripped of his titles and rank. He became a mercenary, and
eventually—solidarity being a first priority in sustaining ancient dynasties—he was accepted back into the fold, but only as a serene highness
instead of a royal highness and only if he took the name Battenberg,
which was considered inferior to Hesse by that royal *Who's Who* of the
nineteenth century, the *Almanach de Gotha*.

The Battenbergs were an exceptionally gifted couple, and they had a
number of children, the first of whom was called Prince Louis. He was
born in Graz, Austria, on 24 May 1854. When he was eight his parents
took him to stay with Queen Victoria at Windsor Castle. The links
between the English Hanoverians and the German Hessians were very
close. Young Louis fell in love with England, and above all fell in love
with the British navy, which was peculiar for a boy from a land-locked
German state. When the Queen's sailor son, Prince Alfred, came to stay
at the Battenberg palace in Darmstadt, Louis asked him, "Would it be
possible for a foreign prince to serve in your navy?"

Prince Alfred thought it an admirable idea. So did Queen Victoria,
the most important person of all among Europe's royal families. And so
the sentimental, home-loving Louis, at his own wish, detached himself
from his family and was prepared by a tutor for entry into the Royal
Navy, with all its ancient traditions and customs, its special language
and protocol, its clubbish exclusivity and harsh practices.

Louis was a pretty boy, with a lot of dark-brown hair, a vulnerable
demeanour, a German semi-royal title and, of course, a strong German
accent. Here was ripe game for bullying, and he was bullied relentlessly. His position was made worse because, at once, he was obliged to
accept special privileges. Even his first ship was a royal ship, a frigate
prepared for a Mediterranean cruise and tour of Egypt with the Prince

and Princess of Wales as passengers, and a suite of titled people on board. Louis longed to conform with the established training routine and way of life of a naval cadet, for all its harshness and strictness. Instead, he found himself alternately mollycoddled and treated roughly in the gun room by cadets keen to teach this young German upstart a lesson or two.

At one time during those early years, Louis was tempted to throw in the towel and return to Darmstadt. The rough treatment was one thing, and he learned to stand up for himself. But, brought up in a household in which the arts were cultivated and curious minds and conversation about science and philosophy encouraged, Louis found the philistinism of his fellow officers almost intolerable. Nevertheless, to resign would be to admit defeat, and this was contrary to Hessian tradition. Louis overcame his misery and loneliness, and was sent to North America in a two-decker battleship. There he had a chance to travel, and to fall in love, frequently and ardently. However, his greatest love affair was with the U.S.A. Like his son later, Louis revelled in the freshness, the open-mindedness, inventiveness and the warm hospitality of the people he met in Detroit and Chicago. He was to come back many times to New York and enjoy the people and the way of life.

While he loved America all his life, it was to England that he surrendered himself over the early years of manhood. He affected the latest fashions and became known as something of a dandy, cultivated English mannerisms, read the latest English books, became an authority on genealogy and titles, and, as his friends would remark, "became more English than the English." He grew a full beard, which was almost as standard as the uniform in the Royal Navy, and was generally regarded as one of the most handsome and eligible bachelors—and a serene highness as well.

The structure of Victorian society made it almost mandatory that his friends be naval officers and the titled and grand. His closest royal friend was the Prince of Wales. Louis became one of "Bertie's" fastliving "Marlborough House Set," though he rarely drank or gambled to excess; he accompanied the Prince on a great tour of India and no doubt shared his mistresses. He certainly had a passionate and long affair with Lillie Langtry, by whom he had a daughter.

It is a truism that the wider one is detached from the harsh, petty realities of life, the less the imaginative processes are exercised. Thus,

Louis came to take for granted the special privileges of his rank and title, his social life with the Queen and her family on the one hand and the Emperor and Empress of Russia on the other. These royal connections were slightly discomfiting to his fellow officers, and obstructive to the forming of friendships. In part because of them, Prince Louis never did "fit into" the Royal Navy. The famous Admiral "Jackie" Fisher wrote that Louis had only three friends, including Churchill and himself. This was typical Fisher exaggeration. But the few friends Louis had tended to be close ones. The vast majority of serving officers, from the upper-middle classes and the aristocracy, tended to choose more orthodox friends, more British friends.

Another barrier was Prince Louis's unashamed professionalism, which was very German and very un-British. When Prince Louis entered the Royal Navy he was appalled at the conscious encouragement of the cult of the amateur. He did his best to conform, tried to learn the "language" and imitate the style. He acquired the nickname "old soul," a popular contemporary endearment for a male friend, but so overworked by Louis in an effort to conform that the name stuck. Like his son, he could not help being a professional to the core.

Prince Louis made insufficient effort to cure his German accent, and failed to see that regular visits to his German castle and his German naval relations—his brother-in-law was an officer in the German navy, which was growing in size and hostility—could be misinterpreted. If it was not a lack of imagination, it was an instance of incredible stupidity in a man of superior intelligence that he failed to recognize the danger signs.

When at last this in many ways extraordinary, clever and charming German-naturalized-Englishman decided that he had had enough of mistresses and that he needed a steady companion, he had a love affair with another German, his own cousin and fellow Hessian, Princess Victoria of Hesse.

Mountbatten's mother, Princess Victoria was the eldest child of the future Grand Duke Louis IV of Hesse and Princess Alice. She was born in Windsor Castle in 1863, the first of the Queen's grandchildren to be born in England. The Queen herself assisted during the long labour. She had only recently lost her husband, Albert (at the Queen's insistence, Victoria's second name was Alberta), and wrote: "Oh, could my adored one have only seen her, lying so happily with her little Baby in her arms!"[1]

Princess Victoria gave early signs of brilliance, and when she was only six, her mother wrote of her wonderful facility in learning. She was tomboyish, physically vigorous, endlessly curious, a fanatical reader. Even as a girl her face was more interesting than beautiful. Later she was to write: "I just had my mind. I accepted that I was not beautiful."[2]

Queen Victoria had unknowingly been a haemophilia agent, a disease that is transmitted through females but only strikes males. One of her sons, Prince Leopold, suffered from it. Two of her daughters, Alice and Beatrice, were also carriers, and both passed this blood disease on to several of their male Hessian children. "Our poor family seems persecuted by this disease!" the Queen once cried in despair.[3]

Haemophilia was early diagnosed in Princess Victoria's second brother, Prince Frederick. He suffered greatly through his brief childhood. At the age of three he had a bad fall, which might have proved fatal to any child; in his case, the unstaunchable bleeding ensured his death.

Tragedy on a greater scale struck the unfortunate family five years later, in 1878. Princess Victoria contracted diphtheria. The disease rapidly spread to all but one of the family. Teams of nurses and doctors fought to save their lives. Queen Victoria, frantic with anxiety, despatched Sir William Jenner to Darmstadt. But nothing could save little Princess May, and her mother, Alice, herself succumbed.

The Grand Duke was among those who recovered. But, being a bluff military man with no knowledge of bringing up children, new and heavy responsibilities were suddenly thrust upon Victoria's fifteen-year-old shoulders. There were, of course, nursemaids and teachers in the palace, presided over by an Englishwoman, Miss Mary Anne Orchard. But Victoria was, in effect and at once, a replacement for her mother.

Victoria accepted these responsibilities with the equanimity of one born to rule. Supported from afar by her grandmother Queen Victoria and visited frequently by the Queen's children, especially the haemophilic Uncle Leopold, whom they all adored, Victoria continued to run the Darmstadt palace, until she fell in love with Prince Louis of Battenberg and agreed to marry him. He was twenty-eight, a handsome lieutenant, world-travelled, charming, bronzed, tall—a fairy-tale prince.

Victoria was nineteen, quick-witted, showing no signs of the burden of responsibility she had carried since her mother's death. And unlike Louis, she was in love for the first time.

She had met her English naval cousin several times before. Once, she remembered, he had rowed her around the lake at Buckingham Palace, dressed in morning clothes. She thought him fascinating. Now, in the beautiful spring of 1883, they became engaged; and Louis wrote to his cousin, naval friend and shipmate, Prince George (who was to become George V): "My dearest Georgie, I have a great piece of news to tell you. Our mutual cousin Victoria has promised to be my wife . . ."

The wedding in April 1884 in Darmstadt was a grand occasion indeed. Even Queen Victoria, who hated visiting Germany, agreed to come.

The Battenbergs' first child was born at Windsor, Queen Victoria again giving comfort during the long labour. The infant was a girl, Victoria Alice Elizabeth Julie Marie, to be known as Princess Alice. Some five years were to pass before it was learned that she was deaf. (This beautiful and brilliant princess was destined to marry into the Greek royal family and experience more unhappiness and tragedy than her mother, but also to bear four girls, and then—like her mother, much later—a boy, the future Prince Philip, Duke of Edinburgh.)

Because of their father's profession, the Battenbergs led a nomadic life, often in rented houses in England or at the naval base of Malta, broken by long visits to the Russian and Hessian courts, at Darmstadt, the summer residence Schloss Wolfsgarten, Heiligenberg, Balmoral or Windsor with the Queen. Like most naval people, it was a life of trunks, of train and carriage rides accompanied by ladies-in-waiting and servants.

There were two more Battenberg children, Louise in 1889, and George three years later. Victoria, and her aging grandmother, assumed that that was the end of the family. By June 1899 Louis was a senior captain, with much work of reform and organization behind him, and he had just been appointed Assistant Director of Naval Intelligence at the Admiralty.

Victoria was enjoying a summer visit with her family at Wolfsgarten. Two of her sisters had married into the Russian royal family, Ella to Prince Serge, and the solemn, mystical and utterly beautiful Alicky to the Tsar himself. Another sister had married the Emperor of Germany's brother, Prince Henry of Prussia; and the woods and lawns of the *Schloss* rang with the cries of numerous princes and princesses, from crawling infants to leggy adolescents.

The Battenbergs returned to London in October. The South African war had just broken out, and the streets were filled with marching troops singing jingoistic music-hall songs, and bands playing "Soldiers of the Queen." Louis had rented a house in Grosvenor Gardens, close by Buckingham Palace. By mid-December Victoria learned for sure that she was expecting another child. She let herself in with her special key to a back gate of the Palace and told the Queen, who was delighted. Then the family took the train to Sandringham, where they stayed with the Prince of Wales, himself destined to become King Emperor in a year's time. Uncle Bertie was thrilled. He loved young children. When they returned to London, he took them all to the pantomime.

The Queen lent the Battenbergs Frogmore House on the grounds of Windsor Castle in the New Year, 1900. Louis travelled up to London to his work in Whitehall. Alice was fourteen, Louise ten and Georgie seven. Mountbatten's birth on 25 June followed a swift labour, and he gave his mother little trouble.

Infant photographs show an irresistibly attractive face, with the clear eyes and long, strong nose already evident. In most of them, he is being held by one of his sisters or by Georgie. When he was two, his mother wrote to her lady-in-waiting: "Baby has been more defiant and swaggering than ever lately, and he and his father have had some serious differences, productive of much loud howling."[4]

Mountbatten never liked being corrected or proved wrong, and when scolded as a small boy, he became moody and sulky. He was still under six when, after being rebuked, he was seen marching about the house with a cardboard sign hung around his neck with "I A O" scrawled on it.

"And what does that mean?"

"It stands for 'I am offended.' I shall wear it every time I am offended."

In a household in which everybody talked, mostly at the top of his or her voice and incessantly—especially his mother and younger sister—Dickie listened thoughtfully, something he always did, although no one ever enjoyed talking more. But at first he was inclined to be quiet and cautious. As a little boy he was not daring. Later he was quite sure that the story about his choice of future career was true. His aunt, the Empress of All the Russias, had asked him what he wished to be, suggesting in turn "a sailor like your father," "a soldier like your uncle," and finally "perhaps an engine driver?" All were turned down peremptorily and in turn as too dangerous, for ships always sink; soldiers are shot; and "the engine might go over the embankment."

Incarcerated in a closet by his mother for some misdemeanour, he was told he would be released only when he was good. Later his mother became anxious and insisted that he must be good now, and let him out. "I am not good yet," he said defiantly, repeated the offence and marched back into the closet commanding to be locked up again.

Half an hour passed before he shouted, "I feel I am good now."

Dickie was deeply attached to his pets, of which he always had a great number, from a lamb and squirrel and white mice to more orthodox ponies and dogs. He idolized his elder brother, and when he learned that Georgie had lost a £5 tip at Osborne Naval College, he saved up his pennies and hocked all his toys to his mother. He could not bear to hear of the suffering of others, and natural catastrophes filled him with undue concern.

Dickie loved uniforms and dressing up and acting in pantomimes. His interest in the theatre and music hall and amateur theatricals came early, and lasted throughout his life. "I suppose I've always been a bit of a showman," he used to say.

By the age of nine he was a perky, passionate, sentimental, spoiled but thoroughly engaging little boy. Apart from a short period at a day school in Eaton Square, his only formal education had been given him by his mother. Victoria loved teaching, had taught her older children at home and always wanted to be a teacher. Speaking once of his early childhood, Mountbatten said, "My mother taught me everything. I had a proper school desk, with my weekly timetable pinned up inside. She was a far better teacher than one could hope to find in any expensive private school. What is more, lessons were fun. I never dreaded them, I couldn't wait to get back to them. Every lesson was interesting, and there was nothing she didn't know about."

Victoria had a special interest in history. "She always taught me history in an international context. It was parallel history, not vertical history. Kings and queens and dates were much less important than movements and social trends." It was the same with geography. Mountbatten continued, "Not rivers and climates and cities and exports, but people and places. As to languages, we were such an international family that they were no problem, except French. I never learned German. I spoke it at the same time as English. My nurse was German, and I never knew which language I was talking, and was completely bilingual until I was about thirteen. At Heiligenberg my aunt Alicky, the Tsarina, talked English to me and the rest of the family, Russian to her servants, German to our staff. So did Uncle Nicky, the Tsar, and all the children. It was completely natural and taken for granted."

This multilingual fluency posed problems to Dickie's eldest sister. When it was finally realized that Alice was deaf—due to thickened Eustachian tubes and therefore inoperable—her mother taught her to lip-read as if it were just another subject in her curriculum. She was an unusually intelligent and quick girl and soon learned to lip-read in German, French, English and Greek so that she could keep up with any conversation. If she missed anything, she was told firmly, she was to give no indication of it, and certainly never ask people to repeat what they had said. "You'll soon pick up the flow of conversation again."

Just as Dickie was a "semi-royal" boy, so was his education partly like those of male members of the royal family at that time, and partly orthodox. Where it differed from both was in its strongly feminine influence. His mother and sisters, and his governess, and the adoring housemaids, figured far more in his life than his brother and father, whom he tended to admire from afar.

This indulgence that he enjoyed, and the femininity of his surroundings, for the first nine years of his life, was to have a powerful effect upon him. It was one reason why he found it difficult all his life to see his fellow-men on an equal level. He tended to overadmire them, as he did his father and brother, and other of his men relations, or consider them antagonists who had to be defeated, and nearly always were.

But Mountbatten was always convinced that he had the best possible initial education. When he went to school at nine years, he was not ahead of his contemporaries. Latin average, mathematics just about adequate. "But I knew far more about things that don't get marks in exams, and my understanding of history and my knowledge of the world was far ahead of everyone else's," he would claim, with characteristic immodesty.

This included such special skills as how to address those who were very grand yet closely related, like Russian grand dukes, German princes and the King of England. The King was to be addressed in a letter "His Majesty the King, Buckingham Palace, London" and it should begin "Dear Cousin George" and end "I remain Your dutiful and obedient cousin, Louis Francis Battenberg," the "of" before Battenberg not being necessary.[5]

Lockers Park, headmaster Percy Christopherson, was a preparatory school for the rich and wellborn at Hemel Hempstead in Hertfordshire, the school motto, "Do well and be Happy." It was sound and steady and was accustomed to managing royalty. Dickie's elder brother had been there, and so had a number of his princely cousins. But here he came up against his first serious rebuffs from the outside world, and his overfeminine upbringing so far had not equipped him to deal with them. There was a certain amount of mild bullying, and no doubt he overreacted to it. There are references to punch-ups and bruises in his letters at this time, and to a severe cut on the chin from a fight with a future admiral. He was poor at football, which counted against him, and only average in his lessons. He ran afoul of his French teacher, a man by the name of R. C. Craig, of seemingly modest accomplishment and understanding.

At length, Dickie complained to his mother about a particular incident with Craig. She wrote back a wise and understanding letter. She was not overprotective towards her younger son. Nor did she always take his side. Dickie may have been spoiled by his brother and sisters and family and the staff, and often by his mother, too, but she could be firm with him, moulding his character into a blend of the best qualities of her own and her husband's: kind without being patronizing, behaving with all classes equally, talking to them naturally no matter what their background and upbringing and education, envincing interest in everything—apathy and idleness being two of the worst sins, compassion and understanding two of the worthiest characteristics to cultivate.

Victoria herself had benefited, on the English side of the North Sea, from the puritanism and severe self-discipline of her grandmother's reign, and on the German side from the emancipated liberalism and appreciation of the arts of the Hessian courts. For example, she detested English cooking but admired English novelists, Dickens especially; hated English acceptance of discomfort and cold in winter but admired English inventiveness and parlimentary democracy. Her lucidity, her enquiring mind that never ceased questioning everything, her enthusiasm and determination to convert others to her way of thinking, her natural acceptance of leadership, all these she passed on to her younger son.

She wrote to him at school regularly, expressing her love unselfconsciously and accompanying it with advice on a wide range of subjects. "Do not talk to the other boys too much about it," she tells him before the funeral of his uncle, King Edward VII, when he would be taking a privileged part in the proceedings. Also, "you will try hard not to think about it when your thoughts are needed for your work."[6]

His mother's influence and love were strongly present all through Dickie's life, until she died at the age of eighty-seven. Until he left Lockers Park, she remained the dominant parent. It was Victoria who ran his life. His father was now a more distant figure, often absent at the Admiralty or abroad, engaged on affairs of state and security at the highest level. Dickie would see him when he was ashore at Dover, where they stayed at the Burlington Hotel, or at Sheerness, or on board his flagship in the Mediterranean where Dickie was the idol of the ship's company, and—now in civilian clothes—in London when his father went to the Admiralty as Second Sea Lord at the end of 1911.

But the emphasis of parental influence shifted inevitably and naturally when Dickie entered the Royal Naval College at Osborne on the Isle of Wight, donned the cap and round jacket of a naval cadet, and left childhood behind as Cadet Prince Louis of Battenberg, or, to avoid confusion, "the young Prince Louis."

"It never at any remote moment ever entered my mind—it never even occurred to me—I had no other plans whatsoever—than go into the Navy." With his father nearing the top of the Navy, his brother already a midshipman, the family solidarity as strong as it was, no other career was conceivable. The Royal Navy was, in his eyes, quite simply the greatest service in the world, and he was destined to remain on active service duty, from cadet to Admiral of the Fleet for fifty-two years, until 1965.

Life at Osborne was tough for all the cadets. It was part of the process of "knocking off the rough edges," of "bringing down to size," and the other convenient contemporary clichés that covered the shaping of pliable youth to a common pattern for a life demanding discipline and initiative, self-restraint and responsibility, self-assurance without arrogance. Bullying was the crude beginning of the process, the first hacks with a blunt blade. It was not actively encouraged, nor was it discouraged, unless it went beyond reasonable limits. It was then considered inevitable, as today it is universally condemned. Certain new cadets could at once be picked out by the older cadets as particularly ripe game, and who riper than this serene highness, slim in build and vulnerable in appearance, with a German-born father who was also—now—First Sea Lord?

They went for young Dickie, this little prince with the pretty smile, and bloodied his nose. Dickie was ready and forewarned, by his father and brother. "They'll try to knock you about, Dickie. You know what to do. If you don't stand up for yourself . . ."

Dickie did. Sixty years later he recalled, "Admiral Sir Percy Scott had an odious son called John d'Urban Scott. I had known him at Lockers Park and disliked him very much. He was a term senior to me, and started to bully me at once, and knocked my cap off. So I knocked his cap off and we had a fight, and I won."

At the time, he wrote to his mother jubilantly: "A lot of chaps in second term egged me on to fight him, which I did. . . . and I've become a hero."[7]

Osborne taught him no more useful lesson than that it pays to make your mark firmly and at the outset; a lesson that he applied in every command, from his first to Supreme Commander South-East Asia. But the period as hero was brief. Some of his fellow cadets found his style brash and cocky, others were fearful of being thought ingratiating to the King's cousin and the First Sea Lord's son. On the first of many occasions in his service life, Mountbatten was lonely.

One day the young First Lord* of the Admiralty came on an official

---

*The First Lord was the civilian head of the Admiralty, a political post appointed by the Prime Minister. The term is now obsolete. The First Sea Lord, working under the First Lord at that time, was the professional head of the Royal Navy.

visit to Osborne. Winston Churchill was already nationally famous as the son of Lord Randolph Churchill and grandson of the 7th Duke of Marlborough, as a hero of the South African war and as a dynamic politician. At present he was working effectively in harness with Dickie's father in preparing the Navy for the coming Armageddon. In another generation and another war, it would be Dickie's turn to work with Churchill, and no one would have a deeper and more profound influence on the shape of his career than the statesman who now stood to address the assembled cadets before leaving.

"Do any of you have any request to make?" he asked at the end.

Dickie was the first on his feet. "Please, sir, may we have three sardines for Saturday supper instead of only two?"

"I'll see to that," Churchill assured him.

These were the first words they ever exchanged. The sardines were never forthcoming. In later years Mountbatten used to say, "From that time I never trusted him."

Dickie was not doing any better academically than he had at Lockers Park. By contrast with Georgie, he was considered slow. But although Mountbatten always said that his older brother was much cleverer than he, the difference actually rested more on their approaches to learning than on their relative intelligence. Georgie went straight at a subject and always came out top. But Dickie's mind, according to Dickie, had more profundity. He would survey a problem, from every angle, consider the implications and the consequences of each approach. Later he became very quick at this assessment process, but he never skipped it. He may not have been as clever as Georgie in the literal sense, but his mind was broader and more imaginative.

The contrast between term time at Osborne and holidays at the Russian or German palaces and castles, or at Mall House in the Admiralty, the First Sea Lord's official residence, was striking. One week it would be "show a leg" at six-thirty in the morning, a race naked to a cold bath, exercises, a Spartan breakfast, a series of lessons in mathematics, signalling, seamanship and knot-tying, interspersed with games, at which Dickie still did not shine. The next week he might be with his family in the fairy-tale splendour of Heiligenberg surrounded by adoring servants and rich German food, with visits to and from loving relatives, rides and dances and fancy-dress parties.

There are a number of photographs from the last summer at Heiligenberg, 1913. They show the boys in British sailor suits, the nine-year-old Tsarevitch in a Russian sailor's uniform, the girls in flounced, high-neck frilly silk dresses and wide-brimmed straw hats against the sun, babies with nurses in big prams, little children holding the hands of older children, numerous pets, and in the background waiting open carriages for a visit to Darmstadt or Wolfsgarten.

In other photographs Dickie—already fascinated by uniforms, medals, decorations, orders and badges of rank—is wearing the uniform of one of the Evzon Guards given him by the King of Greece, or the Cossack uniform presented to him by the Tsar, or the miniature Hessian Life Guards uniform, a present from another uncle, the Grand Duke of Hesse.

"At Heiligenberg," Mountbatten once recalled, "there were tennis courts and all sorts of games like diabolo, and we went on picnics up into the hills and forests, and we had ponies to ride. And then in the evenings we had more games. I remember I wore my cutaway coat for the first time, and it was much admired by my cousins and I was terribly proud. There were a lot of us, and it was really just like any other family."

The Russian royal family was there in full strength, and Dickie fell seriously in love for the first time, at the age of thirteen, when he came under the spell of the Tsar's daughters. Olga was eighteen, Tatiana sixteen, Marie fourteen and Anastasia twelve. "I was crackers about Marie and was determined to marry her," Mountbatten recalled when he was an old man. "She was absolutely lovely. I keep her photograph on the mantelpiece in my bedroom—always have."

Then there was Nicky, the Tsar, looking so much like Louis's old shipmate, Georgie, now King of England, but much gayer and more irresponsible, simple and family-loving. And his behaviour to the pale, vulnerable, laughing little Tsarevitch, the spoilt darling of them all, was very different from George V's to his sons. This was well known among all the party at Heiligenberg, as was the story about Lord Derby approaching the King and asking him if he could not be more friends with his children and make them less afraid of him. After some thought he turned around and said, "My father was afraid of his father, I was afraid of my father, and I don't see why my children shouldn't be afraid of me."

There was none of that Hanoverian nonsense at Heiligenberg in the hot summer of 1913, or at any other time. It was all love and happiness. The Grand Duke of Hesse, Uncle Ernie, who had succeeded to the title eleven years earlier, had had one disastrous marriage but was now happy with "Onor," the former Princess Eleanore of Lich. Their first child, Don, the heir to the title, was just seven—one more Hessian destined for tragedy. "They were all charming, every one of them," Mountbatten recalled. "Even that crazy lunatic, my aunt the Empress [of Russia], was absolutely sweet and charming."

At one point that summer Mountbatten overheard his father say to his mother (for Victoria was always expected to put everything right), "Alicky is absolutely mad—she's going to cause a revolution. Can't you *do* anything?" And Victoria replied, "Well, I am doing all I can." It was not enough, and this was the last time that Dickie would see any of the Russian royal family.

Another portent of doom for the Hessians was the new invention—flying. Both Dickie's father and the Grand Duke were great enthusiasts. As early as 1906 the Grand Duke had taken up the family in a Parsifal airship from the grounds of Wolfsgarten. Dickie had been told he was too young for flying, but at the last minute Uncle Ernie found they were short on ballast, and had reached down and dragged the boy into the sketchy gondola.

There was more flying after that. Three years later Dickie had been taken to an international exhibition of heavier- and lighter-than-air machines at Frankfurt. In that same year, 1909, Messrs. Wilbur and Orville Wright wrote to the British Admiralty to enquire if it might be interested in their flying machines. When Louis, who did so much to support the creation of a Fleet Air Arm, went to the Admiralty in 1911 as Second Sea Lord, he found a copy of the reply, which he later enjoyed quoting as an example of the refusal of the Navy to move with the times: "Gentlemen, I am commanded by my Lord's Commissioners to the Admiralty to acknowledge your letter in which you enquire whether you can interest the Admiralty in aviation. I am to reply that their Lordships can see no possible advantage that aviation could have for the Royal Navy."

In 1912 Uncle Ernie took up many parties from Wolfsgarten in the Zeppelin *Victoria Louise* for flights around Hesse, with champagne and caviar. Dickie had already flown for the first time in an aeroplane, a very primitive naval machine of the first unit formed, in which he sat straddled across the fuel tank, clutching two wire struts. Many years later Mountbatten could not help looking back to this time. He wondered how his parents would have reacted if they had known that in one Anglo-German war Zeppelins like the *Victoria Louise* would drop bombs on London, and in the next, descendants of Dickie's first British machine were to wipe Darmstadt virtually off the map.

The last summer of peace for Europe and for the Hessians at Wolfsgarten and Heiligenberg faded into early autumn. In one final pilgrimage, the families moved north with their great quantities of luggage containing dresses, suits and hats for all occasions, guns and rods and racquets, uniforms and orders and decorations. Dickie already had the first of the countless number of decorations he was to acquire: the Coronation Medal from King George V, which he wore proudly and for which he got mercilessly teased at Osborne. With them came their ladies-in-waiting and servants, and their pets, the smaller held in arms, the rest in special cages. They stopped first at the family seat of Prince Henry of Prussia, Grand Admiral of the German Navy, who in twelve months' time would be Britain's bitter enemy. There was plenty of naval talk—there always was—and the latest types of ships were discussed. But it was all immensely friendly, in spite of the fact that Germany now had almost as great a fleet of dreadnoughts as Britain, built in scarcely more than a decade, and with only one enemy in view.

Prince Henry, a Prussian through and through, brother of Kaiser Wilhelm II, had married Dickie's aunt Irène, who, like the Russian Empress, had one haemophilic son and had already lost an earlier one at four years from this disease.

Then it was Kiel. Dickie saw the Russian royal yacht, *Standardt*, anchored in the harbour amongst a host of German men o' war, from great grey battleships to dark little torpedo boats. "It was a beautiful yacht, with every conceivable comfort. We all went on board and were given the most lavish cabins—very different from Osborne, where we slept forty to a hut."

It was a last fairy-tale cruise in a fairy-tale vessel, through the Kiel Canal, which had been constructed to facilitate the German fleet's passage from the direction of one future enemy in the east to the other in the west. The Russian yachtsmen, who spoke no English, played with the children, and took special care of the Tsarevitch, for whom one small fall could bring weeks of pain and anxiety. There were boat rides, swimming and paddling on the Baltic coast. Then the party broke up. The *Standardt* proceeded up the Baltic, the Germans returned to Germany, the Battenbergs to England.

Even before he entered Osborne, Dickie had been aware of the dangers that threatened Europe. In the evenings and at meals, the talk was often of the political and defence maneouvrings of the nations that were to align against one another as the Allies and the Central Powers. And it was highly informed talk. No one was better connected to the top politicans and defence chiefs than Prince Louis. "I remember standing in the main hall of Buckingham Palace," said Mountbatten, "before all the really important people left for the coronation of my cousin, George V, in 1911. My father turned to me and said, 'Now, pay attention. I am going to introduce you to a very great man, Field-Marshal Lord Kitchener. Have a good look at him, because in the war that is inevitably coming, he will be the great soldier because they will call him back to run the Army.'

"I remember looking up and seeing this great figure and shaking the hand that was offered to me. My father and Kitchener got on very well, far better than Churchill and Kitchener."

After Louis became First Sea Lord, Churchill was often at Mall House. Dickie remembered the plump figure with the clever pixielike face, the darting eyes, the slight lisp, the brilliant conversation, the inevitable cigar. "He seemed incredibly young even in my eyes, but he and my father were marvellous together. They complemented each other so well—my father with his unsurpassed knowledge of the service of which Churchill was political head, and Churchill the canny political animal, very devious, bursting with energy and determination, learning as hard as he could."

Dickie knew from his father that war was inevitable, and imminent, but the immediate demands and events of life at a naval college filled his mind. While his father hastened to develop a proper Naval Staff, which he had brought into being belatedly and against a reactionary tide in the Navy's hierarchy; while he developed a plan for insuring merchant shipping in time of war; while he gave his blessing to the development of an air arm and the further development of new fighting ships like the submarine and new weapons like the mine and torpedo, and dealt with the multitudinous tasks of running the greatest navy in the world, his youngest son was working at mathematics and seamanship, navigation and pilotage, algebra and small-arms practice, on the Isle of Wight.

Dickie was doing better, but his marks were still not brilliant, and he was generally regarded by his instructors as slow and dreamy. "I got beaten yesterday with some cow-hide for passing out water at lunch before Grace," he wrote to his mother jauntily. "It warmed my stern up a bit." There are references to falls and cuts and bruises—an unusual number even for his age. Some of these no doubt were a consequence of fights. Certainly the bullying continued, and certainly he defended himself stoutly. Long before the crisis of the summer of 1914 developed, the innuendos about his father's German origin were being hurled at Dickie. On 21 June he wrote bleakly to his mother: "I have only got one real chum left now, Graham. Stopford got so ragged about being chums with me that he has chucked it."[8]

Dickie was anxious for the term to be over. Then, after a test mobilization of the Navy's reserves and an inspection of the Fleets by the King, he would go to Russia again with his father to join Victoria and his sister Louise, who were already there. While his father conducted preliminary negotiations for a naval treaty with the Tsar and his naval advisers, he could renew his affair with darling Marie.

Three days after Dickie's fourteenth birthday, the Archduke Francis Ferdinand of Austria and his wife were assassinated at Sarajevo. The mobilization in Britain, the first for years and an uncannily prescient piece of planning by Louis, went ahead, and this time it included all the cadets at Osborne and their seniors at Dartmouth Naval College.

Amidst all the activity of transporting some 20,000 civilian part-time sailors from all parts of the country to their allotted ships, and of assembling 59 battleships and battle-cruisers, 133 cruisers and destroyers and countless smaller craft at Spithead, Cadet Prince Louis of Battenberg found himself on board the great battle-cruiser of his elder brother, Lieutenant Prince George of Battenberg, and sharing his cabin.

From the decks of the *New Zealand*, Dickie participated in the royal review, the greatest since the coronation. "It took more than six hours," wrote Churchill, "for this armada, every ship decked with flags and crowded with bluejackets and marines, to pass with bands playing and at fifteen knots before the Royal Yacht, while overhead the naval sea-planes and aeroplanes circled continuously."[9]

"Men o' war were to be a part of the fabric of my life for the next half-century," Mountbatten once said, "but I would never again see a sight like this. No one had beaten us at sea for centuries, and how could they now, against all this might? That's what was going through my mind."

His account written at the time to his mother in Russia was more prosaic: "Papa arrived and we had church, after which we had lunch with the skipper. After lunch we went onboard the 'Enchantress' [Admiralty yacht], and saw Winston Churchill, Mrs. and Miss Hogier [Hozier] or something, also Admiral Jellicoe and the Fourth Sea Lord, and Admiral Hood etc. Georgie took the female Winston Churchills back to the *New Zealand* for tea."[10]

His father returned to the Admiralty to face a series of decisions as crucial as those which had confronted Lord Barham in the Napoleonic Wars. Not only was he certain that there would be war; he knew that it was imminent. Nerves were on a knife edge in all the chancelleries of Europe, and every decision had to be closely examined for any possible reaction from abroad. The Navy's reserves were due to be demobilized and sent home on 27 July. Without them, the fleet would be gravely weakened if—as many feared—the German navy sprung a massive surprise attack.

On Sunday, 26 July, Louis was alone in his office at the Admiralty. Churchill had gone to the seaside to join his family. The Prime Minister and the Foreign Secretary and most of the Cabinet were absent from London, too. ("Ministers with their weekend holidays are incorrigible," Louis exclaimed to Dickie a few days later.) On Friday the Austrians had sent a threatening ultimatum to Serbia. For Britain to cancel the demobilization of her fleet reserves would inevitably be seen as an overture to war.

After an unsatisfactory telephone conversation with Churchill—the line was bad—it appeared that the decision had been left to the First Sea Lord. When the telegrams arriving in London suggested a heightening of the crisis, Louis took the calculated risk of reversing the demobilization. The vast machinery of sending out the messages, of cancelling trains and reversing the dispersal of all the personnel, the recovery of some who had already left, was set in motion. Louis informed the

Foreign Office of his decision and on the next morning drove to Buckingham Palace to explain to George V what he had done and why. Later, on Churchill's return, Louis was praised for his timely action. The fleet, told to "stand fast," was ready for war.

Dickie arrived in London from Osborne a few days later. The older Dartmouth cadets had remained on board their ships, and many were to die in one of the Navy's early disasters, but the junior Osborne cadets were considered too young and inexperienced for war. It was an exciting time to be in Mall House, but Dickie was disappointed that there would now be no visit to Russia, no chance to see Marie. His mother and sister were already on their way home via Norway. His father was even more concerned with state affairs than ever. Feeling at a loss for companionship and occupation, Dickie took the bus to Selfridges and bought some white mice and a cage with his pocket money. Pets had always been a comfort.

On the evening of 4 August 1914, father and son, admiral and cadet, with forty-six years between them, dined alone at Mall House. The silver and the mahogany table at which they sat glinted in the candlelight. The butler silently supervised the single naval servant in his white jacket as he waited on them. They could hear the sounds of cheering and shouting from the Mall and Trafalgar Square. Londoners were celebrating the start of a war with Germany that would result in the death of a million soldiers from Britain and the Empire, and the maiming of a million more. For Louis, it was the blackest day of his life. His adopted country would be fighting his homeland, and he knew from his highly informed position that this was going to be a long and cruel war.

"I felt half excited and elated, half sorry for my father, and very sorry that I was only fourteen," Mountbatten remembered. "All the boys at Osborne knew that it was going to be a quick, crushing victory over Germany, and that there would be a huge battle in the North Sea which we would easily win."

Now he learned the real truth from his father: that it would not be over by Christmas, that the German fleet was very powerful, in some ways more powerful than the British. They discussed the political situation that had led up to the crisis, the progress of the German army against France and Belgium, the organization of the Navy to transport safely the small British army across the Channel, the likely use of submarines.

It was a typically masculine conversation, with Dickie—as always—encouraged to say his piece. Then his father rose to proceed to the Admiralty War Room, to check on the latest situation and issue a series of last-minute orders, and Dickie went to his room and played with his white mice.

No one, not even Louis, had predicted that the first three months of the war at sea would bring so many setbacks, losses and disasters. While the Osborne cadets were still on their summer leave, the Navy won its only victory in Louis's term of office, in a chaotic skirmish close to the German coast when three German light cruisers and a destroyer were sunk. After that, the news was all bad. Two powerful German men o' war, the *Breslau* and the *Goeben*, evaded a vastly superior British force and reached Turkey, which promptly came in on the German side. Three big cruisers were sunk by a single submarine on the same day in the North Sea, with great loss of life. A powerful force of German cruisers in the Pacific was causing havoc to shipping, and the *Emden* had begun her long and famous cruise of destruction.

The British press, restive at the absence of another Trafalgar, began to ask questions about the management of the war at sea. Inevitably, fingers pointed at the German-born First Sea Lord. Spy stories were rampant. Prince Louis had made many enemies in the Navy among those who were jealous of his influence in royal circles and irritated by his German thoroughness and accent, neither of which he took great pains to conceal. It was recalled that he had made frequent trips to Germany almost up to the outbreak of the war, that he had visited his relative, Prince Henry, Grand Admiral of the enemy fleet, that he even had the ear of the Kaiser. Those who were ignorant or envious began to mutter, "Once a German always a German."

The campaign of suspicion and denigration built up rapidly, and found eager ears at Osborne, where almost every cadet had relatives high in the Navy. Dickie was at first stunned by the implications, and then outraged. "What do you think the latest rumour that got in here from outside is?" he wrote his mother. "That Papa has turned out to be a German spy and has been discreetly marched off to the tower, where he is guarded by beefeaters . . . I got rather a rotten time of it for about three days as little fools insisted on calling me a German spy."[11] Others called him "a bloody Hun."

Dickie's mother was not surprised to receive this letter. Churchill, recently returned from Belgium, where he had been supervising the defence of Antwerp, recognized that his partner would have to go, for his own political future was at stake as well as the Royal Navy. On 27 October a highly valuable modern dreadnought was sunk by a mine—another blow among so many and one that brought the German battle fleet almost to equality in numbers.

Even the Prime Minister, who admired Prince Louis so much, even Victoria herself, knew there was no alternative. "With uncomplaining dignity worthy of a sailor and a Prince," as Churchill described it, Louis did as he was told and resigned with a letter which began: "I have lately been driven to the painful conclusion that at this juncture my birth and parentage have the effect of impairing in some respects my usefulness."[12] But in his heart he was hurt and bitter. "The hurt showed in his tired, lined face," commented the Prince of Wales.[13] He had given his whole working life to his adopted nation and her first arm of defence, and he was being tossed aside at the supreme moment of crisis.

"It is the penalty of serving a democracy," wrote Victoria, for whom the humiliation was almost unbearable; "the 'man in the street' is mighty." But she did not spare her words on the government which "with the exception of Lord Kitchener, few greatly respect or trust."[14]

Letters of sympathy and outrage poured into Mall House from shipmates—ratings to retired admirals—and from friends and relatives and people of eminence. The mood was summed up by Lord Selborne, recent First Lord, who described the end of Prince Louis's career as "nothing short of a national humiliation."

The Admiral lingered on for seven years to die prematurely of a heart attack. That was the medical diagnosis. But his family knew that his heart had been broken on that October day when the German armies were still marching on Paris and the threat of the German fleet was even more dangerous than the French fleet's had been in Nelson's time.

When, forty-one years later, Winston Churchill, complaining bitterly, appointed Lord Mountbatten First Sea Lord, it was said that justice had been done, a great wrong righted. In company with the clichés came the anecdotes, some apocryphal, others true. There was, inevitably, the story of young Mountbatten, in 1914 Cadet His Serene Highness Prince Louis of Battenberg, seen standing at attention on the parade ground under the flagpole at Osborne Naval College. He had just heard the news of his father's resignation, and as he saluted, the tears poured down his cheeks.

Mountbatten loved stories about himself. His appetite for them was insatiable. "Oh yes," he said about this one and many others, "yes, that's right—perfectly true." Certainly it is true that his father's dismissal had a devastating effect on him.

But when he was asked about the special vengeful thrust that drove him to become a post-captain (i.e., full-grade captain) at thirty-six, a great war leader at forty-three, commanding all three services—American, British and Imperial—in the Far East, and First Sea Lord at fifty-four, he would say, "It's a curious state of affairs. I must obviously have had a great urge, impelled on me by my father's example, and the fact of his tragic resignation. Too many people say they have heard me say in the past, 'I am going to right a great wrong,' or something like that, for it not to be true."

Without doubt, Mountbatten's appointment as First Sea Lord was the culminating point of his professional life; more important than his great war appointments; a greater moment than his acceptance of the Japanese surrender in Singapore, and later his appointment as the last Viceroy of India with supreme power over hundreds of millions of people. Toward the end of his life, when presented with proofs of the family history containing a bare list of chief characters (representing a cross between *Debrett's Peerage* and the *Almanach de Gotha*) against his own name he firmly added: "First Sea Lord 1955."

If Mountbatten found it uncharacteristically difficult to express the reason for his lifelong determination to achieve this appointment, and his satisfaction in its fulfilment, others may attempt to do so. It was to restore the family honour and its name in the annals of history, and to complete an interrupted tour of family duty.

"We are not going to mope or hang our heads," declared Victoria, when the blow fell. But the psychological shock was profound, and her husband never fully recovered. From working sixteen hours a day at the very centre of the war machine, bearing as great a burden as anyone in high command, he was reduced to idleness and impotence. He retired to the Isle of Wight, where they had a house, from which he emerged from time to time to go to London on family business, or perhaps to visit the wounded in hospital. He took up medal collecting as a hobby and painted—he was a good artist. Victoria, who never could bear idleness, worked energetically on the garden.

Churchill did not survive for long without his partner. He and Louis had complemented each other ideally—two aristocrats with wide-ranging, progressive minds, the older admiral instructing yet restraining the clever young politician's excesses. Ironically, Louis's "German view" and his understanding of the German mind had been invaluable to Churchill and the Board of Admiralty.

Like his mother, Mountbatten always loved speculating on the "if's" of history. "What would have happened if my father had been an Englishman?" he once said. "To begin with, he would have suffered under no pressure, for he was made completely on edge by these attacks and very nearly had what we now call a nervous breakdown. If he had been English, the two of them would certainly have survived those early months. Don't forget that the annihilating victory at the Falkland Islands took place only five weeks after his resignation—and it was he who urged the sending of battle-cruisers after Von Spee. He and Winston would have worked hand in hand for the duration. What's more, he would have worked marvellously with Kitchener, who was the world's most hopeless administrator. There would have been no Dardanelles nonsense, no 'wilderness' for Winston, and success and honour for them both . . ."

Some years ago Mountbatten had a talk with Lady Soames, Churchill's youngest daughter, which was not an "if" historical discussion but touched on the relationship between their fathers. "My belief," said Mountbatten, "is that in 1911 your father was young and immature but full of dash and go, and when he went to the Admiralty, was full of desire to do things, but was at first frustrated by 'Tug' Wilson, Bridgeman and Co. But he fell for my father in a big way when he was appointed Second Sea Lord. The Admiralty was in an almighty mess, but he saw that my father was progressive and open-minded, and above all, his ideas were in tune with your father's."

Mary Soames expressed agreement with this; and Mountbatten continued, "I believe, too, that your father recognized that mine had a direct link with the royal family, which was always useful. Now, when war became imminent, my father must have discussed the dangers of his position if there was a war with Germany. I am quite sure he said, 'Look, I think I should be replaced now.' But your father would not agree. Why not?"

Mountbatten was not satisfied with Mary Soames's belief that it was because he liked him so much. "I know he did," Mountbatten persisted, "but that's not a good enough reason. I think you've got to search deeper. I think Winston realized that my father was the sort of person who would allow him to operate without causing a mutiny in high quarters. He knew that he could leave the Admiralty in his safe hands when he went off on those ridiculously long cruises. This he could not have done with any other admiral at that time. He was essential. And when war came, he begged my father to stay. And my father was flattered and made the very great mistake of staying on. And the moment my father went," Mountbatten continued, "Winston had to find someone else in a hurry, and went back to that old has-been, Jackie Fisher, which was an act bordering on lunacy."

Prince Louis's comment was, "They will blow each other out of office." And he was right. Within a few months the young politician and old salt were at loggerheads over the Dardanelles. Churchill got his way, and Britain floundered on the beaches of Gallipoli. By mid-1915 they were both out.

When Dickie heard the news, he wrote plaintively to his mother: "What are things coming to? Do you think they'll want Papa back?"

THE GOLDEN COUPLE

$\mathcal{A}$ young naval officer, injured and in hospital," wrote Dickie, "desires correspondence." Then he signed the letter "Battenberg" and sent it off to the local newspaper.

In a way, it was true. He had had another accident, this time breaking his ankle while making one of those valiant efforts to master a new sport—in this case skating—in half the time anyone else had achieved. Bored, deprived of attention, he was in bed in the sick quarters with his foot in a cast. The letters came pouring in, some proposing marriage. He sent them off to his brother, suggesting that they should be distributed around the *New Zealand*'s wardroom. In this way some of them were, presumably, answered.

There is no early evidence of Mountbatten's eagerness to forward his career after the dismissal of his father. "I was a slow starter," he once explained. At Dartmouth he failed to become a class captain, a rank suggesting potential officer qualities. He finished Osborne thirty-fifth of eighty, a mediocre rating. At Dartmouth he was distinguished only for his single-stick fencing, an unpopular sport in which he figured second. A contemporary described him as "very hard-working, passionately interested in military decorations, and rather worried about the condition of his complexion."

The Dartmouth course was reduced from two years to one in the emergency circumstances of war, but Dickie—to his chagrin—was still at the college when the Battle of Jutland was fought on 31 May–1 June 1916. His brother, in charge of a heavy gun turret in his battle-cruiser, had already fought at Heligoland Bight and at the Battle of Dogger Bank in 1915, and was in the thick of this massive engagement.

The Germans inflicted the greater damage but were thankful to escape. Georgie told his envious, admiring younger brother how his was the first big ship to sight the enemy, how they had disabled two and sunk one of Admiral Franz von Hipper's battle-cruisers, and how lucky the *New Zealand* had been to escape unscathed in the prolonged gunnery duel, at one time steaming through the falling debris of the 26,000-ton *Queen Mary* after her magazines blew up.

The battle-cruiser commander, Admiral Sir David Beatty, was Dickie's hero, and he had no time at all for the insignificant commander-in-chief, John Jellicoe, "without style and looking like a frightened tapir. Beatty had dash, élan and loads of style," Mountbatten claimed. "I loved the man, his cap jauntily aslant, really going for the enemy, giving the order to close Hipper's ships after two of his own had blown up."

Dickie's father was more cautious in his evaluation of Beatty. He had appointed Jellicoe supreme commander and admired his coolness, judgement and exceptional intellectual ability. But it was the Battle-Cruiser Squadron that saw most of the action, and in answer to Dickie's pleas, Louis pulled strings to ensure that he was appointed to Beatty's flagship, the *Lion*, when he had qualified.

Dickie had another accident before his final examinations—a broken leg this time. He took the exams lying in bed, and finished eighteenth out of eighty. Then there was a last crash course of three months at Keyham; and now, showing his true mettle, he passed at the top. "This is the proudest moment of my life," remarked Prince Louis when Dickie entered the room wearing his midshipman's patches for the first time. And suddenly one sees a jaunty, handsome boy looking out at the world with eyes that are bright with intelligence and enthusiasm for what life has in store for him, and none of the unease of later years.

After her battering at Jutland, the *Lion* was under repair. Dickie joined her on the day she came out of dock, and almost at once was in action to prevent the German fleet from bombarding Sunderland. This was not to be another major battle, but the desperate pursuit, the gunfire and the brushes with danger were all that Dickie could ask for. At sixteen, he saw naval action in the North Sea, something few could claim. On 19 August he also saw the new face of warfare at sea, an experience that was to prove invaluable later. The air arm took a considerable part; they sighted half a dozen German Zeppelins, and the danger was less from shell fire than from mines and torpedoes.

Daily life in the *Lion*'s gun room was less pleasant. Gun-room bullying was as old as the Navy, and the beatings were more serious than at Lockers Park or even Osborne. "Things had not changed much since Nelson's day. We slept in hammocks, of course, and we slung them wherever we could find room—mine was six inches under a bright police light, but you can survive anything. I just slept with a handkerchief over my face.

"Then there were still 'stunts,' when we became the playthings of the sub-lieutenants in the gun room. Suddenly one of them in the middle of dinner would stab his fork into the table or a beam, which meant every snottie [midshipman] had to get out quickly. But before most of us could do so, the subs were at the door with canes, beating us out, and hard, too."

Beatty was made aware that his flagship was particularly notorious for bullying when one snottie, suffering the popular "sport" of cutting hammock ropes, broke his back on the steel deck and was permanently crippled. "Things got better after that, but it was still not a soft life."

The war at sea changed its nature in 1917. The German navy, despairing of ever beating the British fleet in a full-scale gunnery action now that the disparity in numbers had become so great, turned increasingly to submarine warfare against Allied shipping. An earlier and very effective U-boat campaign against merchantmen and passenger liners had been halted by the pressure from neutral America after powerful protests at the loss of American lives and trade. Now the campaign was reopened, with devastating results. Methods of fighting the U-boat were still primitive, and many hundreds of thousands of tons of shipping were sunk and many thousands of lives needlessly lost before the Admiralty could be persuaded to make use of the old safety measure of sailing in convoy. In the month of April 1917 alone, 545,000 tons of merchant shipping were lost, bringing desperately needed food and arms or reinforcements from the Empire.

Jellicoe was now at the Admiralty, Beatty had become the commander-in-chief, flying his flag in the *Queen Elizabeth*, and Dickie was still serving with his hero. But just as many of the German big ships' crews were seconded to the U-boats, so Grand Fleet personnel were being transferred to the new small craft designed to destroy these U-boats. Dickie was appointed to the new 600-ton *P. 31*, armed with light guns and depth charges, for patrol and escort work. Sub-Lieutenant Lord Louis Mountbatten, no longer a prince, was now second-in-command over a crew of fifty petty officers and ratings.

The year 1917 was terrible for everyone in Britain, and it produced a mixture of hopelessness and fury. Decorated heroes on leave out of uniform were scorned and given white feathers. Everything German was vilified. While some called for peace, others called for the abdication of the "German" King. In 1914 a "German" had run the Navy; he had been got rid of, but could he not still be a seditious influence? And what of the German Tecks, Queen Mary's family, and the King, whose grandfather had been pure German?

The Prime Minister recognized the growing danger, and made known his anxieties to the King. This was hardly necessary. George V knew what was going on and was properly outraged. Socialists were loudly proclaiming against "an alien and uninspiring court." "I may be uninspiring," declared the King, "but I'll be damned if I am alien."

A change of name, ruling out all German connotations, was clearly called for. The trouble was, no one was sure what the royal family's name was at present. The King was a Saxe-Coburg-Gotha, but that was not his name. It was the King's secretary, Lord Stamfordham, who in an inspired moment produced a name that no modern public relations firm could have improved upon: Windsor, so English, so safe, so steady, so immediately traditional. As solid as the castle. And Prince Louis, summoned to court from the Isle of Wight by his cousin, simply anglicized his family name to Mountbatten. "I have very serious news of far-reaching effects on us all to tell you," Louis wrote to his children, concluding that "all this is very terrible."[1]

Dickie did not appear to take the news very seriously. Always in a fever of interest about titles and protocol, he asked his mother, "Will my children be 'misters' or 'honourables'? Can I marry without asking the King?"[2] He learned that he was simply Lord Louis Mountbatten, younger son of the 1st Marquis and Marchioness of Milford Haven, the new title of Louis and Victoria, no longer a prince, no longer a serene highness.

For Louis, so proud of his title and breeding, it was "a terrible up-heaval and break with one's past." His wife grieved for him. But she had been brought up under the enlightened liberal philosophy of the Hessian court, and in England she had become a socialist. George Bernard Shaw was her god, and she had no difficulty in reconciling this with her rank and support of the monarchy. Why should she not be a plain "Mrs."? "I would prefer to be a 'citoyenne,' " she wrote to her lady-in-waiting on the news of the name change. But she thought it her duty to think of her descendants, and gave up only her German titles so that she became simply a peer's wife, along with all those wives of "bankers and lawyers and brewers," as she scathingly referred to those she considered jumped-up title-grabbers.[3]

Dickie shared his mother's anxiety about their relatives in Germany, and especially those in Russia, after the revolution and surrender. At about the time of the name change, Victoria and her sister Irène, the wife of Grand Admiral Prince Henry, thought it politic to exchange their maids, Victoria's being German, Irène's English. This was ef-fected through neutral Holland, and each brought news to their new mistresses. The sisters' admiral husbands now also had two sons fight-ing at sea against their cousins. There is nothing on record to show that Victoria thought this extraordinary.

Her German sister, Victoria learned, was growing thin. Of her Rus-sian sisters, she heard little, and she feared greatly for them, although she was supported by the belief that the Prime Minister, or perhaps the King, would intervene to rescue them. At one time, early in 1917, the Foreign Secretary, Arthur Balfour, proposed to send Louis to Russia to see and reason with the Tsar before it was too late. Louis, she believed, would have done a marvellous job, would perhaps even have fore-stalled the revolution; and would have brought back news of Ella and Alicky. But the Prime Minister vetoed the idea and sent Lord Milner, who was a disaster.

Two months later, in March 1917, Dickie wrote to his mother: "How awful about what has happened in Russia. I suppose Uncle Nicky is quite safe, though I can't understand why he has abdicated."[4] And Marie? The beautiful Marie he planned to marry after the war? She was under guard, he had read, along with her mother and the other children.

Victoria was relieved that the Tsar had abdicated, for "no one can tell how far the revolution may go," and his sister was less likely to be assassinated as an ex-Empress. After the murder of her husband, Prince Serge, twelve years earlier, Ella had founded a religious nursing order and given her whole life to her convent. Surely she would be spared.

Rumours of the fate of Dickie's Russian relations multiplied as hard news diminished, and it was not until September 1918 that Victoria, "in a kind letter from George Rex," heard that her sister and brother-in-law and their entire family had been murdered, "removed for ever from further suffering." Dickie and his mother continued to retain some hope for blameless, saintly Aunt Ella. But two days before the war ended, news of her horrible, long-drawn-out death at the bottom of a mine shaft reached England.

Queen Victoria had done all that she could to dissuade her grand-daughters from "going to terrible Russia." And now both of those mis-guided princesses, and all their families, were dead, one of the worst in the long record of Hessian tragedies.

Many years were to pass before Dickie learned how bitterly his mother felt about the failure of Prime Minister Lloyd George to raise a finger to save her Russian relations and his determination to dissuade George V, whose position was still weak in spite of the change of name, from intervening on their behalf. A politician's fear of losing trade-union and working-class votes by showing support for the victims of the Communist revolution had, she believed, caused this tragedy. "Just because the poor man was an emperor," the King commented. As Victoria never forgave Churchill for dismissing her husband, so she never forgave Lloyd George for staining his hands with her family's blood. Nor did the King forgive himself for his weakness and his failure, which haunted him and Queen Mary for the rest of their lives.

Lloyd George also judged it politically inadvisable to make any friendly gesture towards Louis, a foreign-born prince, at the end of the war. He ensured that Louis was not invited to the formal surrender of the German fleet, and a few days later Louis was asked if he would like formally to retire, in spite of the promise made when he resigned that he would be reinstated after the war.

Later Dickie heard his father exclaiming bitterly to his mother, "But they promised me. It was a condition of my resignation. I said that I would go if they made me a member of the Privy Council to show that I still had the trust of Cousin George and the government, and if I was allowed to hoist my flag again—preferably in the Mediterranean."

"Yes, I know, dear."

"The first was a request, the second a condition. You know how much it meant to me—the Mediterranean, the premier command. That's what I so much wanted."

His wife replied soothingly, "But that was not four years ago, it was four hundred years ago. Everything has changed in that time, you must see that." And again she enumerated the end of dynasties and empires, the revolutions, the changes in the old map of Europe.

Louis was only sixty-four, but the repeated blows to his German pride had beaten him physically and mentally. "I think he is beginning to show his age rather," wrote Victoria. Dickie had noticed it too. The admiral with the quick, decisive mind whose fleet always won at manoeuvres, the steady, painstaking First Sea Lord of 1913, had grown old before his time. Dickie had got permission to take him on a routine anti–U-boat patrol across the Channel shortly before the end of the war, proudly showing him all the new gadgetry the *P. 31* boasted. Louis loved the experience, always loved being at sea, but Dickie had to recognize that this was not the same man who had stood so proudly on the bridge of his flagship the *Prince of Wales* and directed evolutions of the Atlantic Fleet.

While his father was aged by the long, hard war, his younger son had become a man, even if he was still only eighteen. He was over six feet, taller than his father, and had filled out, and grown unusually strong. His complexion, which had so bothered him as a cadet, was clear and attractively bronzed by his long periods at sea. He was, in the expression of the time, "quite crashingly handsome."

As Sub-Lieutenant Lord Louis Mountbatten, full of brightness, practical jokes and a schoolboy's quick repartee, he was already developing the winsome appeal—part vulnerability, part boyish cockiness—that caused people, especially women, to be drawn to him in any gathering. The magnetism of the mature man of achievement was already there—visible if still undeveloped.

The voice had the fashionable timbre of the upper classes of the 1920s, but was characterized by its speed instead of the more common drawl. He was quick to pick up nuances, and the eye that was always eager to recognize a pretty girl was already on the main chance, too. He drank the usual, quite considerable, amount for his generation but rarely got drunk. He would drop the most amusing and interesting conversation if something relating to his profession came up. It was already apparent that the Navy came before everything else in his life, but that did not exclude his having a very good time.

Like most sentimental young men, he fell in love easily and had his heart broken easily. He could be teased up to a point, so long as the subject was frivolous. If it hinted at some failing on his part, he did not like it and let it be seen, by an expression or gesture. In his social and his professional life, it was clear that to be a winner meant more to him than it did to most people. His days of dreaming and absent-mindedness were over. He did everything—taking up a new game, learning to operate new equipment, studying photography, improving his French (still his only weak language), driving fast—as if his life depended on his doing it better than anyone else. No one had ever seen a young man so competitive. His determination to win was so powerful that he almost always did. But some shrewd observers murmured the word "insecure."

Any suggestion made to him in old age that he was in the least insecure at any time in his life was invariably brushed aside. Yet it seems evident that Mountbatten's swashbuckling style always concealed doubts about his abilities and achievements. It must be remembered that during his most susceptible years he saw almost all of his great and powerful relations brought down: the Tsar, the Kaiser, the Grand Duke of Hesse, the King of Greece, and even, nearly, Cousin Georgie, George V King Emperor. And far above the fate of all these rulers was the fate of his father, whom he hero-worshipped and who had been publicly and appallingly humiliated and destroyed by slow degrees. Surely the evidence that even the best and most powerful could be defeated by turns of fate and injustices perpetrated by man was a cataclysmic revelation for a young man whose worst fear was defeat and humiliation.

It is unlikely that he ever acknowledged this fear, even to himself. His resolve was always to be *totally* self-confident one day. As an old man, he believed that he had succeeded so well that he could actually say, "Many people express surprise that I accomplished what I did with my background. What they don't understand was that my upbringing and background were far more liberal, progressive and far-seeing than any average British aristocratic family's.

"When I was a boy I thought that the intelligence of all those about me was normal in life. It came as a great shock to me when I went out into the world and discovered that this was not true at all. This led me from quite an early age to feel a lack of reverence towards, say, great politicians with their supposedly great brains. This made it much easier for me to feel at least their equal when I was in their company."

Mountbatten may have felt their equal, or their superior, but there were those who knew him well who could still discern the unease in his eyes from time to time.

At the age of nineteen Mountbatten faced his first royal review, with apparent equanimity. George V had expressed a wish to come on board and inspect his little *P. 31*, so the ship was smartened up at Sheerness and steamed up the Thames to Whitehall. The King's movements were always news, and so, already, were Lord Louis Mountbatten's. Reporters and photographers swarmed over the *P. 31*—"interviewers are assailing her already," reported Victoria, "and Dickie is in agonies at every scratch."[5]

George V, "our sailor king" who always adored any man o' war, came on board at eleven o'clock one morning, went everywhere belowdecks and asked about all the anti–U-boat gadgetry ("Didn't have those in my time") and expressed satisfaction with ship and crew.

Mountbatten loved the ship and was reluctant to lose her. In 1919 she lay at Portland naval base awaiting "c & m"—care and maintenance. Just before the Admiral was due to arrive to inspect her and check that, like the others of her kind tied up alongside her, she was ready to be put in mothballs, Mountbatten ordered the entire company into a locked boiler room and hung a warning notice on the door: "Wet Paint." The Admiral, seeing the *P. 31* apparently unmanned and silent, did not even go on board. "So your ship is in 'c & m,' is it?" Glancing at the *P. 32*, Mountbatten confirmed, "She's next door to it, sir."

By this means the *P. 31* remained in commission and took part in the Baltic operations of 1919–20. But not with Mountbatten as her second-in-command. He was ordered ashore.

A great number of junior regular naval officers were axed at the end of the war, the first to go being those with private incomes. By happy chance, or intervention (Mountbatten would never say which), he and his brother were not affected. But the Board decided that those whose education at Dartmouth had been cut short should go to the university for a year to polish their brains while the peace following "the war to end wars" set in.

Christ's College, Cambridge, in the beautiful autumn of 1919 was as remote a world as anyone could imagine from the dangers and discomforts of the war at sea. Smart young Mountbatten, always in uniform and already sporting his first row of ribbons—one day there would be ten—threw himself into the parties, the Union debates, and his chosen subjects: history of geographical discoveries, and ethnology. But no one seemed to do much work in the aftermath of the war. Cambridge was full of young men like himself who had escaped with their lives and even younger men who had just been too young for the trenches. There was an air of unreality and overexcitement.

Mountbatten had a £300-a-year allowance from his father, a 5s.-a-day pay and a small car. It was ample. He was elected to the Pitt Club and the Union. There was to be a debate with Oxford on "The Time Is Ripe for a Labour Government." Mountbatten, defending the motion, of course, was allowed to invite a guest. Characteristically, he telephoned Winston Churchill, now Secretary of State for War, who agreed to come. The Duke of York (the future George VI) and his brother the future Duke of Gloucester sat on the cross-benches. This was to be no commonplace debate. Mountbatten's contribution at the end was forceful and direct. "Sir," he began, addressing the president of the Union, "in my humble opinion, what previous speakers on both sides of the House have said up to now is tripe." Churchill liked it. "I trust," he remarked, "that the last speaker will show as great facility in dealing with admirals on their quarterdecks as with his opponents on this platform."

Mountbatten fell in and out of love at parties in London and Cambridge and the great houses. His greatest love, "far surpassing all the others," he declared later, was Audrey James, the richest and most popular debutante of the season. "I saw her photograph in the *Sketch* one day and thought she was the most beautiful girl I had ever seen. I met her at a dance soon after, and we both fell madly in love. We were engaged in two weeks."

His mother watched these affairs with a wordly but wary eye and a good deal of indulgent amusement. But she did not in the least approve of the engagement. "You are far too young and poor, Dickie." The family had lost all their Russian possessions, worth several hundreds of thousands, and when Louis was reduced to selling Heiligenberg, the mark had crashed, inflation was wild and he received only a nominal amount for it.

The love affair prospered through that autumn and winter, and they made firm plans for their wedding. Mountbatten was certainly in love, but even through this passion he kept a steady nautical eye open for advancing his career. Emulating his father in cultivating the friendship of his cousin and the future sovereign when he was a lieutenant, Mountbatten had already warmed to the company of his cousin David, Prince of Wales.

The Prince had been born just six years before Mountbatten, the first son of the heir to the throne. After the usual confined "family" up-bringing—no school, few friends, many relations—he had been hurled into the harsh and spirited life at Osborne, where—like Mountbatten—he was quite severely bullied, found life difficult, and to the chagrin of his father, did only indifferently. His fear of his father developed early, and even by the standards of his generation, grew to a threatening size. After graduating from Dartmouth, he had served at sea in H.M.S. *Hindustan*. To his distress, because he was now enjoying the Navy, this was his only commission, and a brief one at that. His grandfather died in 1910, and the new King made him Prince of Wales. Now he must undertake educational travel around Europe, the study of statesman-ship and politics, a time at Oxford.

He was very lonely. His nearest brothers were away at school most of the time. In the months before the outbreak of war, he acquired a strong taste for parties, from small intimate ones to great balls when he "danced the night away." The taste never left him. Then came the 1914 war. At first, as he put it, "my trophy value exceeded my military usefulness,"[6] and he was not allowed even to go to France. But by sheer persistence, he got first a staff job at H.Q., and then appointments nearer to the front, so that several times he was close to the fighting and risking his life. He was appalled by what he saw but responded warmly to the comradeship.

On the night war was declared, while Mountbatten was dining alone with his father at the Admiralty, a short distance up the Mall, another prince dined with his father at Buckingham Palace, also discussing the political and military situation. It was not until after the war, when the age gap seemed so much narrower, that Mountbatten and David came to know each other better. They laughed at the same things, talked a great deal about girls and parties, their time during the war, and their future. The fact that David was heir to the throne and his father not very fit was an aspect in their relationship that was never discussed, but undeniably it played a part. For Mountbatten, cultivating powerful people was part of the competitive game of his life, as natural as a golfer's urge to improve his handicap. He never lost this feeling, and shortly before his death he paid a call on Mrs. Thatcher, who had just become Prime Minister.

In 1919 the Prince went to Canada and then on to the United States. He loved both countries. On his return, Mountbatten asked him if he could accompany him on any future tours as his naval A.D.C. The Prince agreed that this was an admirable idea, but then appeared to forget all about it. Plans were made for a longer tour in 1920 to the West Indies, New Zealand and Australia, but nothing was said to Mountbatten. Then he learned that the Prince would be at a ball, to be given by the famous society hostess Lady Ribblesdale, to which he, rather surprisingly, had not been invited.

At the last minute he telephoned a friend he knew was going and asked him how well he knew his hostess. "Can you arrange to have me invited tonight? It's very important that I see David before he goes away."

"What do you want to see him about?"

Mountbatten said he would tell him later, but that it really was important.

The matter was arranged, with some difficulty, and Mountbatten was invited to share the tour with his cousin, not as A.D.C. but as flag-lieutenant to the Prince's chief of staff, Rear-Admiral Sir Lionel Halsey, in the modern great battle-cruiser *Renown*.

There was a farewell dinner at Buckingham Palace, and on the morning of 16 March 1920, Mountbatten called at Mrs. Dudley Ward's house to pick up the Prince and accompany him to the station. The Prince of Wales was in the throes of his affair with this kind, understanding and utterly discreet woman, the wife of the Liberal M.P. and Party Whip, William Dudley Ward. Now his imminent departure with the prospect of a long separation was too much for him.

The Prince was in tears on the way to Victoria Station, Mountbatten recalled. "Have you ever seen a post-captain cry?" he asked him, who was always moved by this story.

"I don't think I have."

"Well, you'd better get used to it. You may see it again."

From that March morning until their return seven months later, Mountbatten's constant presence and support, his cheerfulness and ebullience, were a blessing for the Prince. A friendship was cemented that lasted until the latter's death. Mountbatten was at nineteen, in the words of the Prince, "a vigorous and high-spirited young man who became the instigator of many an unexpected diversion outside the official programme."[7]

But it was not only Mountbatten's cheerful effervescence that was such a tonic for the Prince during the longest and most arduous tour any member of the British royal family had ever made. The Prince of Wales was subject to fits of depression and self-doubt. He could easily be overcome by a desperate loneliness, and he often said that he would do anything to change rank and place with Mountbatten. The King had always found it difficult to show his approval of anything his eldest son did, and even far from Windsor Castle in the middle of the Pacific, the Prince would receive disapproving letters from him. Something was always wrong; it always had been. If it was not the overinformal poses in which he allowed himself to be photographed, it was something else. Mountbatten gave him fresh encouragement, told him he was marvellous. And he himself enjoyed every minute of it.

"You've no idea what a friend David is to me," he wrote home. "He may be six years older, but in some respects he is the same age as me. How I wish he wasn't the Prince of Wales and then it would be so much easier to see lots and lots of him! He is such a marvellous person, and I suppose the best friend I have ever had."[8]

At sea, it was nearly all fun, with endless games and high-spirited pranks; "crossing the line" a formidable and furious ceremony of pills and lather and shaving with an outsize razor and ducking and pronouncements by King Neptune. On land, however, it was nearly all gruelling work. Everybody wanted to meet the handsome young Prince, above all the ex-servicemen for whom the tour had primarily been arranged. Everywhere the Anzacs (the old Australian and New Zealand Army Corps) were out in strength, and with handshakes so strong that the Prince was obliged to resort to using his left hand.

The New Zealanders were quiet and warmly hospitable. The Australians proclaimed their welcome loudly and roughly with touching that left the Prince and his party painfully bruised. There was a strong anti-monarchist, extreme-left element in Australia that had to be coped with, too, as well as the proverbial Australian sensitivity to criticism and supposed patronage. "The Australians must be handled with care," the Governor-General told the royal party on their arrival. That was not always easy, but the lusty welcome left the right overall impression with both young men. "I had a fine time," concluded the Prince. "I liked its bigness and its courage."[9] Mountbatten liked the country for the same reason, and in later life returned many times, eventually buying land in Western Australia which he enjoyed visiting.

Mountbatten arrived home in mid-October 1920. He had been away 210 days, travelled 46,000 miles, shaken tens of thousands of hands, played tennis in Trinidad, surfed off Waikiki Beach. "I learned a tremendous lot on this tour," he told a friend later, "I think really that I came of age, though I still wasn't twenty-one." This was because, he claimed, he had met so many people far outside his usual circle, had seen so many places, and had also carried responsibility on his shoulders.

Mountbatten had found time (he always did) for a number of passing flirtations on the trip, but now he was determined to make firm plans for his wedding. Audrey had other thoughts. Her fiancé had been away too long, long enough for her to brood on the respective charms of great wealth or a title. She had chosen the first, as represented by the cotton king Major Dudley Coats. She broke off their engagement, and Mountbatten soon discovered that the story going the rounds of London was that Audrey James had preferred the arms of Coats to coats of arms. At first Mountbatten took the rebuff badly, but as one of the most eligible bachelors in the country it was easy to heal the wound.

Mountbatten fell in love, as he did most things, with amazing speed. "It does not matter how often you are in that state," his mother told him, "as long as somewhere in your heart you keep the knowledge of the difference of a love which I hope may come to you only later on and which is one of head and heart together for a girl you will want to make your wife."[10]

Then in July 1921, at a Claridge's ball given by Grace Vanderbilt, Mountbatten met a girl quite as lovely as Audrey James "and about ten times more lively and intelligent." She was introduced as Edwina Ashley, the granddaughter of the enormously rich international banker Sir Ernest Cassel, promoter of industry, railways, dams and projects of all kinds that had made great profits in a time of boom and rearmament in the late nineteenth and early twentieth centuries.

Cassel was one of those shrewd and amusing Jews whom King Edward VII had loved, ennobled and then milked for his favourite charities. His wife had died young, leaving him with a daughter who married Wilfred Ashley, a grandson of the Earl of Shaftesbury. Ashley joined the Army, became a colonel and later went into politics. They had two daughters, Edwina Cynthia Annette in 1901, and Mary four years later. Their mother was always delicate and died in 1911.

Edwina led a restless and often unhappy childhood, the first sixteen years at Broadlands, the great family estate in Hampshire. She desperately needed a mother, and the nursemaids and governesses, and later her schoolteachers, found her difficult to handle. Her father married again—a vicar's daughter, Muriel Spencer. She was more like a wicked stepmother in a fairy tale than a surrogate mother for Edwina.

Life became impossible at Broadlands. Edwina begged to be allowed to live with her grandfather in London, and Cassel gladly agreed. He had four country estates, and in London lived in a gigantic and hideous edifice in Park Lane called Brook House. Edwina, already a very practical organizer, became his social secretary. After her coming-out ball, she followed the usual ritual of balls and dances and dinners and country-house parties. When she met Mountbatten at the ball given by Grace Vanderbilt at Claridge's, the fusion of minds and hearts was (they both later agreed) instantaneous.

The scene might be stereotyped, but there was nothing standard about Edwina's beauty. The wide-apart, clear, intelligent blue eyes, the shape of her mouth, the rapidly changing expressions that crossed her face, the set of her head on her long neck: even an undiscerning eye must at once recognize that here was no standard debutante beauty. Mountbatten saw that he was dancing with an exceptional young woman, to whom he increasingly warmed as they talked.

At this time Edwina was rather shy and introspective. She found Mountbatten's decisiveness and firm views, his ambitiousness, his compulsive need for fun and action marvellously complementary to her own needs. His Hessian breeding, her own measure of middle-European Jewish blood, their exalted backgrounds with so many royal associations, placed them a little apart from the usual run of aristocracy and together gave them an edge on anyone else. Brains, beauty, youth—everything, and not an impediment in sight. Or was there?

For Cowes Regatta week, Edwina was invited to stay with Sir Godfrey and Lady Baring. The instantaneous flash of love between her and Mountbatten was at once recognized by many other people, too. Parties were rearranged to ensure that they were both present, every hostess hoping to claim that she was the real matchmaker of the greatest romance of the year. Cornelius and Grace Vanderbilt had invited Mountbatten on a ten-day cruise in their schooner, *Atalanta*. Edwina joined the party at the last minute, and so, for the first of countless times, they went sailing together.

"It was a wonderful cruise in this huge yacht," Mountbatten said, recalling his courtship, "a very happy time. But what happened after was better still. My parents were living at a house called Fishponds at Netley Abbey. The Crichtons [Nona Kerr, Victoria's lady-in-waiting, had married an Army officer she had nursed in the war, Richard Crichton] lent it to them. I took Edwina to meet them and my father fell head over heels for her. She fell for him, too. He took me aside and said, 'Edwina is the most remarkable and charming girl of this generation that I have met. She's got intelligence, character, everything. Now, you're very young, but if you do decide to marry her, you have my wholehearted approval. She'll make a wonderful wife for you.'" In view of what was shortly to happen, Mountbatten was always thankful that he had, at this comparatively early stage of their courtship, "taken her home." Victoria approved, too, in spite of her prejudice against titled bankers.

His father went to sea again in the late summer of 1921, for the first time as an Admiral of the Fleet. The King had approved of this gratifying promotion and also awarded him a second G.C.B. (Knight Grand Cross of the Bath). Now Mountbatten had his captain's approval to celebrate by inviting him on board the *Repulse*, sister ship to the *Renown*, for a bracing North Sea cruise. It had been ten years since Louis felt the vibrating deck of a great dreadnought beneath his feet. He loved every minute of it, the camaraderie, the war reminiscences, the salty stories told over the port after dinner, and the wardroom pranks among the junior officers.

"We had delightful weather and I think Papa thoroughly enjoyed himself," Mountbatten reported to his mother. "I know the Ward Room here have thoroughly enjoyed having him." But he added ominously: "Papa succeeded in catching rather a bad cold" and "during the night Papa got lumbago."[11]

When he was well enough, Mountbatten put his father on the train from Invergordon and returned to his ship. That weekend he was to go to stay with the Duke of Sutherland at Dunrobin Castle with the Prince of Wales, the Duke of York, the Archbishop of Canterbury and several others, including Edwina, to whom he planned to propose.

On Sunday, 11 September, late in the afternoon, a telegram arrived for Mountbatten with the news that his father had died at one-thirty from a heart attack following influenza. He had not been at all well when he arrived in London, so he had gone to his club, the Naval and Military in Piccadilly. Victoria and daughter Alice had delayed their departure for Paris to visit him again, only to be told that he had just been found dead by a chambermaid.

Without any shame, Mountbatten would describe how he burst into tears as he read the telegram. "I loved him deeply, and it was the most terrible shock. Everybody was marvellously kind, especially David and Edwina. Somebody telephoned the station and found that the only train of the day had already left, and I wanted to set off right away in the car, but Edwina said, 'You can't possibly—it's six hundred miles.' And of course she was quite right; it was only a small car, too.

"Later in the afternoon," Mountbatten continued, "I remember the Prince of Wales saying again how sorry he was and how cut up I must be. 'How lucky you are to have had such a marvellous father!' Then he added, 'If I heard my father had died I wouldn't be able to conceal my delight.'

"The Archbishop said, 'We might have a short service before dinner in your father's memory—what do you think of that?' So I said, 'That's very kind.'

"We didn't say anything to the servants, and I got a couple of cushions for David and Bertie to kneel on as they were wearing kilts, and we knelt down. Then when we were in the middle of the service, the doors were flung open and in marched the butler with a cocktail shaker followed by two footmen with the ingredients. It was six o'clock. Everyone was rather put out but I thought my father would have approved."

Mountbatten never proposed that weekend. By an extraordinary coincidence, Edwina's grandfather died ten days later. This death had profound consequences for both of them.

Mountbatten read of Cassel's death in the newspaper a few days after his father's funeral. "There it was, in cold print," said Mountbatten, " 'Death of multimillionaire. Edwina Ashley, great beauty of the year, now richest heiress.' Over seven million pounds. Result: the question I was going to pop that very day, I didn't pop. Marriage now was out of the question. My mother, when I asked her, also thought I shouldn't marry her. She said, 'It never really works when the woman has so much more money than the man.' From being all for the marriage, she turned against it."

Mountbatten later said that he had had no idea that Edwina was going to be so rich, and neither did she. But many people refused to believe that the two were quite as innocent as they claimed to be. The extent of Cassel's fortune was well known. He was, quite simply, one of the richest men in the world, and his possessions and style of living demonstrated that he did not care who knew it. Edwina's father was rich in his own right, so it was unlikely that he would receive any share of the inheritance. His two granddaughters were the obvious beneficiaries, and Edwina was especially close to him. Even if Edwina was not to be sole beneficiary, it seemed likely that she would inherit a great deal.

Shortly after Cassel's funeral, Mountbatten saw Edwina to tell her that he was leaving the country for many months. "David has asked me to go to India and Japan with him—he says it will take my mind off my father's death. You must come out and join me—cheer things up," he suggested lightly. They parted in the last week of October 1921.

The second empire tour seemed far less promising in prospect than the first had been. The Prince of Wales had been sternly enjoined to do as he was told this time. "You seem to have evolved a new technique of your own in the carrying out of your Commonwealth missions," George V told him, "and while I do not altogether approve your informal approach, I must concede that you have done very well. But you must not forget that India is entirely different from Canada, New Zealand or

Australia. What went down well with the white people in those three Dominions will not go down at all in India. You are to do exactly as *they* tell you."[12]

At Aden a huge banner above the cheering crowds asked the Prince to "Tell Daddy We Are All Happy Under British Rule." It was immediately evident that this was not so in Bombay, where the *Renown* dropped anchor. The welcome was formal and lavish but there was little support from the general population. Gandhi had ordered a strike, there was rioting, and the police opened fire on the mob. In other Indian cities only a few people came out to welcome the royal party.

"I must at once tell you that I'm very depressed about my work in British India," the Prince wrote home to the King, "as I don't feel that I'm doing a scrap of good."[13] Even Mountbatten found it hard to keep the Prince's spirits up in the face of boycott and violence. "The pomp and ceremony," Mountbatten reported, "could not disguise the desperate poverty, the prevalence of disease and the regularly returning nightmare of famine."

One day Mountbatten suggested to his cousin that they go and talk to Gandhi to show him that they understood and sympathized with his position and, if possible, to convince him that they should all be friends. The Prince agreed, and the idea was put to the government officials. It never got up to Viceroy level. Officialdom was outraged—a twenty-one-year-old lieutenant who had been in India only a few days telling them how to run the country! When Mountbatten, undismayed, asked if he could go alone, this, too, was firmly refused.

Years later Mountbatten wrote: "I wonder whether a meeting would have done any good? We *might* have established a useful contact." In the event, with the continuing troubles, Gandhi was clapped into prison. And that did not do any good either. Later, in Allahabad, the authorities locked up Jawaharlal Nehru, already a strong supporter of Gandhi and Congress Committee member, as well. The result was a total boycott of the royal processions and all formal events. The city might as well have been abandoned. "It was a spooky experience," wrote the Prince.

It was better in the princely estates, of which there were more than five hundred. Here the welcome was spontaneous and enthusiastic, and the hospitality of the maharajahs and nawabs was lavish. Mountbatten bagged his first tiger in Nepalese Terai in December, and learned to play polo.

Mountbatten always claimed that three of his lifelong loves stemmed from this four-month tour of India. One was for India itself, for its contrasting life styles, smells and sounds. The second was for polo. Polo was an expensive sport, and he had never had the opportunity to play it at home. Now he had all the ponies and facilities he could ask for. The Prince watched his first efforts with amusement. "He was determined to learn," he wrote, "and his initial appearance on a pony startled the Indian cavalry officers and my staff. But Dickie was nothing if not analytical; and undaunted by his inexperience, he persevered."[14] This unselfconscious determination was typical of him. However, the Prince's conclusion that "his interest in the manifold problems of India was confined to that part of the country bounded by the white boards of polo fields" seems wrong. It was to be Mountbatten's fate all his life to have his ebullient, light-hearted enthusiasm for whatever he was doing off-duty mistaken for a frivolous attitude towards duty itself, which he invariably took very seriously indeed.

The third love was Edwina. Mountbatten had kept up a steady correspondence with her. Her letters and the distance between them helped weaken his decision that marriage between them was impossible, and encouraged him to beg that she join him. "Come out! This is a marvellous country," he wrote to her. He was further encouraged by the Prince, who was fascinated by Edwina, and always pooh-poohed the idea that her great wealth was an impediment.

In fact, Edwina was flat broke. Cassel had stated in his will that her allowance of £300 a year was to continue until she was twenty-one, or until she married; and this allowance was almost exhausted. It never crossed her mind that with the imminent expectation of millions, she might be able to borrow enough to pay for her passage to India.

Eventually "Auntie Grannie," her grandfather's sister, lent her £100. Then she had to get her father's permission to go to India. It was reluctantly given and only on condition that she was chaperoned. She had booked on the cheapest ship she could find, and for that reason it seemed unlikely that any of her friends or relations would be on board. They were not. But by careful study of the passenger list, she discovered the name of an acquaintance who said she would be delighted to "look after" Edwina.[15]

Mountbatten's brother Georgie, now the 2nd Marquis of Milford Haven, took Edwina to Southampton to see her off on the long (and as it turned out very primitive) passage to the East. Georgie was all for the match and, like the Prince of Wales, had tried to persuade Mountbatten to forget his scruples about the millions and marry this adorable, intelligent girl. During the war Georgie himself had married Countess Nada de Torby, daughter of the Grand Duke Michael of Russia, and was no longer short of money.

"I'm so miserable," said Edwina. "It all seems to have gone sour. I don't think I ought to go."

Georgie would have none of it. "He absolutely worships you. Everything will be all right, you'll see." And he kissed her good-bye.

Edwina never minded roughing it. Like most young women of her class, she had experienced the full rigours of boarding school. But it was not only childhood training that led her to ignore physical discomforts. She possessed a fakir's sense of detachment from pain and exhaustion, which proved of inestimable value in her mature life but was to kill her prematurely in the end.

Her voyage was extremely uncomfortable, and it was burning hot in the Red Sea. But she loved it all. She had never travelled out of Europe before, and the magic of Malta, which she was to come to know so well later, the mysteries of Alexandria, the hot smell of sand at Aden, enchanted her.

At Bombay she said good-bye to her chaperone, and found a modest hotel. It was out of the question for her to join the royal party, so she had to find a cheap place to stay in India. Typically, she at once telegraphed the Viceroy on the strength of an old invitation he had sent to her grandfather. Lord and Lady Reading, still in the throes of the royal visit and the problems of nationalism, invited her to stay with them.

The Prince of Wales and his entourage had reached Delhi when Edwina arrived in Bombay. She still had 750 miles to cover and enough money left for only a third-class rail ticket. She was prepared to travel fifty-natives-to-a-compartment, along with bedding and animals, but the ticket clerk at the station told her that it was quite impossible.

"She telephoned me from her hotel," Mountbatten later recalled, "and the line was very bad, but she seemed to be telling me that she was coming to Delhi on a third-class ticket because she was broke. I said 'That's impossible. You simply can't do that.' And she said rather sadly, 'That's what everyone says.' "

More suitable arrangements were made through the Viceroy's office, and Edwina arrived in Delhi in early February. The Prince's duties at the capital were the most gruelling of all, and for much of the daytime Edwina had to amuse herself in the magnificent temporary Vice-Regal Lodge. In the evenings she joined in whatever was going on. "She got on marvellously with David, of course, and everybody loved her," Mountbatten recalled. "She loved dancing, and there were balls or dances most nights. David was flat out for us to get married. But out of courtesy he telegraphed the King for his permission and I told my mother that I intended, after all, to pop the question."

Mountbatten's diary entry for 14 February 1922 read: "After dinner there was a small dance. I danced 1 and 2 with Edwina. She had 3 and 4 with David, and the fifth dance we sat out in her sitting-room, when I asked her if she would marry me, and she said she would."

It was St. Valentine's Day, the windows were open and looked out onto the magnificent gardens. The air was heavy with rich scents.

There was a mixed reception to the news of the engagement. The Prince of Wales was, of course, the first to congratulate them, and agreed to be best man at the wedding. Lady Reading, the Vicereine, was doubtful. "I am afraid she has definitely made up her mind about him. I hoped she would have cared for someone older, with more of a career before him."[16] Inevitably there were those both in India and in English society who commented on the advantage to a "penniless" young naval officer, known for his ambitiousness, of claiming a pretty young girl so soon after her inheritance of a vast fortune. There were, too, uncharitable comments in wardrooms of H. M. ships, where most officers lived on their meagre pay. To the great masses, who read about the engagement in the popular papers, this was a fairy-tale romance. "The friendship of the young couple has been remarked upon for some time," ran one gossip column. "Both were guests of Mrs. Ronald Greville at Polesdon Lacey last October, not long before Lord Louis sailed for India."

For a number of the more sophisticated people, especially the London "smart set," it was too good to be true, and caustic comments were *de rigueur*.

Temporarily out of earshot of the jealous, ungenerous attacks that were later to follow them like a baying chorus throughout their lives, Mountbatten and Edwina delighted in each other's company, publicly and also in the privacy of a bungalow prepared for the Prince of Wales, the key to which he slipped to his cousin. Mountbatten's mother, concealing her earlier doubts, wrote to say that the news was no surprise. "I am really and truly happy at it as I think you both know your own minds now. May much happiness be in store for you."[17]

In fact, Victoria Milford Haven and Edwina quickly formed a close, affectionate and mutually compatible relationship. Edwina admired the older woman's courage, pragmatic intelligence and wide knowledge of the world, of history and philosophy, and found in her the surrogate mother she had subconsciously been searching for. Victoria on her part was attracted by the freshness, depth and openness of Edwina's mind. And both—the woman of fifty-eight who had been Queen Victoria's favourite granddaughter and had known all the crowned heads of Europe, and the richest young woman in England—were socialists by instinct and conviction for most of their lives.

As a naval wife who had also married young, Victoria felt it necessary to offer advice on that role. It was not always an easy one, she told Edwina. "I hope you will be able to take much pride and interest in his career."[18]

When the royal tour continued, first to Ceylon, then to Singapore and Hong Kong, Edwina had to part from her fiancé—the first of many partings. On 12 April 1922 the *Renown* arrived in Yokohama. Mountbatten was fascinated but disturbed by what he saw and heard in Japan. Since that nation had opened its doors to the West in the previous century, it had become a traditional friend and ally of Britain. When the Japanese began flexing their muscles, it was the British navy to which they turned for knowledge, training and tradition, and to British shipyards for their men o' war. A treaty of friendship had long existed between the two nations, and the Emperor had recently made a state visit to Britain.

But now Mountbatten observed new tides flowing in Japan. Nationalism was unhealthily rife on the one side, while Bolshevik-style unrest was growing among the industrial workers. Japan had been rearming at sea in competition with the United States for a decade and now possessed the third most powerful navy in the world. The treaty with Britain had not been renewed.

Mountbatten was naturally curious about the Japanese navy's organization and the new ships pouring from the new shipyards. All official suggestions that one or two of the new big ships might be inspected were rebuffed in chilly tones by the Japanese authorities. But Mountbatten's unofficial attempt to examine the battleship *Mutsu*, the most powerful afloat, surprisingly succeeded. "Perhaps they thought I was too young and silly to matter," he commented. "But, in fact, I compiled a most secret report for the Admiralty on her armour and underwater armament." The figures were impressive. Everything he saw relating to this new and aggressive nation's defences impressed him. He noted in his diary the martial mood of the rulers. "This," he wrote prophetically, "is the war I fear."

When the *Renown* docked in Plymouth on 21 June 1922, Mountbatten had travelled over 40,000 miles with his cousin and had logged impressions and experiences that were to be of priceless value when he faced two of the greatest challenges in his life in the East.

Edwina was at Plymouth to meet him, vivacious, excited, "lovelier than ever," as Mountbatten described her. "We were determined to get married as soon as possible, and we had already made the arrangements for 18 July. That was a date that seemed to suit everyone."

For an hour or two on that wet, chilly summer day, it seemed as if there had been no Great War, no royal assassinations and abdications, no dynastic toppling, no revolution. George V was present, of course, and Queen Mary, and the Queen Mother, Queen Alexandra. There were also Tsar Alexander III's Dowager Tsarina, who unlike the rest of her family had been rescued (by the British navy); the Prince of Wales (best man) and his younger brothers; princes and princesses representing defunct grand duchies; Princess Alice's four girls (Louis's nieces Margarita, Theodora, Cecile and Sophie) acting as bridesmaids in delphinium-blue dresses. The houses of Windsor and Hesse, of Denmark and Saxe-Coburg-Gotha, of Teck and Greece—all were present at this grand celebration.

During the short period between Mountbatten's return and the wedding, photographers and reporters had stalked the young couple from the box at Newmarket race course to the gates of Buckingham Palace, from Broadlands to Brook House. The *Illustrated London News* austerely reported, along with many pages of drawings and photographs: "The occasion aroused great public interest owing to the bridegroom's relationship to the royal family, and the great wealth of the charming young bride." The tabloids screamed that it was "The Wedding of the Century."

The wealth was reflected in some of the wedding presents piled up at Brook House for the massive reception after the couple's bridal car had been dragged from the church by a gun crew from the *Repulse*. There were: a diamond pendant with the royal cipher in diamonds from Queen Alexandra; many more diamonds from the bride's family; a platinum-and-diamond brooch from the Aga Khan; a silver figure of Atlas supporting a silver globe from the Prince of Wales, with the routes of the world tours he and Mountbatten had made traced upon it.

Edwina had been allowed just one pearl necklace before her wedding. Now she insisted on taking all the jewelry with her on the honeymoon. Mountbatten took a revolver. He also took six months' leave at half-pay, which he could now reasonably afford, and they decided to divide their honeymoon into two halves, the first in Europe, the second in the United States.

It started with a drive from Brook House to Broadlands, which had been made available for them, in the Rolls-Royce that Edwina had given her husband, a Barker-bodied cabriolet Silver Ghost model. They were both worn out after the reception for eight hundred, and Mountbatten later used to enjoy recounting how, for the first and only time in their marriage, neither of them was able to talk. "I had to refill the tank at a garage on the way," he recalled, "and by chance a mutual friend of ours pulled up at the same time. So I said, 'D'you know my fiancée, Miss Ashley?' I saw Edwina holding up her hand with the wedding ring, and with a resigned expression on her face. But I was still so stunned I didn't realize it."

After Broadlands, they took the car across the Channel and drove seven hundred miles through France and Spain to Santander, to stay with Mountbatten's cousin Queen Ena and King Alfonso. Then across to Germany to stay with Uncle Ernie, the Grand Duke of Hesse. Even in the 1920s it was still possible, for the right people, to tour from palace to palace.

In addition to being passionately in love, the couple experienced an unsurpassed sense of liberation. Both, in their different ways, had led circumscribed lives: for Mountbatten, navy discipline since the age of thirteen, and the restrictions imposed by his rank and background; for Edwina, the social confinements of her class and upbringing—she was still not yet twenty-one. Now, travelling around Europe, they felt utterly free, relaxed and emancipated. Mountbatten had, in his usual thorough way, planned a detailed itinerary with the aid of Baedekers. Edwina asked him to throw it away. She had had enough of organization and discipline to last a lifetime. For Mountbatten, it was like asking him to go into battle without a chart, but he agreed to please her. The first night out of Paris they ended up with a narrow bed in a murky attic.

As the gossip columnists described it, 1922 was a golden year for the golden couple. From July to December, Edwina and Dickie, beautiful and handsome, rich, almost royal, charming, intelligent, amusing and privileged, travelled around the world by Rolls-Royce, luxury liner and private railroad car, trailing a golden streamer announcing that this was the jazz age, this was the way we must all live. They were, in the eyes of the public, the personification of fun and life and materialism after the four years of austerity, fear, suffering and death. "They were, quite simply, the most glamorous and sought-after people in society. Everyone loved them," one of their contemporaries said.

Edwina fell in love with America on her first glimpse of New York's skyscrapers from the East River. Introductions were limitless; they met important people wherever they went. They were invited to visit President Warren Harding, and Mountbatten was one of the principal speakers at a Navy League dinner in Washington, packed with admirals and senior officers.

He used to pretend that he was disconcerted by the prospect. He was, of course, not in the least disconcerted. From the earliest age, Mountbatten never had any trouble on a dais. Nor did he have any trouble with the American reporters who followed them everywhere. "What d'you have to say about political conditions in India, sir?" "It's not the Navy's business to talk, you know"—spoken with that charming, intimate smile.

"What do you think about the conduct of the modern woman and divorce, ma'am?" "Oh," replied Edwina blandly, "I just believe in being an old-fashioned wife." And her smile was equally disarming.

Dinner with Jerome Kern on the first night, then to the *Ziegfeld Follies*; the next day a baseball game to meet Babe Ruth; dinners, theatres; then a transcontinental tour on the Atchison, Topeka & Sante Fe in their private railway car.

Hollywood. They were met at Los Angeles and whisked off to Pickfair, the famed home of America's sweethearts, Douglas Fairbanks and Mary Pickford, who were to become lifelong friends.

In addition to an abiding curiosity to see movieland, Mountbatten was keen to learn more of the technical side of film-making. When he received the customary box Brownie as a boy, he learned to get the best from it and became fascinated by photography. During his first voyage with the Prince of Wales he had learned about movies from the *Renown*'s cameraman, and in collaboration they had made a training film to teach fleet manoeuvres to the service.

The Admiralty was not interested in this early effort, but Mountbatten was not in the least discouraged. He bought one of the very early 35-mm movie cameras for his own use. And now he was determined to be the most proficient of cameramen—better than anyone else.

In Hollywood he received the best technical instruction from the best cameramen in the world. Cecil B. De Mille and Charlie Chaplin taught him how to direct and how to act. From this stemmed their most unusual wedding present, a film directed by Charlie Chaplin, starring Jackie Coogan and Charlie Chaplin, Lord Louis Mountbatten and Edwina Mountbatten, entitled *Nice and Friendly*. It is sometimes shown today. Chaplin told Mountbatten he was a terrible actor.

Niagara Falls, the Grand Canyon, Florida, then New York again. A last luncheon given by the New York Press Club. "Can we in America," asked the Hearst columnist and millionaire Arthur Brisbane, "produce a young couple of twenty-two and twenty who could possibly be such fine representatives of their country, and do such an excellent job as ambassadors in a foreign country as the Mountbattens have done here in America?" Mountbatten's response is not recorded. Perhaps for once he did not make one. And so there ended, on a note of mutual affection and admiration just before Christmas 1922, the first rendezvous in the long and ardent love affair between the Mountbattens and America. They went on board their liner loaded with presents, which were then piled up in their suite.

"They danced and played and laughed their way across the Atlantic," wrote one contemporary columnist. No doubt they rested and slept, too, and certainly they planned their lives for the following year. Georgie met them at Southampton on 23 December and drove them to the Milford Haven home at Southsea, where they spent a family Christmas with Nada and the two children, Tatiana and David.

In their absence, the Conservatives had been returned to power with an overwhelming majority. Churchill, who had worked so valiantly for a peaceful solution to the Irish problem, had lost his seat at Dundee and was out of Parliament for the first time in the century. In Ireland the last English troops had left the new Irish Free State, and many people believed that this would mean an end to the murders.

As a child Edwina had spent carefree holidays in Ireland with her sister, Mary, and their Pakenham cousins Joan and Dermot, at a castle in County Sligo in this new Irish Free State. Mountbatten planned to visit it for the first time in 1923. It was called Classiebawn.

FAMILY AFFAIRS

 visit to the Ashleys at Broadlands in the New Year was followed by a return to London, and to work. At no other time in his life was Mountbatten to spend so much time away from his professional concerns. The subject to which he had given most thought was his future in the Navy, and what he should specialize in. In the past six months he had tinkered with wireless sets, learned the special skills of making movies, renewed his love for fast cars (and he could now afford to indulge himself to the full with these expensive toys), read a great deal, talked tirelessly with everyone he had met, all the way from Wolfsgarten to Beverly Hills. Now he was keen to get back to work.

Speaking of these early years and their problems, Mountbatten recalled, "Marriage to a very rich woman, as my mother had said, posed problems. I then realized forcibly that the only hope of standing on my own legs was to work. I couldn't hope to produce the money that Edwina had. So I had to work very hard in the one profession where money doesn't count. I worked like a beaver to excel. My father worked very hard, too. He was ambitious in the professional sense. He always took on the most interesting and difficult jobs, and it never entered my father's mind nor my mind ever to do a job other than at one's best ability.

"My father wasn't well off, he couldn't hope to make money in the Navy. My desire to make good was the same as his, except that I had to make good *because* I had a rich wife."

But this was not the only reason why his standard of hard work was far higher than that of his father, who never worked with the intense, almost manic, zeal of his son, as if pursued by the most dreaded of all spectres—failure.

In his determination to excel, Mountbatten suffered several grave handicaps as well as considerable advantages. The first was privilege. When Mountbatten was a boy sitting for his Osborne examinations, his father had lectured him on the advantages and disadvantages of his privileged rank.

" 'It will affect you in two ways,' my father warned me," Mountbatten remembered. " 'When you are young, it will be wholly disadvantageous. You must realize that anyone who appears to be making friends with you has probably got his real eye on the main chance and is just sucking up. *You*' he went on, 'must take the first step, you must make your own choice. Whenever you join a new ship, you will be under suspicion. Work hard. Be seen to be working hard. If you stick to it, the time will come when people will be prepared to help you. Later in your career, you will find your privileged standing an advantage.' "

It turned out just as Prince Louis had predicted, only worse. One can imagine the voices in the wardroom when Mountbatten was known to be joining the ship. "We'll have to take *him* down a peg or two," "Be turning up at the dockyard in that Rolls-Royce his wife gave him," and from the commander, "I'm not having him flashing his money about the place and talking about dinner at Buckingham Palace."

"I can't tell you what I went through," Mountbatten later recalled. "Every time I joined a new ship, I had to start absolutely afresh. I would probably arrive in the wardroom at the same time as a copy of the latest *Tatler* with pictures of me on leave. You could see absolutely the suspicion and the hostility which I then had to break down. I pretended not to notice it."

It was hard, uphill work, but, "Time was the only cure. I just made myself available for any job, and bit by bit I worked myself into a position. But it was very painful and it took time."

The fact that he nearly always succeeded was witnessed by numerous fellow officers, from his first post-marriage ship to his first command twelve years later. Vice-Admiral Sir Charles Hughes Hallett was a gunnery lieutenant in 1923 when he first met Mountbatten. Mountbatten had been with the ship for seven months and had had a hard time. But now he had settled in, and there were only a few who were still hostile.

"In the service you always ran across a few people who disapproved of Mountbatten—mostly it was from a streak of jealousy, that was all." Hughes Hallett thought him "quite obviously a leader. If anything was going on, he would be at the bottom of it, both entertainment and professionally. At guest nights, he always started up the fun and games. He was the natural leader, with comic ideas."[1]

Hughes Hallett recalled that Mountbatten never had any trouble with the lower deck. "In those days, it was very different. They were naturally fond of people with a handle to their name. The divisional system was introduced about this time, and his forecastle division worshipped him.

"When we were painting ship, I remember Dickie taking up a hammer and chipping away at the old paint. A seaman would rush up and say, 'Oh, sir, let me do that.' So he would hand it over and pick up another. 'Oh, sir . . .' It earned the respect of the men, and the job was done in half the time."[2]

Privilege worked against Mountbatten from another quarter in those days. He wanted to get on at once with his long course, which required experience in destroyers. He therefore got in touch with an officer called David Joel who had served under his father at the beginning of the century and who was now in command of a destroyer. Joel agreed to have him as his first lieutenant, but the Admiralty said no. According to Mountbatten, "They clearly considered that this young fellow had had a hell of a good time with long voyages with the Prince of Wales, and a six-month long honeymoon with his rich wife. So they sent me to the battleship *Revenge* instead. It was the very last thing I wanted. Not only did I not want a big ship, but the *Revenge* was a part of the International Fleet in the Dardanelles to deal with all the Balkan troubles at the time. And wives were not allowed—too dangerous."

Mountbatten came back from Turkey to find his sister Louise in love. She was thirty-four, an intelligent, downright, talkative woman who had spent most of her life at home, with the exception of the war years. "She was not very pretty," said her cousin Princess Alice, Countess of Athlone, "and lacked charm. She was so terribly thin with a little flat face."[3] According to one of her nieces, she now "seemed embarrassed, almost annoyed with herself" for being in love.

Louise was in love with Crown Prince Gustaf Adolf of Sweden. In 1905 he had married Queen Victoria's granddaughter Margaret, Princess of Connaught, who had died in 1920, leaving the Swedish prince with five children. He had come over for the English season, a lonely man who was attracted to the woman he had last met in 1914 when she and her mother were returning hastily from Russia through Sweden after the outbreak of the war. They became engaged, the wedding was fixed for November, and the Swedish navy escorted the groom to British waters for the occasion. The *Revenge* was assigned to meet the Swedish squadron, and in this way Mountbatten appropriately met his future brother-in-law at sea.

The wedding on 3 November 1923 was almost as grand, and attended by almost as many royal figures, as the Mountbattens'. The family, and especially Louise's mother, were very relieved at the marriage, although secretly they found the Crown Prince dreadfully serious and boring. The couple later gave the democratic stamp to the Swedish monarchy by bicycling around Stockholm. They visited England every year, except during World War II, until the King's death at the age of ninety-two—visits that continued after Louise's death in 1965 and were accepted with stoic resignation by everyone from the Queen downwards.

By this time Edwina had completed the reorganization and renovation that would make Brook House less gloomy and less ponderous. Cassel had bought Brook House from Lord Tweedmouth and had given an architect his head, and many hundreds of thousands of pounds, to create from the shell a banker's Buckingham Palace. It took a year to quarry the eight hundred tons of Tuscany marble that faced the main hall and staircase. There was nothing whatever Edwina could do about the marble, but brighter paint and curtains and carpets helped to relieve the Edwardian mustiness.

One hundred guests could sit down in Eastern splendour in the dining room, and they could retire to the Turkish baths afterwards if they wanted to work off the effects of the rich food.[4]

Edwina was half attracted to the place, half appalled by it. Mountbatten loved it. Nothing could be too enormous and ostentatious for him. Once recovered from his early reservations about being married to the nation's richest woman, he had settled down to enjoy her wealth. All his life he possessed a special talent for transmitting to others any pleasure he felt, and this naturally included his delight in having a great deal of money. When Edwina gave him the biggest Hispano-

Suiza money could buy, he emphasized its identity and ownership by getting an "LM" number plate and a special mascot, just in case he might not be identified.

Mountbatten now made up his mind about the specialist branch to which he would dedicate his naval career. Like his father, he believed strongly in the future of the naval air arm, in which, for the present, Britain led the world with the first true aircraft carriers and torpedo-carrying planes, and in 1918, on leave, he had taken private flying lessons. Then the formidable leader of the RAF, Lord Hugh Montague Trenchard, had succeeded in prising from the Royal Navy control of all naval aircraft. It was the worst thing that could happen to the Navy, and Mountbatten saw little future in a career in a branch in which he would have to take an RAF commission. Submarines also intrigued him, but he felt with his highly sensitive antennae that the best future for him lay in signals.

While serving in the *Revenge*, he applied for a course at the Signal School at Portsmouth, and was accepted. He settled down to a long period as a land-based sailor, first at Portsmouth and later at Greenwich. The work was highly demanding, and he never allowed pleasure to interfere with it. On the other hand, his wealth and exceptional energy ensured that he also enjoyed himself with a very full and very grand social life.

He played polo with a string of ponies he had recently bought, went to parties in London, entertained lavishly at Brook House, saw his mother frequently as well as his brother and Nada and their family, dined at Buckingham Palace, and at York House with the Prince of Wales and Mrs. Dudley Ward, and found time to include in his daily round an invariable diary entry: "Amuse Patricia."

Towards the end of his service at sea, on St. Valentine's Day when the *Revenge* was at Funchal, Madeira, Edwina had given birth to a girl. Mountbatten returned to London as quickly as he could. There was a great party at Brook House to celebrate, and Douglas Fairbanks and Mary Pickford came to the christening of Patricia Edwina Victoria Mountbatten.

Neither the baby nor professional work deflected Mountbatten and Edwina's determination to accompany the Prince of Wales to New York in the summer of 1924. They sailed in the liner *Berengaria*, along with a host of their other friends, including Lady Diana Duff Cooper, returning to play her now famed part in *The Miracle* on Broadway. New York was again one long party. So was London, at the height of the season, on their return.

Later, at the end of the Portsmouth signals course, Mountbatten came out with the highest points. The reason, according to Mountbatten himself, was simple. "I was born with an ability to concentrate very hard on a job for a long time," he said, "and then turn for relaxation to something quite different and work just as hard at that. It has proved remarkably useful in my life. When I was Viceroy of India, for example, and working about eighteen hours a day with a great many difficulties to contend with, I would relax at the end of the day by working on my book *Relationship Tables*." Anyone who has seen this enormous genealogical masterpiece, which delineates relationships by coded numerals of his family back to the late eighteenth century, will marvel at the concentration and clarity of thought required to compile it.

This rare talent allowed him to develop exceptional proficiency which put him at the top and simultaneously lead a full social life. The trouble was that it was the glitter of his playboy existence that attracted public attention, and no one outside the service knew how hard he worked to be a winner. But then, Mountbatten made no attempt whatever to disabuse the public from the notion that he was a playboy first and last. All that his friends observed from time to time was the old abstracted expression that might creep over his face while dancing the tango at one in the morning at the Café Royal, and an unusual drying up of the conversation—Mountbatten was working on a problem related to the conversion of Royal Navy wireless signalling from Morse code to voice.

In addition to polo, Mountbatten and Edwina had taken up sailing, their first yacht being named *Shadow I*. Mountbatten also amused himself off duty with a ferocious American Garwood Liberty-engined speedboat which could do 40 knots. Now, he considered, it was time to join the Royal Yacht Squadron, a very exclusive club whose membership was strung about with all sorts of conditions, like being well connected, an obvious gentlemen, and possessing a yacht of suitable size. For a sponsor, Mountbatten thought he should go to the top, and asked the Duke of Sutherland. As described by Mountbatten himself, this is what happened:

The Duke thought that was a good idea. "But what is the size of your yacht, Dickie? They can be rather tricky about that."

It was less than 50 tons, the lower limit. "Well, I still think it's a good idea, and I'll propose you."

Later, standing on the lawn outside the club as a guest, Mountbatten saw the dashing pioneer aviator Claud Graham-White come tearing in in his Garwood Liberty-engined speedboat, spinning around and splashing yachts and people. There were angry protests, and within Mountbatten's earshot one ancient member (no doubt on the committee) said to another, "There's that bloody young so-and-so Dickie Mountbatten showing off again."

His subsequent blackballing created something of a sensation because the club depended on royal patronage. "I'll go and see the King about it—it'll be all right," said his friend Lord Birkenhead, the Secretary of State for India. Others were concerned at this snub, including the club's vice-commodore, Lord Camden. "Next time I'll get David Beatty to put you up—that'll show the Navy approves, and I'll second you."

This was in 1926. Mountbatten now owned the 66-ton *Shrimp*, well above the lower limit. There were rumours that a retired admiral was lobbying committee members to blackball Mountbatten again. He was identified as Admiral Sir Francis Bridgeman, who had been sacked as First Sea Lord by Churchill and superseded by Mountbatten's father. He was known at the time to have sworn vengeance on the family.

The result was a second blackballing, which was almost unprecedented and a real blow to Mountbatten, which he never forgave and never forgot. Many years later, during the war when he was Chief of Combined Operations, he found himself at dinner next to the politician-soldier Lord Mottistone, Lord Lieutenant of Hampshire and the Isle of Wight, a keen yachtsman and Royal Yacht Squadron member.

"What are you doing in London?" Mountbatten asked.

"I'm going to see someone at the War Office. Some damn line regiment wants to requisition the squadron's clubhouse. Can't have that."

Mountbatten told him that by chance he was the one person who could fix it. "It was for the Guards Brigade, a part of Force J. I'll tell them to find somewhere else."

"That's really very kind of you," said Mottistone.

"Kind? Not at all," Mountbatten protested. "If I'd been a member (but I was blackballed twice), I would have been horrified at the club's unpatriotic attitude, and disgusted that the squadron should be the only scrimshankers not to play their part in the war. It amuses me to put you in this unfavourable light."

"Well, I'm inclined to agree with you," Mottistone cravenly conceded. "I think we should *want* to be taken over. And I do hope you will now join us."

Mountbatten shook his head. "Certainly not. If I can't get in by election, I'm not joining by requisition."

Sometime after this, the King told Mountbatten that he really ought to join. He answered, "I can't afford the one hundred guineas' entrance." But the King insisted. "Come along, Dickie, be big about it, and show you don't mind." So he did. But the day the King died he resigned.

Part of the trouble had been that Mountbatten's idea of yachting did not altogether match that of the Royal Yacht Squadron's in the 1920s. He soon became impatient with sailing, which depended on unpredictable wind. He really preferred an engine, the more powerful the better. The newspapers frequently reported his racing, nearly always as the winner. But stories in the popular press did not increase his chances of election to that ancient and splendid club: "*Shadow II* at Bournemouth won an exciting race against Claud Graham-White in *Gee Whiz* over a course of 18 miles under the auspices of the Royal Motor Yacht Club."

In common with numerous Royal Navy officers over the years, the Mountbatten's acquired a house near Portsmouth for convenience while he completed his signals course. Adsdean, however, was bigger than most such houses, and it required eighteen servants to run it satisfactorily. It was of stone and flint and almost as ugly as Brook House (which required many more servants), although Virginia creeper helped to conceal its hideous proportions. Edwina decorated the house throughout in her favourite colours of pink and cream, with a good deal of gilt and French walnut.

Mountbatten loved it, and incorporated in the grounds a special pit for polo practice, with wire netting to catch the balls and full illumination for night use, a paddock and a golf course. They lived there until just before World War II.

The Mountbattens appeared to be settling down to the domestic life of an affluent, rising young naval officer on a shore appointment. Patricia toddled on the terraces, and when she was old enough, learned to ride. But Edwina was soon feeling restless. All her life she was impatient with routine, and feared above all else forming a fixed pattern to her life. She loathed the predictable. Every so often she felt a need to escape, to discover, to travel, to face challenges and risk her life.

The novelist Barbara Cartland, who was a close friend of Edwina's sister and knew them both very well at this time, once explained that Edwina "could be tough when she wanted something because she *always* got her own way, yet she was compassionate in the real sense of that word. She gave the impression that she was really interested in everyone's personal problems. The secret was that she *was* interested and nothing was too small or too unimportant for her to put right."[5]

Other contemporaries recognized in Edwina's bubbling excitement an element of hysteria which took much controlling. One moment she could appear totally selfish and self-indulgent, the next concerned only with the happiness of others. She was a loving mother, and also a severe one with an emphasis on discipline. While her dress and extrovert, extravagant public behaviour represented female emancipation, she was Victorian with her children, instilling in them a sense of high morality while practising a relaxed moral pattern of behaviour herself. She was especially stern with her younger daughter, later keeping her on a modest allowance and insisting that she should work for a living. Her friends mildly remonstrated with her at this, reminding her of her own gay days twenty years earlier, but she brushed aside their protests. Things were different then; now they were living in an age of austerity, and socialist principles decreed that *everyone* should work.

But Pamela had not even been born, and Patricia was still only two when Edwina suddenly decided to indulge in her new-found lust for travel. Her trip to India in pursuit of Mountbatten had given her a heady taste for exploration, and the money which came to her a few months later removed any barrier to her indulging this taste. So, instead of settling down to the comforts and pleasures of Adsdean and Brook House, she slipped quietly away, at the end of the 1925 season, telling only a few friends. Mountbatten heard little from her—an occasional letter from Russia or the South Seas. For four months, she sailed as an ordinary member of the crew of a 50-ton sailing schooner trading for copra among the Polynesian islands. She eventually reappeared, in a daze of satisfaction and contentment and in wonderful health, in the early spring of 1926.

Mountbatten was living at Brook House. He had succeeded in getting into the prized advance signals course at Greenwich. Now he was longing to get out to the Mediterranean, and before the end of the summer he heard that as of 14 December 1926, he would be assistant fleet wireless officer in the battleship *Warspite*, Admiral Sir Roger Keyes's flagship, a plum appointment for a young lieutenant.

The appointment, he was later to learn, almost backfired on him. When Keyes saw the list of new officers who were to join him, he crossed out Mountbatten's name. "I don't want a cousin of the King out here on my staff." He already had Georgie, who was a gunnery commander, in the fleet, and perhaps he thought one was enough. So he wrote to the Admiralty. While the letter was still in the mail, he relented.

"I was thinking about it," he told Mountbatten later, "and I turned up an old file of letters from your father. I realized that he had given me such support as a young man, and shown such confidence in me, that I couldn't do this to his son. So I sent a telegram to the Admiralty cancelling my letter."

The Mediterranean Fleet was the next stage in the career pattern Mountbatten had traced to emulate his father's. Prince Louis as a lieutenant had been appointed to the Mediterranean Fleet's flagship exactly fifty years earlier, in 1876. His commander-in-chief had been the Queen's second son, Prince Alfred. Fleet gossip at the time suggested court influence. Now Mountbatten had to face similar accusations, hinted at in rumours and gossip columns.

Edwina, as always, listened sympathetically to his complaints that whatever he did and wherever he went he was pursued by tales of patronage originating either in her wealth or his royal connections. She told him to ignore them and just get on with the work. "Rise above it, darling," she would say. It was her favourite advice to everyone who appeared to need stiffening.

Because of the constant charge of privilege, Mountbatten was always inordinately proud of achievements that could not be ascribed to outside influence, such as his inventions, which no one could deny him and which, for this reason, tended to be underrated by those seeking to denigrate him. These inventions included the Mountbatten Ruler, which was engraved on compass roses and obviated reference to the compass on the chart; a semaphore machine worked on a typewriter board capable of sending forty-five words per minute; a sub-focal signalling shutter, which again was capable of signalling fast, a much higher speed than by lamp signalling.

These inventions had the mixed reception that met everything Mountbatten did, many of his contemporaries believing that they were invented more for publicity than for the good of the Royal Navy. Then, in 1926, and for his own amusement, he devised in Brook House a facsimile of an admiral's cabin in his flagship. This was built, at great expense, on one floor, with every detail correct. Through the "windows" could be seen a replica of Valletta Harbour, Malta, with buildings and anchored ships all to scale. At the touch of a switch, the scene could be turned to night, with the ships lit up, and at the touch of another switch, the flagship could signal orders to the ships by Morse lamp.

It was not in Mountbatten's nature to keep this schoolboy's-dream-come-true to himself. He brought parties of friends to view it and to witness the movements of the "admiral's" ships. The press necessarily got wind of it, and Mountbatten's welcome of this interest, and the subsequent misunderstandings, were also typical of his confused press relations all through his life. He could not resist their approaches, and then worried about the consequences and the inaccuracies they seemed invariably to perpetrate.

Articles in the weekly picture magazines describing the "cabin," not always accurately, appeared widely. Mountbatten was more distressed at the inaccuracies than the publicity, which he claimed was intended to help the interior decorator and architect who had designed it to get more commissions. But in the end he had to admit that the invitations to the press were a mistake. "I agree that it looked like an advertisement for me, which is unfortunate," he wrote to Andrew Yates, one of his closest friends. Then, defiantly: "If people take it amiss that's there [sic] funeral. Life is far too short to worry about that sort of thing."[6]

And he never did worry for long. In October he despatched his polo ponies to Malta so that they would be ready for play when he arrived. The *Shrimp* was not to be left behind either, and her designer and builder, Peter du Cane, accompanied her through the French river and canal system via Paris, with orders to tuck her out of sight somewhere in Malta until Mountbatten's arrival.[7]

The expectation of hard work, regular polo, sailing and a full social life in Malta filled him with delight. In spite of recent discomfitures, Mountbatten said he was happier than he had ever been before in his life, and perhaps ever would be again. Edwina and Patricia and Edwina's sister, Mary, would be arriving a few weeks later.

Edwina and many of her bright-young-thing friends had discovered work during the general strike, which had begun early in May 1926, soon after Edwina's return from the Pacific. Since she was an avowed socialist, her friends expected her to support the strike, and certainly not to cross a picket line. But every day she was driven from Brook House in her Rolls-Royce to the *Daily Express* office in Fleet Street, where she and Jean Norton, her close friend, operated the switchboard of their mutual friend Max Aitken, who had been Lloyd George's Minister of Information during the war and been made a baron—Lord Beaverbrook—for his work. In the machine room, Lady Diana Duff Cooper helped with the folding. Lord Beaverbrook caught the spirit of Fleet Street's reaction when he wrote: "I think everybody enjoyed the strike—on both sides—volunteers and strikers alike. It was treated in a holiday spirit; and the pickets outside the *Daily Express* office were quite as amused as the amateurs working the mechanical side of the newspaper within."[8]

On a more serious level, Edwina was a witness to the ferocious row that blew up during the strike between Beaverbrook and Winston Churchill, now Chancellor of the Exchequer. Churchill, who had organized and produced an emergency newspaper called the *British Gazette*, wanted to requisition the *Daily Express*'s newsprint and delay the publication of regular newspapers when the strike was over. Beaverbrook resisted, and won, at the cost of a broken relationship for nearly fifteen years.

Three years later Beaverbrook took his two beautiful temporary telephone operators to Russia. To Edwina, there seemed to be nothing incongruous in sailing to Russia, which she admired so ardently for its supposed egalitarianism, in one of the world's most luxurious yachts, or in helping to break a strike by Britain's workers, whom she regarded as ground-down victims of capitalism.

All this was part of Edwina's engaging unpredictability, like the socialist *Daily Herald* left lying around in the house, the only newspaper allowed, while other newspapers were reporting her extravagant parties and clothes and her appearances at court. For example, a month after the general strike: "Some marvellous gowns will be seen at the 3rd Court of the Season at Buckingham Palace tonight. Distinctive even among such an array will be the 'all silver' dress which Lady Louis Mountbatten will wear. It is composed of nothing else but silver sequins—hundreds and hundreds of them."

To many of her friends this inconsistency was treated lightly: "Oh, isn't that like darling Edwina!" Others were puzzled, or outraged.

Six months later, in February 1927, the Mountbattens for the first time became a married couple serving on a foreign station. They were well aware that with their wealth and rank, their youth and reputation, they had to watch their style of living in Britain's famous Mediterranean fleet. Mountbatten, on the c.-in-c.'s staff in the flagship, had heavy responsibilities. His will to succeed, to justify the privileged appointment, was boundless. But he had to face the predictably suspicious attitude of his fellow officers with the certain knowledge that he was being watched every minute of every day.

When the flagship was at sea leading the fleet on cruises and manoeuvres, Edwina would follow in the *Shrimp*, and if the *Warspite* anchored at Nice or Naples, Barcelona or Cyprus, the beautiful white Mountbatten yacht was either already there or would soon arrive to anchor close by the flagship, and Mountbatten would proceed on board, usually with a party of friends. "Edwina got used to following the fleet around," said Mountbatten, "and the Mediterranean is not a bad place to follow it in."

When the fleet was at Malta, Mountbatten spent most of the time ashore, either lecturing midshipmen in signals or on routine office work, and living in their temporary home. Later, inevitably, they acquired a big house, which he shared with his brother. Almost every night there would be some form of entertainment, and the Mountbatten parties were, of course, the most lavish and the most popular among junior officers and their wives.

No one who served in the Mediterranean Fleet in 1927 could be unaware of the presence of the Mountbatten entourage. The evidence of wealth, the reputation that preceded them, the sight of this golden couple cruising among the men o' war in the Piraeus or Alexandria, all singled them out. Many retired officers today can recall them clearly, every memory etched in superlatives. For some, the picture is still marked by resentment, distant echoes of wardroom complaints about the flaunting of their wealth, of seeming slights and echoes of arrogance. For others, it is all admiration for an able, amusing and hardworking young wireless officer with a hospitable and charming wife.

From those midshipmen who attended his classes, there is unstinted praise for his enthusiasm and for his ability to transmit it to his students. No one could fault him as a teacher. No one ever forgot a Mountbatten lesson. A petty officer said, "The reason we admired him so much was because we were never able to put anything over on him."[9]

It irritated Mountbatten to see his students trying to match their note-taking with his own speed, and thus missing much of what he was saying. He decided to ban all notebooks, and instead provided every student with a précis of the day's lecture, which they could then work up into notes. These summaries were later compiled into a textbook on wireless telegraphy, which was used throughout the signals branch of the Navy.

Many of Mountbatten's fellow officers recognized his abilities and enthusiasm, and even the most hostile could not deny him certain qualities or ignore his style. But few of his contemporaries or his seniors believed that he would go very far in the service. "We always thought of him as having married millions of pounds and being mad on polo and pretty girls, and we thought he was a write-off as far as the Navy went," recalled Lieutenant-Commander Peter Kemp, who was a sublieutenant at the time. "We didn't see why he should *bother* to work. If any of us had had such luck, *we* shouldn't have bothered. No, he was becoming the great playboy, and he acted like one. He wasn't going to go far, that's what we said."[10]

There were many different reactions to the way in which he conducted himself with his great wealth, but the most intelligent and fairminded of the officers agreed that he stood up well under difficult circumstances. "It never struck me that Mountbatten had an easy row to hoe as a junior lieutenant," is Kemp's judgement today. "He managed things very well, I think. The only mistake that I can remember was a bit later. The c.-in-c. had to give rather formal and big parties for officers and their wives. By their very nature, they were stiff affairs, which we had to attend as a duty.

"Now, the Mountbattens lived in great style very near to the c.-in-c.'s official residence, and one night they held a huge party on the same night as one of the admiral's. I suppose we all left the c.-in-c.'s party as early as decently possible and walked next door to join a much more hilarious party. It aroused a lot of talk at the time. Looking back, I think it was a rather poor show. But being impecunious sub-lieutenants, we enjoyed ourselves, all right. There was something about those Mountbatten parties . . ."

Kemp did accept that "their ruddy great yacht" following the fleet around got a lot of backs up, particularly the backs of senior officers. Not the lower deck. In those days, a lord and lady in a yacht were not the invariable target of resentment and envy they were to become later.

Just before he left England, Mountbatten had written to a friend that he was looking forward to coming out to Malta, doing some real work and getting in some regular polo. To him, the prompt arrival at Valletta of his ponies was almost as important as the prompt departure of the *Warspite* on a cruise. His polo was less a sport and entertainment than an extracurricular activity into which he threw as much energy and to which he gave as much thought as he did to the development of faster and more efficient methods of signalling.

"I was never naturally good at it," Mountbatten said of his early polo days. "I was not a specially good horseman when I began, and I didn't have a good eye for ball games. I had to plug away at it to be respectably good. But I made a point of studying the game."

From the start, Mountbatten saw a chukker of polo as a close parallel to a naval battle, with all the needs of leadership, decisiveness, speed, communication, manoeuvrability and good fast shooting. As he stood bent over the table at his house discussing the day's performance with his team, the "Bluejackets," moving models around, giving orders and uttering rebukes, spectators were known to liken him to a Prussian cavalry officer after the Battle of Sedan.

Mountbatten was indeed thinking and talking in terms of war, but exclusively of sea warfare, and of a successful polo player as an exact parallel to a successful naval commander. This was evident in the language he employed and the message of his writings. He began first with a duplicated booklet, which was very elementary, but even this contained such commonsense advice to a polo player or gunnery officer as "When knocking about, always aim in a definite direction. Hitting aimlessly may be amusing but it is a very bad habit."

Later he wrote a book that was to become the accepted authority on the game, of which he was as proud as he was of his inventions. It was called *Introduction to Polo*, and he used the waggish pseudonym "Marco." Much of the advice in this interesting book could be introduced, changing scarcely a word, into a naval tactics manual.

As a destroyer commander in war, Mountbatten followed his own sagacious advice to a polo player a decade earlier: "The primary factor in a successful attack is speed. Generally speaking, if you are the stronger side you will be the attacking side, and it will be to your advantage to speed up the game. When you are the weaker side, however, you may sometimes feel that your advantage will lie in slowing up the game and making it 'choppy.' But it will not do you much good to break up your opponent's attack if you do not immediately counter-attack in your turn . . ."

And these homilies to a polo captain could be translated to any captain on his bridge, in peace or war: "He should never criticise something that is done, and can't be undone, in the hearing of other people"; or, "The team should have implicit confidence in the captain's decisions"; or "Never feel that a piece of criticism or advice is too much trouble to give, or that it is too trivial, or that it exceeds your province."

In every respect the book provides an interesting summary of the qualities that Mountbatten regarded as important to good leadership, and his efforts to spread the popularity of the game throughout the Navy did much more than improve the sales of his book. Polo is fast, tough, requires quick decisions, initiative, teamwork and, above all, good shooting. Mountbatten started the Royal Naval Polo Association, persuaded the King to become patron and his sons associate patrons, designed—after months of experiment and study—a new head for the mallet and called it "The Royal Naval Polo Association Head."

Combining two of his enthusiasms, he took movies of his team at play and then screened them in slow motion after practice so that the team members could discuss their faults at leisure. He always carried in his pocket a squash ball, which he crushed in his hand whenever the hand was idle in order to strengthen his wrist muscles—something his nephew Prince Philip imitated when he began four-in-hand riding.

Within months, polo playing at Malta, which had always been a light-hearted game, had developed a highly professional quality, with much higher standards and rather fewer laughs than before. With Mountbatten, it was the score and only the score that counted, and his "Bluejackets" began to pile up the silver cups.

Mountbatten was promoted to lieutenant-commander on 15 April 1928, and at last given a destroyer appointment. Small, fast ships suited his temperament. Nothing gave him greater pleasure than manoeuvring a 35-knot destroyer, making simulated torpedo attacks and retreating under a smoke screen, stalking submarines or acting with his flotilla as a screen to the battle fleet.

The flotilla leader, *Stuart*, was a very fast 1,600-ton ship which had been launched just before the end of the Great War. As flotilla wireless officer, Mountbatten's appointment was a step up, but it did not carry the same prestige as being on the c.-in-c.'s staff. It was at this time that he sought to improve the speed of visual signalling, a destroyer's wireless being especially vulnerable in combat.

Family life and naval life during the late 1920s ran in close parallel for a period and then became widely separated for weeks, perhaps for months. At Malta, or cruising with the fleet, Edwina appeared to have everything she could need for a happy and full life. But her restless mind and her wanderlust were too powerful, and she would often leave her family, sometimes on very short notice. One of these tours took her to Hollywood again, but her first love was for strange and exotic parts of the world, travelling with the most basic luggage—"shorts, six shirts and a dress," reported the newspapers in September 1932, "is all Lady Louis Mountbatten is taking on her Persian Desert trip"—and living as far as possible with the people.

Mountbatten would have arranged a minute-by-minute itinerary months ahead, with cars to meet him, appointments with notable figures, and sojourns at embassies. This was not Edwina's way. Usually with just one friend—Marjorie Brecknock, Jean Norton or her sister-in-law Nada—she would rough it in Persia, Egypt, the West Indies, the more obscure regions of Asia and the Far East, usually returning with treasures from some archaeological dig or a small zoo of wild animals.

Once it was a lion cub; Sabi remained a family pet until she became too large for comfort.

Mountbatten was proud of Edwina's travels, her souvenirs and photographs, as he was invariably proud of all family accomplishments. His love for her was as strong as ever, and he missed her badly during these long absences. But he had learned from his father that a sailor's life entails separations to which you have to reconcile yourself, even if, in Mountbatten's case, it was the wife who left her husband behind.

What he did come to accept with deep regret later was that these long and arduous tours, which took place all through Edwina's childbearing years, necessarily limited the size of their family and left him without a male heir. Edwina treated her body mercilessly and refused to accept that she was in the least ill when most people would long before have taken to their bed and called the doctor.

Edwina had always been unusually afraid of death, a fear that had grown with the acquisition of everything her heart could desire: wealth, a handsome young royal husband, a position in society and in her married life which enabled her to do exactly what she wanted to do at any time. She never told anyone that she did not expect to live to a great age. But the pace of her life, her impatience to pack in experiences of people and places, to learn and to see, all suggest that she was determined not to waste one minute when she might have only a few years left.

Four years passed before she conceived another child. Her rough and restless travels may well have led to miscarriages, and as Mountbatten said, "Edwina was one of those remarkable women who never show they are about to have a baby." In December 1928, Edwina was in Egypt studying archaeology. Mountbatten joined her for the more social side of her trip, then he had to go back to his ship. They saw each other briefly at the other end of the Mediterranean, and from Gibraltar, Mountbatten took time off one weekend to accompany Edwina to Morocco. The sea was so rough before they could return that the regular steamer was cancelled and Mountbatten had to charter a launch to get back on time. Edwina was more than eight months pregnant, but after a night bouncing around on the water between Africa and Europe, she said that of course she was all right and would drive off at once in order to synchronize her arrival with her husband's at Barcelona.

Above left: Princess Victoria of Hesse, Mountbatten's mother, as a young woman before her marriage at the age of twenty-one in 1884.

Above right: Prince Louis of Battenberg, now a naturalized Englishman and "buck about town" as well as a rising naval officer. He was forty-six and a naval captain when Mountbatten was born.

Dickie in "naval uniform" at the age of four in company with his tattered but beloved teddy bear "Sonnenbein."

The naval Battenbergs, father and sons: Dickie the cadet, Prince George the lieutenant, Prince Louis now a full admiral and First Sea Lord, 1913.

Young statesman and mature sailor as partners in 1914, Winston Churchill as First Lord of the Admiralty, Prince Louis as First Sea Lord.

"My dear Prince Louis," wrote Churchill, "I cannot further oppose the wish, you have during the last few weeks expressed to me, to be released from the burden of responsibility . . ."

On board the Russian imperial yacht *Standardt,* in the Baltic. The haemophiliac Tsarevitch, the Tsar, Marie and Olga. The escorting destroyer is of the *Amuretz* class.

The Russian imperial family, 1905. Mountbatten's Aunt Alicky holds the infant Tsarevitch, and the Grand Duchesses are (*left to right*) Tatiana, Marie, Anastasia and Olga.

Mountbatten's favourite portrait of his cousin, the Grand Duchess Marie, whom he hoped to marry.

Above left: Dickie and David at play. A characteristic "snap" of Mountbatten and the Prince of Wales while on the Prince's world tour.

Above right: Dickie and David at work. The Prince of Wales as a captain, Mountbatten newly promoted lieutenant in naval uniform for one of the numerous formal occasions connected with their world cruises on board H.M.S. *Renown,* 1920–22.

Below: King George V considered this widely printed photograph of his son and cousin unsuitable for the general public.

Above left: Edwina with her grandfather, Sir Ernest Cassel.

Above right: Edwina Cynthia Annette Ashley.

Below left: Lieutenant Lord Louis Mountbatten, age twenty-one, shortly before his wedding.

Below right: Edwina—Lady Louis Mountbatten—in 1925.

"The wedding of the year," 18 July
1922, St. Margaret's, Westminster.

The honeymoon. Edwina and
Mountbatten embark in the *Majestic*
for New York.

Hollywood, 1922. Charlie Chaplin breaks the news to Dickie that he will never make an actor. Freddy Neilson sadly agrees.

Edwina "held up" in the film *Nice and Friendly,* which Chaplin made for them as a wedding present.

Dickie and Charlie recovering
after a hard morning's
shooting.

Instant and lifelong friends:
Edwina and Chaplin, 1922.

Above left: Edwina, age twenty-seven.

Above right: Goodwood Races, July 1926. On Mountbatten's left is his sister-in-law, Nada, Marchioness of Milford Haven.

Below: Mountbatten, Edwina and her sister, Mary, at the Highland Gathering, 1923.

Above: Mountbatten with his first Rolls-Royce, Edwina's wedding present to him: a Silver Ghost model, with "signalman" mascot.

Below left: Douglas Fairbanks; Patricia, age seven (today Countess Mountbatten of Burma); Edwina; and her father, Colonel Wilfred Ashley.

Below right: Discussing tactics with the Duke of Gloucester before a chukker, June 1937.

The Royal Navy Polo Team in 1937. *Left to right:* Lieutenant-Commander E. G. Heywood-Lonsdale; Commander C. E. Lambe; Mountbatten; and Commander E.W.B. Sim.

Pranks at Balmoral Castle, August 1936. Mountbatten and King Edward VIII (dressed as a peasant) on the left, Wallis Simpson and Edwina on the right.

The penthouse, Park Lane, in 1937, with furniture by David Joel and a scattering of books, including *Treasure Island, Memoirs of a Fox-Hunting Man, In Search of History* and a biography of Mountbatten's relative, Kaiser Wilhelm II. The model is of his first ship, H.M.S. *Daring.*

Above left: Mountbatten (*second left, front row*) and captains of the flotilla in jovial mood.

Above right: The destroyer commander, Full Speed Ahead. Captain Lord Louis Mountbatten on the *Kelly*'s bridge, 1940.

Below: The *Kelly*, torpedoed and listing, off the Dutch coast, 1940.

The *Kelly* as heroic film fiction, with Noël Coward acting the part of Mountbatten in *In Which We Serve*, 1942.

Three generations of Mountbattens: Mountbatten is flanked by his elder daughter and mother; Edwina wears her St. John Ambulance uniform.

Mountbatten the Chief of Staff and Mountbatten the orator. Among those around the table are Mountbatten (*far left*), Field Marshal Alan Brooke (spectacles, moustache), and Air Chief Marshal Peter Portal and General "Pug" Ismay (*at the far end*). The assembled troops are on the quayside at Bombay.

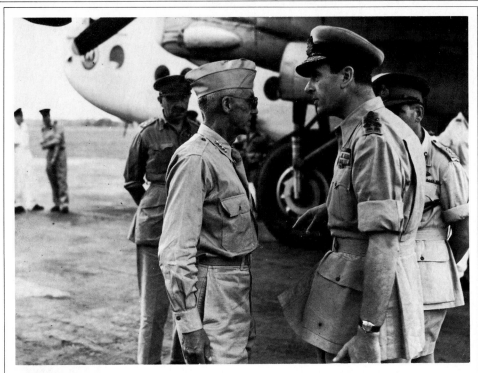

General "Vinegar Joe"
Stilwell and Mountbatten
at Kandy, 1944.

Mountbatten, General
R. A. "Specs" Wheeler
and the Chiang Kai-sheks,
1944.

Edwina drove the six hundred miles over very rough roads by herself in her Rolls-Royce. "I went to meet her at the Ritz Hotel," Mountbatten recalled of the amusing crisis that followed, "and she was looking very fit and ordinary. 'How are you, darling?' I asked her. 'Very well. But I think a young Mountbatten is going to appear at any moment.' So I got busy on the telephone to find a doctor."

The only doctor available in the city was a throat specialist. "So I rang my cousin the queen in Madrid. But Ena was away, so I was put through to King Alfonso. 'You're having a baby! How exciting! I'll tell nobody.' 'That's not really the point,' I said. 'She wants help.' I suppose the line was very bad, but I just heard him say, 'I'll send the military governor.' And so he did."

Within half an hour the hotel was like a royal palace in a threatened military coup, with guards at every entrance and on every street corner, so that even the throat specialist had difficulty in getting through. However, with his assistance and the help of a nun, Edwina was satisfactorily delivered of a girl. She was later christened, in the Chapel Royal, Pamela Carmen Louise Mountbatten, with the King of Spain standing as a godfather. The other godparents were the Duchess of Penaranda, her aunt Crown Princess Louise of Sweden and the Duke of Kent.

On her return to England from one of her long tours abroad, Edwina found herself temporarily responsible for a beguiling, bright, fair-haired little boy who, if not quite abandoned by his parents, had so far led an unsettled life marked by long periods of separation from his mother or father, and most often from both. He was Mountbatten's young nephew Prince Philip of Greece. When Mountbatten's eldest sister, the deaf Alice, Princess Andrew of Greece, gave birth to a fourth daughter, Princess Sophie ("Tiny"), in 1914, he wrote crossly to his mother from Osborne asking why his sister never had a boy. His wish was at last fulfilled in 1921 when Philip was born on Corfu on 10 June while Mountbatten was falling in love with Edwina Ashley in England. Prince Andrew's father, George, was Danish; his mother, Olga, Russian. He was Greek by adoption, and his elder brother was king, off and on. Prince Philip refers to himself as Danish by birth and English by adoption. Mountbatten once said, "Prince Philip is the son of a Danish-Greek prince. His mother was a Battenberg, daughter of a naturalized Englishman. He dislikes being referred to as a Hessian."

All her life, Princess Alice was deeply loved by her family (and especially by her younger brother Dickie), and for most of her life was an object of anxiety. Her mother worried first about her seeming backwardness, and when it was diagnosed, her deafness. When she fell in love with Prince Andrew and married him, they all worried about Andrew's military career in a country that could idolize you as a hero one day and put you up against a wall the next morning. At one time during the Great War, Allied warships threatened Athens in an attempt to strong-arm Greece onto their side, and one of them opened fire on the palace, fortunately missing Alice and the nursery wing. After this, the King had to leave, and Prince Andrew and his family with him. They sought asylum in Lausanne, and Mountbatten visited them there, via Paris, immediately after the war was over.

"He made the greatest of friends with the children after his first shyness at finding his nieces had grown so big," Victoria wrote of the meeting between brother and sister.[11] He found the family, not for the first time, penurious, and Victoria sold some Burmah Oil shares and despatched the proceeds to Switzerland—"I am only sorry I can't see her face when she gets my letter."

The following year, 1920, Greece returned the King to power, and Prince Andrew to the army. Promoted to lieutenant-general, he was boundlessly optimistic when he brought his family to England in the summer of 1922 for the Mountbatten wedding. Prince Philip, thirteen months old, did not attend the wedding, but waved cheerfully from a window to his mother and father as they left in the rain, his father in full-dress uniform of a Greek general.

No sooner had Andrew and Alice and their children returned to Greece than there was a counterrevolution, the family sought refuge in a villa, unsuitably named Mon Repos, on Corfu, from which Prince Andrew was enticed back and then thrown into prison and charged with treason. Five fellow officers were shot after a token court-martial, and Andrew's life appeared to be in grave danger.

Alice, almost demented with worry, despatched telegrams to the Pope, King Alfonso of Spain, Poincaré of France, and her cousin George V of England. At first there was no response from anyone or any government. Then King George, guilt-stricken at the recent assassination of his Russian cousin and all her family and horrified that he might, by reason of political cowardice, have the blood of another cousin on his hands, acted with the decisiveness of a sailor born and bred. He made use of all his considerable royal influence through the Foreign Office. An emissary had already been secretly despatched to parley with the Greek dictator, Pangalos, and a man o' war ordered to Piraeus to display her guns. Prince Andrew was smuggled on board at night, and the warship slipped away the entire family and put them ashore at Brindisi on 5 December 1922.

George V was relieved, and ever after proud of the part he had played in rescuing the family. He did not set eyes on the boy until he was thirteen years old. Prince Philip remembers being at Buckingham Palace in 1934 at the time of Princess Marina's marriage to the Duke of Kent and standing aside for the King. George V paused, looked at him thoughtfully and said, "You're Andrew's boy!"

The family settled in St. Cloud, that favourite haunt for refugees outside Paris. They were not at all well off. An uncle paid for Prince Philip's private education at his first infants' school. Nor did the marriage prosper. Mountbatten, who saw them as often as time allowed, observed some of the characteristics of his late aunt Ella developing in his eldest sister. After her husband had been blown up, Ella had developed a deeply introspective, almost mystical religious tendency, combined with a need to succour the poor and the sick. Now Alice was showing the same tendency. She opened a shop in Paris and dedicated the profits to Greek refugees even more penurious than she. Prince Andrew left for the gay life of Monte Carlo. He was, like his son, never very good at playing the solemn role.

The princesses were looked after by friends, relatives and governesses, and quite soon all married. Prince Philip made one of his visits to England in 1926, an enchanting, precocious and mischievous boy, much loved by his grandmother. Alice was not well and was spending long periods in sanatoriums. Prince Andrew was deeply concerned about his son, whom he adored but was ill equipped to look after. The family rallied round. Victoria agreed to act as a mother, and the part of father was jointly adopted by Mountbatten, his brother Georgie and Harold Wernher, an ex-soldier and now millionaire businessman who had married the sister of Georgie Milford Haven's wife, Nada.

On her return home from her latest tour, Edwina found at Adsdean nine-year-old Prince Philip, who fitted in easily with the routine of life.

Mountbatten and the two girls, now one and six, returned from Malta with the nursemaids.

"Dickie took great pride in his nephew," Edwina's biographer noted, "who was to take the place of the son he would never have. During the holidays the placid and feminine Mountbatten nursery was much enlivened by the appearance of young Master Philip, who, always a tease, imposed his will on Patricia, who soon became his willing slave and imitator."[12]

Talking one day about Prince Philip and his upbringing in England, Mountbatten said, "We all rallied round but there's no doubt that my mother took the main burden. Andrea [Prince Andrew] was in no position to help, nor was his mother. Andrea was a charming and delightful person, but he lived abroad until he died in Monaco at the end of 1944—after the invasion. He was a great Anglophile and wanted Prince Philip brought up as an English boy. When we asked him about his career and suggested the Navy, he liked the idea—but on no account the Army.

" 'I have been driven demented in my career,' he told me. 'First of all I became a serious soldier—a cavalry soldier—then about 1910 the Greek government said it didn't want a prince serving in the armed forces, so I was thrown out. Later, I was allowed in again. Then in 1917 I was thrown into exile, came back and thrown out finally. Just look at my life!' he would exclaim. 'I was a keen professional soldier, and have been thrown out three times. I don't want that to happen to Philip.'

"Apart from my mother," Mountbatten continued, "it was my brother and I. We did it to a certain extent together. I looked after him as far as his naval career was concerned, and later did the whole job single-handed."

There was, from the start, a wonderful compatibility and understanding between the two. Prince Philip admired his uncle greatly and was more than ready to shape himself in Mountbatten's likeness, while Mountbatten always claimed that he recognized from Prince Philip's earliest years that he was "abnormally intelligent." Princess Alice, Countess of Athlone, considered him more intelligent than Mountbatten—"and that's saying a lot."[13] Asked when he first saw signs that his nephew was going to become an exceptional person, Mountbatten replied laconically, "Out shooting one day, when he was eight or nine. It was rough. The way he coped told me.

"Prince Philip," Mountbatten declared on the same occasion, "is an absolute Mountbatten and not a bit Hanoverian, and his children have a degree of intelligence quite lacking in King George V, King George VI or any of those people at all. Prince Charles, too, is an absolute Mountbatten. The real intelligence in the royal family comes through my parents to Prince Philip and the children.

"The Queen, of course, is a marvellous person. Her ministers are always surprised at how well-informed she is. She is extremely sound—not brilliant—and that comes from her mother. There was great worthiness in King George VI, King George V and even Edward VII, but that old Hanoverian line was becoming dimmer and dimmer, so that they could not even pass their exams."

Mountbatten's shaping of Prince Philip the man, and his destiny, is always regarded highly in any estimate of Mountbatten's achievements. Some people think it was the greatest thing he did. Julian Amery, the distinguished diplomat and politician, regards Mountbatten's "coaching of Prince Philip" as deserving of his highest credit marks, helping to make him into a personality disassociated from the old establishment, someone acceptable to all shades of political thinking (except the lunatic) and to all classes.[14]

Surprisingly, a modesty about himself and his achievements is something Prince Philip acquired over the years when Mountbatten was such a powerful influence in his life. This writer once described him as "a remarkable man." Prince Philip would have none of it. "Hough refers to me first as 'a remarkable man,' which is faintly ridiculous as I am only in a remarkable position."

Prince Philip's education after Cheam preparatory school was discussed with Prince Andrew. Mountbatten had for some time thought that Kurt Hahn's school in Schloss Salem near Lake Constance was the right place to develop to the full Philip's evident qualities. Mountbatten and his brother sent him there in 1933. He thrived but didn't like what he saw of the influence of the new Nazi regime, unlike his grandmother, who for a while wholeheartedly approved of it—deceived by the word "socialist." When Hahn escaped to England and thence to Scotland to set up Gordonstoun, Prince Philip followed him there.

It was in Prince Philip's third year at Gordonstoun that two more tragedies struck at the House of Hesse. In October of 1937 the Mountbattens were in London for what was expected to be a specially joyous wedding. In February 1931 Prince Philip's prettiest sister, Cecile, had married George Donatus ("Don"), hereditary Grand Duke of Hesse. In the next few years they had three children, two boys and a girl. Early in 1937 Don's younger brother Louis ("Lu") had met and fallen in love with an English girl, the Honorable Margaret ("Peg") Geddes. In October the Grand Duke died, and his younger son's marriage in London was postponed to November. The family took off for the event from Frankfurt on the afternoon of 16 November in a Junkers trimotor—the hereditary Grand Duke, his wife, who was expecting another child, the late Grand Duke's widow, the two boys, their nursemaid and the best man. Coming in to land at Ostend en route, the plane struck a tall chimney concealed by mist, crashed and burst into flames. Everyone on board was killed, and the Hessian family, which traced its roots back to Charlemagne, was all but wiped out.

Mountbatten recalled that black November evening. "Lu and Peg had gone out to Croydon to meet the family, and they learned the news while they were waiting. I had sent two cars to collect them all. They came back with just the engaged couple, prostrate with grief. We all went round to Peg's father's house—Lord Geddes—and had a ghastly family meeting. My mother said the wedding ought to go ahead, not in four days time with all the formality and publicity, but the very next day while they were still in a state of shock. She was absolutely right, of course. I stood in as best man. Then the married couple went to Ostend to the scene of the crash, and on to Darmstadt. What a honeymoon!"

There was a double tragic postscript to the catastrophe. Lu and Peg adopted the surviving infant girl, who had been left at home. Eighteen months later she died, "as if the hand of Hessian fate had signed the cancellation of her reprieve." And as the years passed, Lu and Peg found that they could not have children, so the Hessian Darmstadt dynasty was threatened with extinction.

At Gordonstoun, Kurt Hahn broke the news to Prince Philip. Five months later he had to break the news of another tragedy to his pupil, and this time it was even harder for Prince Philip to bear.

In a family tight-knit with loyalty and affection, there were no ties closer than those between Mountbatten and his elder brother Georgie. People who saw the two of them in the Mediterranean Fleet on a professional level, Mountbatten a signals lieutenant, Georgie a gunnery commander in the *Warspite*, recognized at once the brotherly affection

and the contrast Mountbatten the millionaire playboy, Georgie the
diligent professional. "He was a brilliant chap," said a sub-lieutenant
who served with him. "We expected great things from him and not
much from his younger brother."[5]

Mountbatten agreed: "Without trying at all—and his brain was lazy
as well as brilliant—he would come in first or second in his exams. If he
tried at all, he always came out top."

In the winter of 1937–38 Georgie Milford Haven contracted cancer
of the bone and died after much suffering on 8 April. It was a terrible
blow to the whole family. "I was absolutely shattered," said Mountbatten. And Prince Philip, to whom Mountbatten was more than ever a
father, was also heartbroken. It was one sadness too many for Georgie's
mother. Patricia Mountbatten, now thirteen, calling to say good night
to her grandmother, found Victoria at her desk attempting to write
letters, the tears pouring down her lined cheeks. No one had ever before
seen this tough, competent, ever-rational granddaughter of Queen Victoria crying.

4

SIGNALS OF DANGER

*M*ountbatten chose the signals branch in the Royal Navy in which to specialize because all his life he was interested in communications—in the widest sense. Signals meant much more than the first and vital operation of keeping ships in touch with one another. It embraced the narrower but vitally important subject of officers keeping in touch with the lower deck, of ships' companies keeping in touch with their families, of sustaining morale by keeping ships' companies entertained and in touch with the news of the day.

As fleet wireless officer, Mountbatten was in the central listening post of some seventy men o' war, in touch with every unit wherever it might be in the Mediterranean, in touch with international and domestic news, and with local fleet news, from a seaman with a sudden attack of appendicitis in a tug to preparations for a gunnery practice in a 30,000-ton battleship.

From the day he took up the appointment, Mountbatten began an elaborate programme to increase the efficiency of wireless communications throughout the fleet. From the signals H.Q. at the Castille in Valletta, he kept the fleet telegraphists tuned day and night to the various frequencies used by the fleet. Often he would examine the strips as they came from the machine and despatch comments, favourable or unfavourable, to the operator responsible for the transmission. In this way he simultaneously demonstrated to them his own indefatigable energy and his interest in their work. Over a longer period of time he even got the telegraphists' status and pay increased at a time when economies were the order of the day.

On one occasion Mountbatten organized an elaborate and spectacular demonstration of the efficiency and importance of signals in the
big lecture hall in the Castille. It was an electronics pageant extending
over three days so that everyone, from the commander-in-chief to ordinary seamen stokers, could attend. They all did, too; the show was a
sellout. Like a master of ceremonies (which was exactly what he was),
he stood before the audience and asked for a message to pass through to
the Admiralty. Back would come the reply from London within seconds. With war planes circling over the island and submarines stationed at the harbour entrance, he would initiate a mock exercise—
"Enemy sighted!" "Commence to attack!" The first naval action in a
war was simulated in sound, with the W/T operators working away
publicly on the stage like a chorus in a musical. It was the best show in
Valletta and had the members of the audience on the edge of their
seats. It did no harm to Mountbatten's standing, either.

On a more serious level, when the threats to service pay suddenly
became real in 1931 as a result of the economic crisis, Mountbatten's
role as fleet wireless officer proved of importance in helping to prevent
the spread of disaffection. On 15 September, the Atlantic Fleet muti-
nied at Invergordon. It was the first fleet mutiny since the mutiny at
the Nore in 1797, which resulted in the hanging of twenty-four men.

Mountbatten was the first officer in the fleet to hear the news. The c.-
in-c. was Admiral Ernie Chatfield, Beatty's old flag-captain at the Battle of Jutland; his chief of staff was Sidney Bailey; and the flag-captain
was Captain Davenport. The fleet was dispersed on its first summer
cruise, and the conclusion reached by Mountbatten, which was backed
by his assistant, Micky Hodges, was that there must be no communication between units of the fleet and that the units must remain dispersed.

"The cause of the Invergordon Mutiny, which was a severe cut in
pay, would certainly have led to mutiny in the Mediterranean Fleet
too," Mountbatten recorded of this critical occasion. "And the reason
for that was that most of the officers were in full sympathy. They knew
how close to the bone the men's families were living. Davenport said his
men would never mutiny—it wasn't possible. I didn't argue. I went
straight to Bailey and said, 'There is exactly the same feeling here as in
the Atlantic Fleet. I'm stopping all W/T communications, and if you
bring the fleet together, there'll be a mutiny, I'm warning you.' "

Mountbatten was told that if it was as serious as that, he had better go and see the c.-in-c. "Chatfield was a very remote man. When I saw him, he already had my views through Bailey and Davenport, who was absolutely furious with me, just as if I was some mutineer myself.

"Chatfield was upset too. 'If what you say is true, how is it that I've never been told?' 'Perhaps because they're scared, sir,' I said. 'Scared? Why should they be scared?'

"So I explained to him that the Navy had suffered from promotionitis ever since the postwar cuts when two out of three junior officers were forced to retire. 'Nobody can afford to say what they think anymore.' Then I said something like this: 'Imagine, sir, H.M.S. X. A mutiny on board is feared. The Officer of the Division, if he knows, is going to pretend to himself that things aren't really that bad and won't say anything to his commander. If the commander does suspect it, he won't risk his promotion by telling the captain—he'll be too busy sucking up to him. The captain's in the zone for promotion to rear-admiral, so he's not spilling the beans to you because he thinks you may be the next First Sea Lord [Chatfield was] and he's not going to tell you.'

"So Chatfield looked hard at me and said, 'This is a terrible condemnation. How is it that you've got the courage to tell me when nobody else has?' 'That's very simple, sir. By a pure fluke I was allowed to stay on in the Navy. I had private means. I don't need to buy my promotion by silence. What I do care about is the truth, and that you should know it.'

"It may be coincidence that I was promoted next shot. Later, I learned that there were symptoms of mutiny at Malta, and that a few rifles were taken from the half deck of a cruiser and ditched. How did I hear? Through the telegraphists, of course."

Mountbatten always claimed that he saved the Mediterranean Fleet—the premier fleet—from mutiny in September 1931. As it was, the Invergordon Mutiny brought about a cancellation of the pay cuts and led directly, four days later, to a report from the Bank of England that foreign credits were exhausted. With even the Royal Navy unsteady, international confidence in Britain evaporated. On 21 September an act suspending the gold standard was rushed through Parliament, and the pound tumbled.

A year later Mountbatten was dealing with an altogether more agreeable W/T occasion. The BBC had developed an Empire Broadcasting Service which King George V was due to inaugurate with a talk to his people on Christmas Day 1932. The C.-in-C. Mediterranean ordered that all fleet personnel should listen to the speech. The only way to do this was to build a new high-frequency receiver high up on the island, linked by a cable to a ship which, in turn, would retransmit the broadcast on the medium band used by ships' sets.

The equipment had to be brought from Britain, and the last pieces arrived only on Christmas Eve. In a characteristic race against time, which might have been set up for one of Mountbatten's more flamboyant shows, everything was linked only minutes before the voice of George V came over the ether. It was heard perfectly, with none of the fading associated with long-distance reception at the time.

With an elaborate series of street and café loudspeakers, also wired up, half the native population of Valletta heard the broadcast, too. The days of satellites and transistors were still decades away. To many who heard the modulated tones of the King Emperor, in the steets and on shipboard, the achievement seemed like a miracle, which pleased Mountbatten, who liked to perform miracles.

On one of her Hollywood jaunts, Edwina had seen and heard the first of the "talkies" which had created such an entertainment sensation. Through his earlier sponsorship of movie projectors in the fleet, which developed later into the Royal Naval Film Corporation (Patron H.R.H. the Duke of Kent), Mountbatten had made the Navy film-mad. The early conversion of the projectors to link up with talkie transmitters was brought about entirely through Mountbatten's ingenuity and had been the means by which the medium-wave transmission had been picked up for the King's broadcast.

The conversion, according to the company in England that made the equipment, would cost not less than £400. This was a ridiculous figure, which the Admiralty would not for one moment countenance. "I thought the Navy deserved to have the talkies Edwina had told me about as soon as anyone else," Mountbatten recounted when talking of this period. "Sooner if possible. So I did a very simple thing. I designed a loudspeaker system myself which could be made for eighty-five pounds. Most of the parts could be had as spares from the Fleet Repair Ship, anyway. It worked very well. I used to visit ships and help with the installation."

.   .   .

1932 a copy of the Sunday newspaper *The People* for the
ninth of that month arrived in the post at Casa Medina. The
fleet was in harbour, Edwina had been there since the previous August,
and the family was complete. Mountbatten had been promoted to
commander four months earlier and was awaiting an appointment to
his first ship. He had also, more anxiously, been awaiting the packet
that arrived that morning.

Friends in London had already warned the Mountbattens by telegram that a scandalous article about Edwina had been printed in one
of the Sunday tabloids, and they were expecting the worst. They were
both hardened to the often malicious tittle-tattle of the gossip columnists in both England and America. But they had never read anything
like this before. Mountbatten said, "We'll have to get on to the solicitors."

"Do you really think it's necessary?" Edwina asked. "If we sue for
libel, it'll mean the whole thing coming up again. I'll have to go to
London and you'll have to get leave."

"We'll do what they say. But I don't think the paper should be
allowed to get away with that."

"Behind the Scenes" was a gossip column which had run for some
time in *The People* under the by-line "The Watcher." In this issue it was
headlined

FAMOUS HOSTESS EXILED
SOCIETY SHAKEN BY TERRIBLE SCANDAL

I am able to reveal today the sequel to a scandal which has shaken Society to
the very depths. It concerns one of the leading hostesses in the country, a woman
highly connected and immensely rich.

Associations with a coloured man became so marked that they were the talk of
the West End. Then one day the couple were caught in compromising circumstances.

The sequel is that the Society woman has been given the hint to clear out of
England for a couple of years to let the affair blow over, and the hint comes from
a quarter which cannot be ignored.

To almost anyone who followed the gossip columns, "the woman"
could only be Edwina and the "quarter which could not be ignored"
could only be the Palace. To the more knowledgeable, "the coloured

man" was Paul Robeson, whose *Othello* had recently taken the West End by storm.

The solicitors recommended that the Mountbattens issue proceedings for libel against Odhams Newspapers, the publishers of *The People*, and they both returned to London on 6 July to give evidence. The case came up before the Lord Chief Justice, Lord Hewart; the defendants retained Sir Patrick Hastings; and Norman Birkett, who had until recently been held with a retainer for Odhams, acted for the Mountbattens.

Birkett opened the case strongly: "It is not too much to say that it is the most monstrous and most atrocious libel of which I myself in all my experience in these courts have ever heard. Your Lordship," he continued, "may think that the word 'scandal' at the top of the article, coupled with the words 'the hint comes from a quarter which cannot be ignored,' puts it beyond all doubt that the writer deliberately intended to defame Lady Louis Mountbatten."

Later, Birkett asked if "in the very exceptional circumstances of this case," Lord and Lady Louis Mountbatten might go into the witness box.

The judge agreed. Mountbatten was first. He was anxious to clarify at once the real reason why Edwina was living on Malta. He therefore merely made a statement that he was serving in the Mediterranean Fleet, and that his wife and children were, consequently, living there.

Edwina followed him into the box. Birkett said, "The second paragraph in this publication deals with a coloured man. Is there one single word of truth in the allegations there made?"

Edwina replied loudly and firmly, "Not one single word. In fact, I have never in the whole course of my life met the man referred to."

"Your friends have named to you the coloured man supposed to be referred to in the paragraph?"

Edwina agreed that they had, although Paul Robeson's name was never mentioned in court. Edwina confirmed again that "the whole thing is a preposterous story."

For the defendants, Sir Patrick Hastings made an unqualified apology—"genuine and deep regrets." As a point of principle, Edwina refused all damages, which would certainly have been heavy. The case attracted enormous interest, and their wiser friends wished they had ignored the article, believing that the whole thing would have been forgotten in a few weeks.

The truth was that Edwina did know the coloured singer Leslie Hutchinson. All West End society loved Hutch, whose sentimental songs and piano playing enchanted night-club audiences. Moreover, Edwina had rather foolishly given him a cigarette case with her name engraved on it. She did not always sufficiently consider the consequences of her actions, and regarded "proceeding with care" as only half living. But she cannot be blamed for taking out libel proceedings, although these brought the matter to the attention of people who did not regularly read the tabloids, among them the royal family. It is very doubtful that the attention of King George and Queen Mary would have been drawn to the article, which was only one of numerous scandal stories printed every week, if the case had not come up before the Lord Chief Justice and been so widely reported in *The Times* and the *Daily Telegraph*. On the day after the hearing Mountbatten, his mother and Edwina drove to Buckingham Palace for luncheon. This was read by many people as a gesture of sympathy and solidarity by the Crown. But in fact, George V and Queen Mary were not at all pleased about the business, and there was a noticeable cooling of relations for some time after the case, which Edwina strongly resented.

There were other "very exceptional circumstances of this case." Members of the Bar unconnected with it were curious to know how the Lord Chief Justice's Court was open at 9:30 A.M. to listen to the case which—because no one had been informed of this almost unprecedentally early hour—meant in effect that it had been heard *in camera*.

They also wondered if Edwina could really have succeeded in proving that she was the person referred to, and whether Odhams Newspapers, if informed beforehand that Edwina would not accept damages, had not been strongly tempted to give the required apology, whether or not they were guilty of libel, especially if she had agreed secretly to pay all the costs.

Later there was gossip about the Earl of Sefton, who fell in love with Edwina, although no one was sure how she felt about him. She and Hugh Sefton would often be seen dining out with "Poppy" Baring and Prince George—a steady foursome at a time when dining alone with any man other than your husband was still not acceptable.

Perhaps Mountbatten should have accepted earlier that Edwina—rich, emotional and physically volatile, often alone in London, easily bored and with a range of friends as wide as the Mediterranean—was likely to have affairs. Perhaps he preferred the sailor's licence of the blind eye, even to himself. When some three years after he was married he could no longer ignore what was going on, when everyone knew except him, it hit him very hard. He told Barbara Cartland, his close woman friend of his last years, "I was terribly upset and found it hard to believe. I had never looked at anyone. It was an awful shock."

In 1919, on his way to Switzerland to see his sister Alice and her children, he had stopped off in Paris and—encouraged by the future Duke of Gloucester—visited the usual places in the traditional English gentleman's style. There were plenty of flirtations on the town with the Prince of Wales, but Mountbatten was an innocent in love and remained an innocent all his life.

Women were always more important than men in Mountbatten's life, and he was always at his best with them—amusing, teasing, charming, informative. With women there was no sign of the need to dominate which was always there in masculine company. Barbara Cartland declares that he could not live without women around him when he was not on duty or at sea. "He adored amusing women," she says, "and liked them very feminine and well-dressed, with small wrists and high heels."

Mountbatten knew that he was at his most agreeable with pretty women around him, and when he was in a position to do so, he always arranged for them to be on his staff. Everyone who worked with him from the time he became head of Combined Operations remembers them today—"an absolutely smashing lot!" Their contribution to his success and the outcome of his campaigns was as great as that of any of his advisers and staff officers (and a great deal more than some of them), who tended to joke patronizingly among themselves about "Dickie's harem."

Women who knew him well agree that the sexual act, in itself and in isolation from the exciting hurly-burly and challenge of professional life, was never of importance to Mountbatten. This writer can testify that he liked to hear about it from others, enjoyed joking about it, enjoyed hearing about the sexual experiences of his male friends and

s. He was, in short, a man who enjoyed the sexual act more in
and anecdote than in fact and practice, and the voyeur strain
w... ronger in him than in most men. When he became reconciled to
Edwina's infidelities, he liked to hear about them from her. Because his
sense of family pride was so strong, he even came to be proud of her
powerful sexuality, which also fascinated him, no less because he was
wholly unable to satisfy it. Twelve years after Edwina's death, her
letters to Jawaharlal Nehru, the great Indian statesman, were discovered by Mountbatten's family, and he revealed eager impatience to
read the passages detailing their affair.

Mountbatten also enjoyed the company of young men, especially
when he was older. They posed no competitive problems either, and he
enjoyed charming and flattering them, too. If he willingly accepted—
even preferred—relationships with women without active sex, the
thought of closer relations with men was something he never even con-
templated. "He wouldn't have risked his career," his defendants
against widespread posthumous accusations of homosexuality declared.
Indeed he would not. But he was by nature, constitution, upbringing
and morality remote from irregular relations with other men.

Mountbatten could not bear the callous manner in which some of his
contemporaries treated their mistresses. His friendship with the Prince
of Wales survived the abdication crisis with ease. It survived only with
difficulty the Prince's treatment of Mrs. Dudley Ward, who had been
his faithful and discreet mistress for nearly seventeen years. After an
anxious period of nursing her critically ill daughter, she telephoned St.
James's Palace in the usual way, only to hear a tearful voice on the
switchboard at the other end announcing the end of the affair in these
words: "I'm terribly sorry, ma'am, I have orders not to put you
through to His Royal Highness."

There were periods early on in the Mountbatten marriage when both
were miserable, and the misery always stemmed from her affairs. They
were, at times, better apart, and the opportunities for separate lives
were always there. "The real tragedy was," Mountbatten often said,
"that we were closer than we had ever been and were getting on marvellously just before she died, and were looking forward to growing old
together because we had everything in common."

.   .   .

On the last day of 1932, Mountbatten got his first command. He could ask for nothing better. It was a destroyer, and a brand-new one, the *Daring*, one of the "D" class of 1,400 tons, with a speed of 35 knots, and an armament of four 4.7-inch guns and eight 21-inch torpedo tubes. "Here I am in my first command—a bit dazed but feeling very grand," he wrote to his mother.[1]

"A captain is God Almighty," he said in his biographical television series. "He can do exactly what he wants with his ship. You can make Easter Sunday into Good Friday. You can shape the spirit of the ship to your own ideas. You can make yourself hated or loved. And for all this, they pay you—pay you for doing the most wonderful job in the world."

Mountbatten rapidly worked the ship's company up to a high level of efficiency. "*Daring* by name, and daring by nature—that's us," he told his destroyer's company, and used a quote from the sixteenth-century geographer Richard Hakluyt as the ship's motto: "We have made every sea the highway of our daring." "Ah, pride before a fall," he was telling himself only weeks later, remembering the wonderful letter Nelson wrote to Fanny from the *Vanguard* when he was blockading the French fleet in Toulon and met a disastrous storm: "I believe firmly that it was the Almighty's goodness, to check my consummate vanity. I hope it has made me a better officer . . ."

Far from making every sea the *Daring*'s highway, his flotilla was ordered out to Sinapore to swap ships with the China Station flotilla, which had old destroyers built in a hurry during World War I. There was much gloom in the flotilla at the prospect of exchanging their new wonder destroyers for the old "tin cans," but Mountbatten would have no depression in his ship. It was the sort of situation in which his natural resiliency was shown at its best. At Singapore, where they took over H.M.S. *Wishart*, named after some nonentity of an admiral, he called up all hands and spoke to his men: "We have just left behind a ship with a great name. We have now got the only ship in the Royal Navy with an even greater name. Our new ship is named after the Almighty himself, to whom we pray daily, 'Our Father wishart in heaven.'"

The flotilla sailed back to the Suez Canal and the Mediterranean, through the Indian Ocean at 10 knots to conserve fuel and the old turbines. To keep the men amused and interested, Mountbatten started a ship's newspaper, organized a band and had competitive games every day and evening entertainments. Rolling through those hot, sulky seas at snail's pace, a ship's company could easily become slack and bored. There was no time for either in the *Wishart*. When they finally arrived at Malta, Mountbatten had a tight, happy ship in which he knew every man by name.

There were flotilla exercises as well, but no opportunity on the voyage for gunnery practice. The Captain (D)* was an old shipmate of Mountbatten's father, a gunnery enthusiast called H. T. Baillie-Grohman. At the beginning he had taken a bleak view of Mountbatten, and (like Roger Keyes) had to be converted slowly to a pro-Mountbatten way of thinking. When Mountbatten had first been appointed to the *Daring*, Baillie-Grohman had called him to his cabin. "I told him," Baillie-Grohman said before he died recently, " 'Look, Dickie, it's all right for you. But please remember in this flotilla that there's hardly one of us with two brass pennies to rub together. So, be a good chap and watch it.' He did, too; he really behaved very well, and there was no sign of that early extravagance I had seen when he first came out."[2]

Mountbatten was to have a brush with this officer later. He liked Baillie-Grohman but thought he lacked the final polish of a leader. When they arrived at Malta it was a Friday morning, and Baillie-Grohman had been looking forward to taking the flotilla straight out for target practice to show his and the flotilla's keenness. Instead, he was frustrated by the impossibility of drawing targets before Monday morning. The flotilla leader made a signal to all destroyers which was brought to Mountbatten by his yeoman with a long face. "I know how anxious you all are to get on with working up," it ran. "You share my disappointment that we shall not be able to do so until Monday. Please inform your ship's company."

Mountbatten read it with dismay. But as he had shown earlier with this crew, he believed strongly that bad news could always be phrased cheerfully. So, there and then, he rewrote his senior's message to all hands: "We have just reached out destination after seven weeks at sea. The Captain (D) believes that we have now become experienced seamen quicker than any other destroyer flotilla in peacetime. Although

*"D" for destroyers—an important service distinction.

he is now very anxious to start working up, he has very kindly arranged for us to have a full weekend in harbour to rest and recuperate."

The notice was received with cheers, and the liberty boats were soon on their way . . .

The working-up gunnery practice began promptly at dawn on Monday, the flotilla's crews buoyant and enthusiastic after their forty-eight hours of shore leave. Mountbatten had given much thought to destroyer gunnery and from his father's as well as his own experience had, as often happened, reached an unorthodox conclusion. It had for a long time been common practice—he called it a fetish—for destroyers to go in for fast shooting with the standard 4.7-inch guns. Baillie-Grohman was of the orthodox school, which was more romantic than practical: the "Jutland image" of racing at the enemy, then helm hard over, torpedoes away, guns blazing. Mountbatten held that one would in fact make more hits if the guns were laid with more deliberate care and fired less frequently. The *Wishart*'s showing at target practice appeared poor, and many of his fellow commanders wondered what had happened to Mountbatten's usually keen and competitive destroyer. Then the results began to come in. The *Wishart* came out on top by a wide margin and had expended less than half the shells of her opponents.

The summer regatta, the most important contest of the year, was still three months away, but Mountbatten was already actively preparing for it. Early in June he addressed the ship's company on the subject. "A ship embarking on the regatta with a will to win," he told his men, "is a ship with a healthy morale bred into her—and the guts needed for winning a pulling race will be invaluable in war." He told them that the *Wishart* was going to win everything—no question of that. Not just gunnery, but boxing and football, pistol and rifle shooting. And *all* the races. He told them that they were going to be Cock of the Fleet. And they believed him.

All through that summer the training continued relentlessly. The summer cruise brought no relief. "I had a 'dry-puller' installed on the forward deck," Mountbatten said, recalling those days, "and every morning I mustered the crew on the fo'c'sle for dry-pulling exercises. Every man would have to pull so many strokes. It was quite hard going, but it prevented them getting slack at sea." ("Slack" being a relative word in the *Wishart*.)

Mountbatten had been doing some more calculations. He took the distance between the place where the first oar and the last oar entered the water, and the distance between their seats, recorded the strokes per minute, got out some graph paper . . . Thirty-eight and a half strokes a minute produced the best results. "It was quite simple. But no one had thought of doing the sum before. We kept to that figure for the whaler."

The regatta took place on 4 September, the high point of the Mediterranean Fleet's year, with the whole fleet watching, and the wives and families of officers and men who were on the island, and most of the population of Malta, too. The whaler races had all the drama, the cliffhanger uncertainty almost to the end, of a Hollywood thriller. The performance might have been scripted by Mountbatten himself. "If you don't win, I'll derate the lot of you!" he called out to his petty officers. There was no need. At the end of the long day his blistered, weary men were the winners. There were ferocious celebrations on board that night. A live cock was lashed to a spar high on the *Wishart's* mast. A telegram from the King was read out. It was all very stylish.

At the end of the commission, when he said good-bye to the *Wishart's* company, he said, "When we arrived at this station, I said we would win every trophy that was to be won. As you all know, the *Wishart* triumphed in every game except football, and in football we lost every match. I feel that I was directly responsible for this because I quite forgot to specify which trophy I meant to win, the silver cup for the best team or the wooden spoon for the worst. We won the spoon, so I can safely say that I fulfilled my promise."

This little speech is typical of many that he made throughout his professional career—humorous, flattering, unpatronizing, affectionate, and, you can be sure, with a spontaneous ring to every phrase.

Within seconds, Mountbatten could hold the attention of a bunch of cynical newspapermen kept waiting in the cold for too long, as he could a company of demoralized soldiers isolated for weeks in the Burma jungle, weary of canned food, mosquitoes, damp heat and the ever-present, ever-unseen danger lurking around them. Like a trouper who has trod the boards for years, he was consistent and never failed. In a moment the audience was warmed, encouraged, amused and given new self-respect and new will.

Although his men adored him, many others felt that his success could have been tempered with a measure of modesty. And modesty was as remote, on that summer afternoon, as a cloud in the Mediterranean sky. Just a touch of humility would have provided the antidote to a rankling resentment. Why did a man as clever and as sensitive to the feelings of others, who could read the mood of those around him with such speed and accuracy, not apply that antidote? Why did he not recognize that his style of total professionalism, of showy bravado, was not always liked by the British, whose feelings about success and winning are so confused, contradictory and totally mystifying to many foreigners? Was it because he *was* a half-foreigner that he failed to see what was happening? Would an orthodox public-school education, with its force-feeding of a diet of shame at too much success and shame at failure, and a great deal more bullying than at Osborne or Dartmouth—would that have helped?

Again, one must look at his father and observe the parallel and similarity. Prince Louis had made insufficient efforts to get rid of his German accent and failed to see that regular visits to his German castle and his German naval relations at a time of growing international distrust might be misinterpreted. His son failed to comprehend that a beautiful rich wife, an enormous white yacht and a flashy Hispano-Suiza might be misunderstood as the provocative flaunting of wealth and privilege before the less wealthy and less privileged.

The royal connections of both Prince Louis and Mountbatten, and in Mountbatten the great wealth, were also slightly discomfiting and obstructive to the forming of friendships. Neither father nor son quite "fitted into" the Royal Navy, even though both were exceptionally able officers. But just as Prince Louis could have entered the wardroom of a German battleship in 1908 and at once been accepted as a fellow officer, so Mountbatten could have served in a German pocket battleship in 1938. Disregarding politics (which the German navy largely did), both men would have felt comfortably at home, more comfortably than in their own service, just as their German fellow officers would have felt comfortable with them, and their uninhibited competitive professionalism.

It was this same professionalism which led Mountbatten to take a fresh, unorthodox view of the Navy's matériel and equipment. Once again like his father, who served on the committee responsible for the revolutionary battleship *Dreadnought* of 1906, Mountbatten for his part did much for destroyer design in the 1930s. From a curious and trivial incident relating to the improvement of his own comfort in the *Daring* he came to know A. P. Cole of the Royal Corps of Naval Constructors, a brilliant designer.

Mountbatten, who had never much enjoyed an austere way of life, was disappointed to find that the very up-to-date *Daring* had no basin with running hot and cold water in the captain's cabin. So he engaged some Maltese dockyard workmen to fit one. They ran the outlet pipe into the waste pipe of the wardroom bathroom on the inboard side of the ship and then through a bulkhead. In the middle of all this work, while Mountbatten was ashore, Cole came on board, went to the captain's cabin and saw the men working at what looked like a hole in the ship's bottom.

As Mountbatten reported the event to a friend later, "The next I knew of it, I was summoned to the Vice-Admiral, Malta. Cole was there repeating the charge, in front of me, that I was interfering with the structure of my ship without permission and making a hole in the bottom. I said, "You're a liar. I am doing nothing of the kind, and I think it is amazing that you should snoop about in a captain's cabin without permission, and then report him for something he has not done.' I ended by saying rudely, 'No wonder constructors are not allowed to wear naval uniform!'

"The Vice-Admiral then kicked him out and ordered him to report and apologize to the C.O. *Daring*. It was the best thing that ever happened. We became great buddies after this and I had a powerful ally in the Naval Constructors."

It was Mountbatten and Cole who were jointly responsible for the single-funnel, two-boiler design, and Mountbatten alone who conceived and had installed the all-covering bridge right across the ship, with a deep drop covering the catwalk, a slanting roof and a windscreen, which allowed (for the first time) the bridge personnel to remain dry in any conditions. It marked the end of the era when a destroyer captain was supposed to go into action soaking wet and half blinded by spume. This was more like driving a car with full visibility even in a rainstorm.

Before the "Mountbatten bridge" there was the "Mountbatten station-keeping device." Destroyers are nimble, manoeuvrable, very fast ships which normally work close together in flotillas. They are not unlike a squadron of bombers flying in formation. To keep correct station, therefore, is one of the most difficult and important priorities. Adapting a device he had seen in a French battleship, Mountbatten conceived his "station-keeping device," which, together with its cousin the "line-of-bearing keeper," which was also Mountbatten's invention, were installed in all classes of destroyers completed on the outbreak of the war. As usual, most commanders hated them at first and later came to rely heavily upon them.

The imminence of two very different crises became evident during Mountbatten's time with the *Wishart*. The first involved the Prince of Wales, who had dropped Mrs. Dudley Ward for Lady Furness, wife of the shipping magnate Christopher Furness, and then in 1931 had met Wallis Simpson. Mountbatten, as the Prince's confidant in all things, learned soon of his growing affection for the American divorcée, and of the royal family's concern. Mountbatten's mother saw evidence of the strength of their mutual affection at the time of the Silver Jubilee in 1935 and wrote complainingly to Mountbatten of the way Mrs. Simpson insisted on showing this publicly.

Before leaving the Mediterranean, Mountbatten and Edwina saw the Prince and Mrs. Simpson several times, at Cannes, Monte Carlo and Leghorn. They were apparently inseparable, and it was clear that this affair was different from any that had gone before it. There was a new expression of fulfilment and happiness in the Prince's face. He was relaxed and easy with this American woman, who on first acquaintance concealed a clever mind and steel determination beneath a seeming naïveté.

The two couples made a bright, brittle foursome, watched by curious and envious eyes in the more expensive and exclusive resorts of the Mediterranean and the Adriatic, the target of snapshots for the gossip magazines. Edwina intuitively scented serious trouble. Mountbatten was simply pleased to see his old friend happy with a woman who, at last, appeared to give him complete satisfaction. The thought that, with his father's death and succession to the throne, she would press him to marry her did not cross his mind.

On 2 October of that year Mussolini invaded Abyssinia, setting in motion the series of invasions and annexations that led to the world war four years later. Britain and France at first reacted strongly, and sanctions were imposed on Italy. There was a real likelihood of war, and the Mediterranean Fleet was placed on a war footing, its main base moved from vulnerable Malta to Alexandria. The *Wishart*'s flotilla, however, was left behind in Grand Harbour to keep the flag flying. The old destroyers were considered expendable, to commit what damage they could if they were attacked. The "do or die boys" they were called by the other units of the fleet as they sailed east. Edwina, typically, became the wireless announcer, her optimistic voice bringing cheer to the islanders and the Navy—what was left of it.

Mountbatten liked to speculate on how they would have fared against the full might of Mussolini's fleet. It was a very modern fleet, with many exceptionally fast and well designed ships. "We should have put up the best show we could, and have done some damage. Judging by the Italians' performance when war did come, our flotilla would have easily outfought any destroyers we came up against. But a lot of their cruisers were much faster than we."

It was presumed that in the event of war the French would be allies. The nearest French base was Bizerte, and Mountbatten was given the task of liaisoning with the French admiral there about docking facilities in the event of Malta dockyards being put out of action.

"I knew him quite well," Mountbatten said of this visit, "and I knew he spoke English. But when I arrived with the *Wishart*, do you know he wouldn't speak a word of English? And he ordered all his staff to talk French, too. Fortunately, I had taken that translators' course and kept my French up. But they were completely uncooperative and extremely rude to us. It was an omen of what we were in for later."

Mountbatten's return to England in March 1936 appropriately coincided with the march of the German armies into the demilitarized Rhineland. Mountbatten believed strongly in air power and knew that it was already changing the face of naval strategy and tactics. He was given a staff appointment in the Naval Air Division. Stationed in London, at the Admiralty, he was in a position to learn the truth about the nation's defences, and by his energy, skill and connections at the highest levels, to influence events far more than any other thirty-six-year-old naval commander.

Edwina had kept Brook House going all through the years of the Depression at an annual cost of around £20,000. Even by Cassel standards, the lawyers thought this unduly extravagant. Now, amid a thunder of publicity and falling rubble, it was torn down and a block of luxury apartments erected in its place—under the old name. The top two Edwina kept for herself, as a superduplex and London's first penthouse.

From the outside, the two towering floors were quite distinct from the rest of the building, but to distinguish them further they were floodlit at night. The penthouse had thirty rooms (five reception rooms could be made into a single ballroom or a cinema seating 150), a nursery wing, kitchens and servants' quarters, all built to the highest standards of comfort and luxury.

Here the Mountbattens lived when "in town" until the outbreak of the war, Mountbatten every morning descending in his pride and joy ("the nonstop fastest lift in London") to deal with the problems brought about by the rapid expansion of the Navy, and the problems of air power in particular.

The first priority in Mountbatten's appointment brief was, as he put it, "to bring the Fleet Air Arm back into the Navy." The RAF's victory after the Great War in retaining joint control over naval flying had been an inefficient and untidy arrangement. The naval pilots were enthusiastic and skilful but were operating with planes fit only for the scrap heap. The air arm was far behind the U.S. Navy, and even more inadequate in contrast with the magnificent Japanese air arm, which, ironically, the Royal Navy had helped build up at the time of the Anglo-Japanese Treaty of Friendship.

One memorandum Mountbatten found on his desk when he came to the Naval Air Division ran:

Can anyone doubt that if we went to war tomorrow, complete chaos would reign in the Navy's Air Services? Where are the machines? Where is the trained personnel? Where is the up-to-date material? They simply don't exist. There is not a squadron afloat today with aircraft of a type which was not in service three years ago. There is not a squadron with a type whose design is less than ten years old.

Unlike Prime Minister Stanley Baldwin, Mountbatten believed (with Churchill) that time was running out, and that unification of the air arm had become urgently necessary. Churchill, as coordinator of all agitators for strengthening the nation's and empire's defences, was Mountbatten's first ally. Early in 1937 Mountbatten sent Churchill an eleven-page memorandum concisely advancing the case for the Navy's plenary control of the Fleet Air Arm at the earliest opportunity.

Mountbatten had always been prepared—even eagerly willing—to use circuitous routes to reach his desired goal. It was the successful arrival that mattered, he argued, whether it was by way of an out-of-office ambitious genius like Churchill or through Buckingham Palace. The Fleet Air Arm Memorandum brought Mountbatten into that secret club of grey figures feeding Churchill confidential information that proved the deplorable state of the defences and allowed him to attack the government with facts and authority.

This group of anxious patriots made a disparate lot, ranging from Cabinet ministers like Lord Swinton and Anthony Eden to the novelist Sir Philip Gibbs, and including admirals and generals. Wing-Commander Charles Anderson was probably closer to Churchill than any other airman and was a steady conveyor of information on RAF defences. Mountbatten concerned himself almost entirely with Fleet Air Arm affairs.

Mountbatten's victory on behalf of the Navy occurred on 30 July 1937, after some bloody skirmishing with the RAF. A tremendous amount of work remained to be done, and the two years remaining before the outbreak of the war were not long enough to complete the changeover, with the result that RAF personnel were still serving in carriers during the early months of hostilities. Little of the modern equipment had come through, no modern fighters were available comparable with the RAF Spitfires, and 150-mph biplanes were the main equipment. As a consequence, many defeats were suffered and many lives were unnecessarily lost in the early months of the war. While at the Admiralty, Mountbatten formed the strong view that the anti-aircraft defence of R.N. ships was inadequate, and he was among those who campaigned against powerfully entrenched opinion for improving them. In January 1937 an expatriate Austrian engineer working for the Oerlikon armament works in Switzerland arrived in London on a sales mission. He had, he claimed, a very fast-firing gun to offer with a very high muzzle velocity using small 20-mm explosive shells. It was, he said, the answer to the German Stuka, the JU-87 single-engine dive bomber.

Mountbatten learned of his arrival, liked the sound of the gun, liked the sound of the man, his own father being Austrian-born too. "I had this man Antoine Gazda in my office at the Admiralty all one morning," Mountbatten said when discussing dive-bombing techniques with this writer, "trying to shoot him down. I used every argument against his Oerlikon gun, but he shot me down instead. I was convinced that this was the weapon which could save ships and lives from the low-flying dive bomber and torpedo bomber. I arranged for a meeting between Gazda and some of the more important members of the [Admiralty] Board, the DNO [Director of Naval Operations], the Controller, my own boss, and so on. On the morning, Gazda turned up with his notes and equipment, but no voice, so I took over, doing a quick conversion from the metres in his notes to feet and yards. It went down all right."

But that was only the beginning of the battle—a battle against entrenched opinion, apathy, conservatism, a belief that the multibarrel two-pounder pom-pom which had been in service for years could deal with anything flying. The trouble with the pom-pom was that it was too inflexible and too slow to bear on the target. The other trouble was that British gunmakers, notably Vickers, saw business going abroad.

Delay and procrastination continued for two years. In the end, Mountbatten persuaded Oerlikon to proceed with an initial order on the expectation that the converted and enlightened Admiral Sir Roger Backhouse would confirm it when he became First Sea Lord. Backhouse almost immediately died of overwork, and Treasury authority was not given for the order until the month war broke out.

It is incalculable how many destroyers and other ships might have survived dive-bomber attack at the Dunkirk evacuation and during the Norwegian campaign if Mountbatten's lobbying for the Oerlikon had been successful earlier, or how many more lives and ships would have been lost if, among all his other tasks and preoccupations, he had not battled so hard and for so long for this deadly cannon when he was at the Admiralty. The ultimate irony was that when he got back to sea, though his own ship was one of the first to be equipped with Oerlikons, they failed to save her against a mass onslaught of Stukas.

There is a famous late-1930s photograph of the entire Mountbatten family in uniform, with the two girls dressed as Girl Guides. It reflects the feeling that was sweeping Britain: The time for play was over. Britain must be prepared. Britain meant business.

"I knew that war was coming, as night follows day, just as my father did by 1912," Mountbatten said of this period. "As a serving officer, there was little I could say in public, unlike Winston, who sometimes seemed to be the one voice of sanity. I had two assets, however. I was of German descent and like my father understood the German mind. I was well-informed, and thanks to my position and my relationship to the court, I had the ear of powerful men—others as well as Winston. This was what my father had meant when he had said that at first my privileged position would be to my disadvantage, but later it would be useful."

Mountbatten recalled a meeting. "I mentioned again and again to Eden and Salisbury my view of the German situation. Then, at the time Halifax was sent out to double-cross Eden in Rome, I had a call from Eden.* Could he and Salisbury come and see me? I suggested Broadlands, being a convenient point for all three of us. We talked at very great length. I remember word for word what I said: 'I have been trying to make you English people understand what I as a man of German descent clearly understand: that this situation is unquestionably going to end in war unless this country can make *really* clear the circumstances under which it would fight. As long as Chamberlain is controlling foreign policy, the issue is cloudy and befogged. You must resign, both of you. You must speak in the House supporting each other and denouncing in unequivocal terms the policy Chamberlain is pursuing. You must say you will not be associated with a policy leading to war, explain the alternative policy, and then intelligent people will rally round you.

---

*The British Foreign Secretary resigned in protest against his government's appeasement policies towards Germany and Italy. Eden's successor, Lord Halifax, visited Italy on 11 January 1939, when Halifax found the atmosphere in Rome "most friendly and easy." But Mountbatten's use of the word "double-cross" was unjust and inaccurate.

" 'Unless you do this, you'll strangle yourself with your old school tie.'

"I know Eden agreed with me. But he never said a word. The rest is history. Hitler never knew, he never understood what the calibre of this country really was, and a bit more than a year later, we had slipped into war again . . .'"

In that same year, Mountbatten attended the Higher Commanders' Course at Aldershot, where he met many of the senior officers of the three services beside whom he was to fight. Seen now in retrospect, it looked as if the hands of fate were moulding events and his career into a shape that would be impelled into a trajectory as unswerving and spectacular as that of a 16-inch naval shell. Ten days before the war broke out, Mountbatten, now promoted to captain, took over from the builders the ship that will forever be associated with his name, H.M.S. *Kelly*. He had been appointed Captain (D) of the 5th Destroyer Flotilla—eight men o' war which found themselves (with Mountbatten's connivance) at the centre of the fighting at sea almost from the first gun blast.

The *Kelly*, of course, was unique. There was no man o' war like her in any navy. What could possibly be more suitable than that she should be fitted out in part as a royal yacht? George VI and Queen Elizabeth were scheduled to make a state visit to Belgium in the late summer of 1939, and Mountbatten had arranged for his new destroyer to be their conveyance. The royal-cabin equipment and fittings were, therefore, of the most luxurious order possible. And so they remained, to Mountbatten's advantage, when the war led to the cancellation of the visit. This time there was no need to fit a makeshift, illicit hot- and cold-water basin in his ship. He had his own bathroom *en suite*.

Instead of the King and Queen, it was the King's brother and his wife who enjoyed the royal-yacht luxuries of the *Kelly*: one of Mountbatten's first wartime missions was to bring home the Duke and Duchess of Windsor from France. Mountbatten had remained in touch with his cousin after the abdication and had even offered to be best man at his wedding, but had been turned down sharply by the Duke, who still innocently imagined that his wedding could be classed as "royal," at which, customarily, there was no best man, only "supporters," in his case preferably his brothers. But Wallis, who was never on easy terms with Mountbatten after the abdication, saw to it that he was not invited to the wedding. She was jealous of David's old friendships and especially jealous of Mountbatten's intimate relations with all the royal family, who had treated her so shabbily. She was suspicious of Mountbatten's role in the abdication crisis, and believed, with reason, that Mountbatten had opposed both the idea of a morganatic marriage and the abdication.

It was indeed hard for the woman who had once believed that she could be Queen of England to observe the solidarity of the ranks that closed around the Court of St. James's after she had—in her eyes—been rejected. With his sharp eye and swift judgement, Mountbatten recognized the compass courses he should steer through the shoals. He knew that he carried what the new Queen would call the stigma of close friendship with the man whose weakness, selfishness and sexual appetite had forced her own beloved husband unwillingly onto the throne.

It was part of the Mountbatten creed to avoid making enemies and to keep friends. In 1937 he accomplished the double task of retaining good relations with the ex-King and developing his amicable but not intimate relations with the new King. In Paris the Duchess of Windsor read with displeasure reports like this one in the *Daily Sketch*:

> By accompanying the Duke and Duchess of Kent to the Westminster [Coronation] rehearsal last week, Lord and Lady Louis Mountbatten showed how skilfully they had maintained their position in the new social reign, despite a long-standing friendship with the King who was never crowned.
>
> With the Duke and Duchess of Kent, they had watched the Duke of Gloucester, as first Prince of the Royal blood, rehearse his bow before an empty chair. When Lady Louis emerged to public view, she was seen chatting vivaciously to the Duke of Kent, while her husband shared a joke with Duchess Marina of Kent.

"I had been agonized for David at the time of the abdication," Mountbatten explained. "I know it was terrible for him. Winston was among those who believed he couldn't live without her. I didn't think that, but I know it was a terrible decision for him. I always thought it was his duty to remain King and told him that he ought to give up Wallis if that was the only alternative. But we remained friends—Edwina and I were too fond of them both for there to be any break." There was a break later, after the war, though Mountbatten was never aware of any cooling off and acted as host when the Duke returned to the country with the Duchess in June 1966 for the unveiling of a plaque in memory of the Duke's mother, Queen Mary.

But in those early, dark days of the war, the *Kelly* arrived in Cherbourg, on 12 September 1939. Churchill, First Lord again, had sent not only Mountbatten on this errand but his own son Randolph. The Duke and Duchess were awaiting them, together with the usual mountain of luggage. The Duke greeted his cousin and shook Randolph's hand, glancing down at the spurs he was wearing. Randolph had dressed in the uniform of the 4th Hussars for the occasion, and the Duke pointed out with glee that his spurs were on inside out and upside down—a gaffe that Mountbatten had been the first to notice but had left for the Duke to point out.

The *Kelly* cast off at four o'clock, and set course at high speed for Portsmouth. "I enjoyed the voyage very much," said Mountbatten. "David and Wallis were very impressed with the luxury, and David said, 'You're doing yourself very nicely, Dickie.' Then he came up onto the bridge with me as it got dark and we approached Portsmouth, and we chatted about old days. Of course, the English coast was blacked out, and I remember thinking back to that evening with my father in the Admiralty, with the crowds cheering for the start of the war." This time he didn't hear a sound above the *Kelly*'s engines . . .

5

THE *KELLY* AT WAR

*I*t was somehow supremely right that Mountbatten's body still bore the tattered remains of a jersey decorated with the emblem of H.M.S. *Kelly* when it was recovered from the sea. The brief fighting career of this ship, retold time and again, made into a musical, fictionalized in Noël Coward's film *In Which We Serve*, grew into a legend in Mountbatten's own time, and has flourished for forty years. The wonder is that the ill-starred ship survived for as long as she did, for she was seldom out of trouble.

The *Kelly* was one of the "J" and "K" class destroyers, which Mountbatten had helped Cole to design, rushed to completion for the outbreak of World War II—modest-sized vessels with a speed of around 34 knots, armed with ten torpedo tubes and six 4.7-inch guns. Unlike the guns of most contemporary foreign destroyers, which were dual-purpose weapons, the *Kelly*'s could elevate to only 40 degrees, and were therefore restricted in their usefulness against high-flying aircraft. Her light anti-aircraft defences were also inadequate, even when later supplemented with Oerlikon cannons.

With her single raked funnel (the configuration to Mountbatten's design) and the black band singling her out as flotilla leader, she looked a fine, modern, businesslike fighting ship, and Mountbatten was tremendously proud of her. "Keep On" was the motto he contrived for her; and that seemed to her company to be peculiarly appropriate as they learned from their captain's first speech that they were going to store and munition the ship in three days instead of the customary three weeks. "We have a job to do. Let's do it."

The "phoney war," from September 1939 until the German invasion of Denmark and Norway in April 1940, may have been quiet for the Army and Air Force. At sea it was action from the beginning, with the German navy recommencing commerce warfare with surface ships and U-boats just as if 11 November 1918 had marked only a pause in the relentless dual between the two navies. The word "phoney" made the Royal Navy furious. Even before she delivered the Duke and Duchess of Windsor to Portsmouth, the *Kelly* had been in action, an anti-submarine exercise turning into the real thing when the ship's "Asdic" (submarine detection apparatus) caught a "ping" and the *Kelly* released a pattern of depth charges.

All that came to the surface was a lot of dead fish and some oil. Mountbatten claimed a "probable." Admiralty Intelligence had a good laugh at that, for they knew that the nearest U-boats were many miles away. But they were already doing terrible damage, sinking the liner *Athenia* on the first day of the war, and the valuable aircraft carrier *Courageous* a fortnight later. The *Kelly* was one of a number of ships that answered the carrier's S O S. Two torpedoes had struck the big ship, sending her to the bottom quickly, with the loss of some five hundred lives. It was cold and rough when the *Kelly* reached the spot in pitch-darkness. The stench of oil fuel, the shapeless bundles of the dead wallowing in the waves, the choking cries of those still alive, all the squalid litter of a sunk ship that was to become feared and familiar in the years ahead, were to be seen by the light from two neutral ships standing by. One of the ships was an American liner. The *Kelly* managed to relieve her of some of the *Courageous'* men and picked up others from the water. At last, after two hours, she headed for Devonport with the shocked and injured sailors laid out in the sick bay.

All through October and November, the *Kelly*, joined now by more of her flotilla straight from the builders' yards, operated patrols against the German submarine offensive in the Western Approaches.* On 14 October, while escorting a convoy, they heard another "ping" on their submarine warning device, a real one this time. The *Kelly* closed in on the submerged U-boat, and plastered the sea with depth charges.

---

*The British Naval Command Area from which the Allied war against U-boats in the Atlantic was commanded and administered. At this time the area comprised the waters south of Ireland, the southern half of the Irish Sea, and the western Channel, with headquarters in Plymouth.

This time there was no doubt. Amid the cauldrons of white foam from the explosions, the smashed U-boat's bows emerged, stood vertically out of the water, remained stationary for a moment like a grey grave-stone to her own dead, and then slipped to the bottom.

The *Kelly* steamed north a few days later, to Loch Ewe in Scotland and then, late in November, to the Tyne. On a foggy early-December day, news of two oil tankers in trouble at the Tyne estuary reached the *Kelly*. She immediately raced downriver in company with another de-stroyer, narrowly missing a collision with a big merchantman. Both tankers were sinking. Mountbatten ordered the *Kelly* alongside one that was burning. It was four o'clock in the afternoon; darkness was falling, restricting the visibility further.

Almost at once, Mountbatten heard a bumping under the destroyer's bottom. It sounded louder to those below, as if someone were hammer-ing the keel from stern to stern. Then there was a huge explosion, and half the ship's company was thrown to the deck. They had blundered into a minefield, steamed right into the centre of it. The *Kelly*, helped by two tugs, limped back to her old yard at Hebburn, where she had been completed in the summer. While she was in dry dock, Mountbat-ten could see the extent of the damage, and could see how lucky they had been. If the mine had exploded on first impact, the ship could have gone to the bottom. As it was, they all had an unpleasant fright, but it was a scare that proved too much for one stoker, who had panicked.

Mountbatten cleared the lower deck and addressed the ship's com-pany. "Today we have been through one of the most trying experiences which can befall a newly commissioned ship in war," he began. "Out of two hundred and forty men on board this ship, two hundred and thirty-nine behaved as they ought to have, and as I expected them to behave, but one was unable to control himself and deserted his post, and incidentally his comrades."

Mountbatten paused. His eyes flickered over the sea of faces, pausing here and there, exploiting every ounce of drama in the situation.

"I had him brought before me a couple of hours ago, and he himself informed me that he knew the punishment for desertion of his post could be death. You will therefore be surprised to hear that I propose to let him off with a caution. One caution to him, and a second one to myself for having failed in four months to impress my personality and doctrine on each and all of you to prevent such an incident from occurring. From now on, I wish . . ."

It went down wonderfully. And he followed it with the news that there would be Christmas leave for all. And when word got around that few of the men had money to pay for their rail fare home, Edwina, who had come to join Mountbatten at the Tyne, was one of the first to hear it. "I think I'd like to pay for everyone's Christmas-leave fare," she said. "Very good idea," said Mountbatten.

The following day Mountbatten and Edwina travelled down to London. Edwina had joined the St. John Ambulance Brigade and closed down the Brook House penthouse for the duration. For the present, their only London headquarters was Victoria's suite in Kensington Palace.

Patricia and Pamela had been despatched for safety to New York, sailing in the liner *Washington* from Galway on 14 July along with Duff Cooper's son, the children of Arthur Christiansen, the newspaper editor, and others who could afford to do so. In later years Mountbatten was always rather defensive about this decision, anxious that the girls should not be regarded as specially privileged when so many of their contemporaries, including their cousins Princesses Elizabeth and Margaret Rose, had stuck it out at home. "With their Jewish blood, they would have been the first for the gas ovens if the Germans had invaded," he would say to justify their departure.

London was a depressing place that December. There were a great many people still against the war, and few manifestations of the patriotic fervour of 1914, though none of the hysteria which had driven Mountbatten's father from office, either. Churchill was back at the Admiralty as First Lord, and he was a joy and stimulus as always when they dined at Admiralty House on 5 December. Churchill had an enormous regard and admiration for Edwina, and they always got on marvellously.

There was a great deal of torpor and pessimism in the city; and once again the references to the "phoney war," and stupid songs like "We're gonna hang out the washing on the Siegfried Line," when nobody was going to do anything of the kind, infuriated Mountbatten.

At lunch he met Eden with Leslie Hore-Belisha, Secretary of State for War. Both politicians were depressed. The Navy, they said, was the only service doing anything, to which Mountbatten concurred, saying that a lot of his friends were being killed, and it was not a phoney war at sea.

"What's the Army doing?" he asked Hore-Belisha.

"It's so lucky," replied the War Minister, "that the Germans are so busy in Poland and not attacking us, giving us time to build up the Maginot Line, making it completely impregnable."

That sounded plausible, but Mountbatten was outraged. "It is an absolute axiom of strategy," he said, "that the same course of action cannot be advantageous to both sides. If the Germans are leaving us alone, it is because it suits them to do so. If we go on doing nothing, when the Germans have tidied up Poland, they'll turn round and mop us up."

Hore-Belisha protested, but Mountbatten persisted in his belief that Britain and France ought to be attacking at once. "It is crazy to do nothing. We'll be picked off *in seriatim*. Look, the French army is riddled with Communists, forty or fifty percent of those called up are Communists and will turn against the government when the Germans attack. The Germans will turn the corner of the Maginot Line and dash through Holland and Belgium, just like last time. Then we'll be finished."

This plea, Mountbatten said thirty-five years later, made not the slightest impression. Nor were the other two in the least impressed by his account of the meeting with the French admiral at Bizerte four years earlier. The French were in fine fettle, stalwart allies, both men insisted.

It was a busy time in London for the Mountbattens, both of them pursuing their causes amid the apathy. A few years earlier they would have been seen, as often as not, throwing themselves heart and soul into parties and following new ideas for diversion and entertainment. Now they were on other errands, more serious pursuits, wearing uniforms with decorations instead of dinner jacket and evening dress, but still driven by the same well-known fire. It was a curious and interesting metamorphosis.

On 7 December, at luncheon with the fashionable hostess Sibyl Colefax, Mountbatten's cause was publicity for the Royal Navy, which he felt it sadly lacked. "The Air Force seemed to bag the whole thing," he claimed, according to another guest, Harold Nicolson. "For instance, the other day a merchant ship was arriving in the Firth from the Argentine . . ."

A German plane, it seemed, had raked the bridge with shells and bullets. "The navigating lieutenant was killed," according to Mountbatten, "and the old captain was wounded by thirty bullets. He picked himself up and said to the signaller, 'Is Lieutenant Jones dead?' 'Yes, Sir.' 'Then bring me a chair.' He sat down and steered the ship in." Later he was found to be dead. "Dickie," Harold Nicolson noted in his diary, "feels that that story ought to have been written up."[1]

A day or two later Mountbatten left London for Portland, where he took over the *Kelly*'s sister ship *Kelvin*. There was a letter from Eden awaiting him, saying that "if anyone else but you had been talking about the Western Front I wouldn't even have bothered to listen. But after you left, I got a careful and up-to-date intelligence report. It is true what Leslie [Hore-Belisha] said. The Maginot Line has been strengthened, the French cannot be turned, you can sleep easy in your bed . . ."

Ten years before this meeting, as a young lieutenant at work on his *Introduction to Polo*, Mountbatten had written: "Whenever you are doing nothing you are doing wrong." The same stricture applied to war, he believed. War was *now*, and nothing was being done. "Now I was really frightened. I had opened their eyes, told them the truth, soundings had been taken, and *still* they couldn't understand. Now I was certain that by the summer of 1940 we should be finished."

Only Churchill, Mountbatten and a very few hard-core realists recognized the dangers ahead in the winter of 1939. There are two equally remarkable aspects of this story about Eden and Hore-Belisha. The first is that the British War Minister at the outset of the greatest war of all time, *and* the brilliant and far-sighted politician who had so recently and spectacularly resigned as Foreign Secretary because the government would not acknowledge the dangers of fascist dictatorship, both suffered from the same myopia a mere four months before Hitler's Western offensive. The second is that they were prepared to listen seriously to a naval captain not yet forty years old with no formal standing in defence or political matters.

After more months of strenuous patrols and convoy work in the Western Approaches, Mountbatten got his *Kelly* back in time for the great offensive he knew was coming in the spring. Almost at once, she was in trouble again. On convoy escort work in the North Sea, she collided lightly with another destroyer, scraping and tearing her side from close to the bows to the stern. She was patched up at Scapa Flow in the Orkney Islands, and then proceeded slowly down the east coast to London for complete repair.

It was twenty years since, at the conclusion of another war, he had brought the little *P. 31* up the Thames for inspection by his father and mother and George V. At the outset of this war, Mountbatten invited George V's son to visit his destroyer. George VI and Queen Elizabeth, and the Duke and Duchess of Kent, arrived for dinner. It was a very Mountbatten evening, an intimate royal family affair. Mountbatten showed off his new if now rather knocked-about destroyer, and with special pride his new movie projector. Thanks to his old friendship with Charlie Chaplin, Mountbatten had managed to acquire a print of Chaplin's new film, *The Great Dictator*, which had not yet been shown in London. And so the *Kelly* became the venue for its British premiere.

Mountbatten and the *Kelly* were back at Scapa Flow before the end of April. Norway had been invaded and hard fought over. As a precursor to later events, Royal Navy dive bombers had sunk a German cruiser, the first major man o' war to be destroyed at sea by air power alone. Narvik had been taken from the German invaders. George VI had written to Churchill as First Lord that he "would like to congratulate you on the splendid way in which, under your direction, the Navy is countering the German move against Scandinavia." [2]

Mountbatten was itching to take part in the furious naval actions that were taking place up and down the fjords: bombardments, actions against German aircraft, and ship-to-ship skirmishes. His opportunity came at the end of the month, but by this time the Germans were in the ascendancy. Air power was proving to be the balancing factor in the combined sea-land operations, just as Mountbatten had feared, and the French and British forces were everywhere being pinned down.

Five thousand troops, under the supremely courageous old eccentric, General Carton de Wiart, were gathered at the little Norwegian port of Namsos, awaiting evacuation, and the *Kelly* was among the warships designated to escort the relieving troop transports. They had no air cover, and Luftwaffe bombers and fighters were present in great strength, ranging deep into the North Sea and watching every move on the ground. The convoy's only cover was fog.

"I asked permission for my division of four destroyers to evacuate the first night's contingent under the fog cover," Mountbatten explained later. "It seemed to me the only way of ensuring success. The moment permission was granted, I began a mad dash along the seventy or so miles of Norwegian coast to Namsos. It was five in the morning. Suddenly the fog cleared, like a curtain pulled aside. A hundred yards ahead was a mass of half-submerged rocks. So it was full astern, and we missed them by yards. It also meant we couldn't continue with our plans, and all that day we played hide-and-seek with the German bombers, in and out of scattered fog banks.

"We tried again at nightfall—or twilight, because that's all you get at this time of the year. We went up the fjord at twenty-six knots, between the snow-capped peaks and the lush valleys with their wooden farmhouses. It was all incredibly peaceful, and I remember saying to myself, 'This can't be war . . .' But it was!"

The last turn of the fjord revealed Namsos in flames. Every building was burning from a German bombardment. "It seemed impossible that anyone could be alive, but there was old de Wiart, one eye gleaming defiance."

"Lord Mountbatten managed to feel his way into the harbour," the general later wrote, "and the other ships followed him in. It was a tremendous undertaking to embark the whole force in a night of three short hours, but the Navy did it and earned my undying gratitude."[3]

"The Germans really missed a trick not putting on a raid while we were taking on board these great numbers of men," said Mountbatten. "There were thousands of them lined up on the jetties."

At dawn the Luftwaffe arrived, and the transports and escort were fiercely bombed all day. The packed French destroyer *Bison* was soon sunk. Most of her wounded survivors were picked up by the big destroyer *Afridi*, then that, too, was destroyed, and nearly all the wounded drowned. The *Kelly*'s gunners claimed one dive bomber and the ship was near-missed time and again.

This was real war, closely fought, deadly dangerous, clamorous, what Mountbatten had spent the last twenty-seven years preparing for. "As we steamed back across the North Sea, out of range at last of the

German bombers, I thought about my father, who never saw any action in all his years in the Royal Navy. I hated war as much as he did, but he would have envied me that action off Namsos, just as he had loved to listen to Georgie's descriptions of the naval actions he fought in the North Sea."

The Namsos evacuation took place on the night of 3–4 May 1940. Five days later, as the German armies opened the offensive that would lead to the collapse of Belgium, Holland and France in a single month, the *Kelly* was at sea again leading the 5th Destroyer Flotilla—"the fighting fifth," as they loved to be called—against a suspected German mine-laying force off the Dutch coast.

It was a quiet, still evening, with banks of mist forming and dispersing, making visibility deceptive and ever-changing. Just after ten o'clock Mountbatten was on the bridge with the officer of the watch. They both saw the faint shape emerge out of the half-light, travelling very fast. It was a German E-boat—a fast motorboat armed with torpedoes and guns—coming straight at the *Kelly*. The track of its torpedo was like a white towline hurled towards them. Mountbatten remembered thinking, as if he himself were immortal, "That's going to kill a lot of people!"

It did not, though. Someone was shouting, "Torpedo track port!" A split second later the dim shape disappeared. The torpedo passed clean under the *Kelly*, dead amidships.

There was no time for relief and self-congratulation. A second torpedo was hard behind it, and this time there was no escape. It struck above No. 1 boiler room, blasting a fifty-foot-long hole, killing and injuring dozens of men below.

Mountbatten was yelling, "Take over secondary steering!"

"No answer from the helm, sir."

They had been steaming at 28 knots. The effect, as the *Kelly* heeled hard over to starboard until the gunwale was almost submerged, was for the seas to pour in with Niagara-like force, tearing at bulkheads, killing, maiming, drowning men in its path. When she was stationary and silent, wallowing uneasily in the swell, no one who had witnessed the explosion and its consequences gave the *Kelly* more than half an hour.

Mountbatten had trained his men carefully in damage control. It was not a popular exercise in the Royal Navy, in which it was considered a bit "off-side" to assume your ship might be sunk or severely damaged. But on a visit to the American naval base at Pensacola, Mountbatten had made a careful study of its damage-control routine under the instruction of Admiral William ("Bull") Halsey and had absorbed the lessons for the benefit of his own flotilla.

Repair parties were at work before the *Kelly* was stationary, rigging emergency lighting, shoring up bulkheads, attending to the wounded. No. 1 boiler room was completely flooded, and water was getting into the second boiler room, too. Weight above the waterline was rapidly disposed of—the ten torpedoes fired safe, the depth charges and ready ammunition for the guns thrown overboard, along with the ship's boats, except the whaler, which was set to tow astern. In accordance with the ship's motto, they were going to "Keep On," though very few of them thought it would be for long. In the darkness, with the seas already rising, the destroyer *Bulldog* succeeded in getting her in tow, and at a crawl, the *Kelly* headed towards home.

Long after midnight, a curious thing happened. Out of the darkness there came at high speed the shape of an E-boat, like the ghost of their assailant. It was no phantom. It was another E-boat. Or could it have been the same one? It collided heavily with the *Bulldog*, ricocheted off her hull, then struck the *Kelly*, shedding chunks of her structure, including the steering wheel (which was brought to Mountbatten the next morning and later became a prized trophy). No one ever knew what became of that E-boat after her spectacular act of self-immolation. She must have gone to the bottom almost at once.

It was a long and arduous tow, and the battle was being steadily lost. Deeper and deeper sank the *Kelly*. Mountbatten shed more tons by evacuating almost the entire surviving ship's company, ten tons of them, he calculated. And now there was nothing more to remove.

The Luftwaffe arrived like carrion crows. First a reconnaissance plane, then Stukas following, bombing the *Kelly* and the *Bulldog*, wheeling in low to machine-gun the last boats taking off the *Kelly*'s wounded crew. Mountbatten cursed himself for having ordered the ready ammunition thrown overboard. The remaining nucleus crew managed to bring up some from the half-flooded magazines, and Mountbatten himself manned a .5-calibre machine gun. "I felt a great deal better for it, too."

The weather got worse. The tow parted, was picked up again. The *Kelly*'s list increased until it seemed as if she must capsize at any instant. Another day ended. Pleas to abandon ship were sharply resisted by Mountbatten. Food and water ran short, and everyone was dead tired.

The next day a tug made a welcome appearance and took up the tow. Mountbatten remained awake and on the bridge for more than ninety hours, nursing what was left of his ship back to the yard that had built her.

"As the procession slowly passed into the river mouth," ran the official history of the *Kelly*, "a great cheer went up from the people of Tyneside who had come out to welcome their ship back home. . . . All the shipyard workers knocked off work with one accord to come and give them a cheer, while at the same time all the ships in the river sounded their sirens."[4]

But those same "yardies" wouldn't touch her until she had been cleaned up. One of the *Kelly*'s chief petty officers was in the worst-damaged compartment after she had been dry-docked: "There were still lots of bodies lying around, and flesh hanging from the pipes and bulkheads. The 'Chief' was looking at what had to be done, and was scarcely able to stop himself being sick, when a voice at his shoulder said quietly, 'It's terrible, isn't it, Chief? But there's nothing we can do to help them now. Let's get on with it.' It was Mountbatten, who took a broom and worked alongside the CPO until the job was done."[5]

The bodies, or what was left of them, were buried in Hebburn cemetery, and a plaque in their honour can be seen there today: "In memory of the 27 men killed in action with E-boats off the German minefields. . . ."

During that ninety-hour tow across the North Sea, history was being made in France and the Low Countries. And in twenty more days, Royal Navy destroyers were bearing the brunt of the German attacks to prevent the evacuation of the British armies, and remnants of the French army, from Dunkirk.

Once again, Mountbatten travelled south to London, leaving his sorely battered ship to be repaired. This time it would take six months. Two double-decker buses could have driven through the hole in her side; she needed an entirely new midships section, a new boiler room and numerous new bulkheads. "Might as well throw it away and start again," one "yardie" was heard to complain.

London was in a state of political turmoil. Chamberlain was on his way out, Churchill was leaving the Admiralty for 10 Downing Street and his long war of near-dictatorial power as Prime Minister—and incidentally replacing himself with a First Lord of the Admiralty who would do exactly as he was told.

Mountbatten now set up his staff and H.Q. at the Country Hotel at Immingham on the east coast, where his flotilla was well placed for the threatened German invasion. During that summer of 1940, the world's attention was concentrated upon the skies of southern England, where the RAF fought off the massed armadas of German bombers and fighters, suffering terrible losses in doing so. It was a public arena, a new form of warfare, and the stakes were high.

But any invasion had also first to break the Royal Navy, and its battles, witnessed by only a handful of participants or shore observers, were crucial, too. Admiral the Earl St. Vincent's eighteenth-century tag still applied: "I do not say that they cannot come. All I will say is that they cannot come by sea."

Mountbatten commanded "the fighting fifth's" operations from other surviving destroyers, the *Jackal*, *Javelin* or *Jupiter*, his presence on board always honing a special edge to the crew's morale. E-boats were a formidable and ever-present enemy, especially at night. German destroyers were active, too, as the numbers of massed invasion barges built up in the Channel ports. Enemy minefields had to be swept, British mines laid.

An officer in the *Jupiter*, Lieutenant John Jones, recalled one especially testing summer night, with the *Jupiter* and *Javelin* covering a force of four minelayers off the Frisian Islands: "I was officer of the watch when the disaster happened. The minelayers *Esk* and *Ivanhoe* were themselves mined, *Esk* with her bows blown right off back to the bridge, *Ivanhoe* with her back broken and partly abandoned. Lord Louis had to make a decision either (a) go on to the minefield and get them off and risk losing *Jupiter* and *Javelin*, or (b) leave them there. If (a) failed and the destroyers had been lost, he would have been blamed for recklessness. If he decided on (b), he would have faced criticism of an unpleasant nature."[6]

No one doubted that Mountbatten would choose the first course. "What a dramatic moment it was for me," Jones continued, "as I scuttled away to my station aft to prepare to tow. Going on a minefield to tow a stricken vessel off it is a test for the strongest nerve. We succeeded in getting our three-and-a-half-inch towing hausers out to the quarterdeck of the *Esk* and got her out stern first, and subsequently safely back to the Humber."

Another of Mountbatten's officers at this time, Allan Noble, remarked crisply of Mountbatten "that nothing was really worth doing unless it was slightly dangerous."[7] "Slightly" is a relative word. Within a few weeks German torpedoes hit the bow *and* the stern of his ship, and the *Javelin* herself had to be towed into Devonport.

By this time—November 1940—some wag at the Admiralty had coined the phrase that there was no one anyone would sooner be in a tight corner with than Dickie Mountbatten, and no one capable of getting you into one quicker. Mountbatten enjoyed the joke when it reached him and cherished it to the end of his life. He never registered that the phrase had a double edge to it. No one doubted Mountbatten's courage for a moment, but there were people in high command who wished that he had a less urgent need to make a splash, and a greater sense of ship preservation. Rushing into minefields and up fjords with only the sketchiest of radar may have been in the best Elizabethan swashbuckling tradition, but it lost sorely needed ships at a time when destroyers were incredibly valuable.

Another body of opinion, however, held that this Francis Drake style was just what was needed at the time, that its value in raising the fighting spirit, of the lower deck especially, more than outweighed the risks and damage it occasioned. This biographer tends toward the second view while accepting that Mountbatten was, from his earliest days, accident-prone, and careless of risks. Many people suffer from an unreasonable number of accidents through their life, from rashness, misjudgement, a poor eye, until—like so many human characteristics—it becomes a habit. For Mountbatten it extended from falls at home and at school, mishaps at Osborne, to accidents all through his naval career, especially on the polo field, of course. It embraced car accidents, due not to lack of skill but to a strong tendency to become distracted, according to those who drove with him. These accidents became habitual, too. He even had railway accidents—he was very proud of these, one returning from Spain at 70 mph, another in Australia with the Prince of Wales, both serious. When later he was given command of a carrier, George VI was heard to utter with a groan of despair, "Well, that's the end of the *Illustrious!*"

Late in November 1940, the *Kelly* was ready for re-commissioning. She was virtually a new ship, manned by a new crew, facing a new war— a war at sea in which the odds were weighted more heavily than ever in favour of the enemy. Since the fall of France, all but a few units of the great French navy were lost, and the formidable Italian navy now faced Britain in the Mediterranean. In 1917, when German U-boats had almost throttled Britain to death, their bases were limited. Now, from harbours extending from the northern tip of Norway to southern France and from the Adriatic and North Africa, German U-boats and several of the fastest and most powerful battleships in the world could range the length and breadth of the Atlantic and the Mediterranean. By any statistical calculation, the odds against Allied survival at sea appeared hopeless.

Once again the *Kelly* and her flotilla were drawn to the busiest and most dangerous fighting zones—first to Scapa Flow, then the Clyde and the Western Approaches Striking Forces operating out of Plymouth. Besides numerous U-boats, the German battle-cruisers *Scharnhorst* and *Gneisenau*, and the heavy cruisers *Hipper* and *Prinz Eugen*, were operating from newly acquired French Atlantic bases, raiding the convoy routes.

All these men o' war were as fast as the *Kelly*, and all had a hundred times greater gunpower. But the *Kelly*'s flotilla pursued the battle cruisers almost into Brest, just missing them, and chased the *Hipper*—or her ghost—as far north as the Faeroes. Perhaps it was as well, this time, that her luck was out. Next it was the weather, and not the enemy, that forced the ill-starred ship back into dockyard hands. All vessels hit the same Irish Sea storm, but it was only the *Kelly* that lost her boats and Carley rafts, her abandon-ship gear and her starboard guardrails.

When she had been refitted and spruced up once more, George VI came to inspect her again, and Mountbatten and his officers had dinner with him in the now more austere wardroom. "We talked about the war and almost nothing else," said Mountbatten. "Like his father, he loved talking Navy—*his* Navy, and always felt comfortable and at home on board one of his ships. The shyness and diffidence seemed to disappear and he was just one of us. Again like his father, he would have loved to come to sea with us and seen some action."

In honour of his visit, the King gave the ship's company all-night leave. The Luftwaffe chose that night to bomb Plymouth. The watch ashore decided they would have preferred Brest harbour and the German shore batteries. But the *Kelly* was able to add her weight of anti-aircraft fire and to use her newly installed Oerlikons for the first time.

Shortly afterwards Mountbatten took the *Kelly* south. She had been intended for the Mediterranean before the war, had even been light-painted for that station. But while the war remained fiercest in the north, she had remained in the North Atlantic, the Channel and the North Sea. Now the *Kelly* followed the worst of the fighting as a worshipper follows the sun.

Postponing indefinitely the invasion of Britain, Hitler was now hell-bent on turning his armies to the east, and in preparation for the Russian war, he determined to neutralize Rumania, Greece, Turkey and Egypt to protect his flank for his drive on the Russian Caucasus. The Italian army and navy should have carried out these tasks, but Admiral Andrew Cunningham had destroyed the Italian battle fleet in Taranto harbour—like a dress rehearsal for Pearl Harbor—and at the Battle of Cape Matapan. The Greeks had contained and then driven back Mussolini's armies, and General Archibald Wavell had thrown the Italian armies out of Cyrenaica with a force of one-fifth the Italian weight.

But in the early months of 1941, German Panzers were seen for the first time in the North African desert, German soldiers stemmed the tide of the Greeks, and the skies were filled with new, more formidable and more skilfully flown warplanes; the Luftwaffe dive bomber had come to the Mediterranean, and the Royal Navy, with only the sketchiest air support, began to suffer savage losses. Once again the price was being paid for an undeveloped and mixed-manned Fleet Air Arm and inadequate anti-aircraft weapons.

Nowhere had the new face of sea power shown itself more clearly than in the Mediterranean. Warships without air cover of any kind were safe only at night or in fog. The mighty air barrages of 1944 and 1945, when battleships were equipped with two hundred and more anti-aircraft guns, had not yet been envisaged. Even the Italian air force could bomb almost with impunity from high altitude, though it rarely made a hit.

The German dive bombers had all but closed the western Mediterranean, and when the 5th Flotilla made Malta safely from Gibraltar, in company with the new 40-knot minelayer *Abdiel* and cruiser *Dido*, there were thousands on the battlements of Grand Harbour to celebrate their safe arrival.

"Except for our brief brush with the Germans at Namsos, we had not seen aerial warfare on this scale before," said Mountbatten. "The Germans and Italians bombed Malta night and day. I saw no point in risking the *Kelly*'s entire company, so I sent half the flotilla's companies ashore to the shelters every night, and the other half manned the guns. I stayed on board every night. A fine story it would have made if the *Kelly* had been sunk with Captain Mountbatten skulking in an air-raid shelter! But in all my life, I've never been so scared!"

It was a relief to get away from Malta, to cast aside for a while the claustrophobia of Grand Harbour, with orders to bombard the enemy-held North African port of Benghazi. The attack was carried out on the night of 10–11 May under very difficult conditions. The destroyers succeeded in damaging a merchantman close to the entrance to the harbour, but all the ships within the breakwater appeared in the uncertain moonlight to be already damaged or sunk. Mountbatten ordered his five destroyers to withdraw shortly after midnight, and almost at once they picked up the sound of aircraft. They were their old enemies, Ju-87 Stukas, coming in vertically to dive-bomb them in the dark, a bold operation no one had ever witnessed before. The destroyers dropped smoke floats, and while these may have confused the pilots, they also added to the difficulties of the gunners, who were unable to pick out their targets properly until the Stukas opened up with their machine guns just before pulling out of their dives. No losses could be claimed by either side, although the harassing attacks continued until they were far out to sea, and everyone must have been relieved when orders were given to call off the attacks.

The final phase in the unhappy career of H.M.S. *Kelly* began in the last days of May 1941. The dust and smoke from the last bombing raid seemed to hang perpetually in the hot air above Valletta. The weather was perfect: hot and dry, with one cloudless day following another. The past weeks had been frustrating for the flotilla, catastrophic for the Allied cause. The war was going badly in Africa, the British had been driven out of Greece after failing to hold the German invasion. The streets of Valletta were blocked by rubble; the people, living underground for much of the time, were demoralized and half starved. The German attack on Soviet Russia, which would add new heart to the Allied cause, still lay a month ahead, and any hope of stemming the German Wehrmacht seemed as distant as the hot Mediterranean sun. In the small world of the *Kelly*, nothing much seemed to have gone right, either.

On the morning of 21 May, Mountbatten was ashore in conference with his commanders for most of the morning. He returned on board after lunch, and ordered the lower deck cleared so that he could, once again, address the ship's company. "I told them that things weren't going too well in the eastern Mediterranean, that the Germans had carried out a large-scale airborne attack—the biggest in history—on Crete the day before, and that our forces there were hard-pressed. I said, 'It's our job to go to support them at once. Make no mistake, things are going to be tough, but we have got to stop reinforcements from getting through. The chief threat, of course, will be from the air. But we've faced quite a bit of bombing already, and I trust that we're about to increase our score.' I ended by saying that I knew they would all live up to my expectations."

Within an hour, the *Kelly* was leading the *Kashmir, Kipling* and *Jackal* out of Grand Harbour—a harbour that held so many memories of regattas and the peaceful to-ing and fro-ing of liberty boats and admirals' barges and whalers and Maltese *dghaisos*. All through Mountbatten's life, and his father's life before him, this island had been the symbol and first bastion of British naval supremacy. For generations, the Navy's finest men o' war from the three-decker ships-of-the-line of Nelson's time, to the 30,000-ton battleships and aircraft carriers, had ridden at anchor here, flying the white ensign. Now the harbour was littered with wrecks, enemy mines often closed its entrance, half the town was in ruins, and the life was being squeezed out of the Navy and the people who lived here.

There appeared to be little hope for Malta as the destroyers steamed out for the last time, the watch on deck going about their duties in white shorts and singlets in the heat of the evening, heading for a battle that would be more ferocious than anything they had so far faced. Steaming east for Crete, no sign of war defaced that first beautiful Mediterranean night, nor much of the next day, which was again hot and clear and calm. A suspected U-boat was depth-charged, a distant enemy reconnaissance plane spotted.

In the evening, as they approached the beleaguered island, high-level bombers were seen by the lookout, and fire was opened on them with the 4.7s. Mountbatten was still on the *Kelly*'s bridge, where he had remained throughout the day and night, and he ordered evasive manoeuvres. Neither side scored a hit, and he called for his dinner—the usual slice of bread and tin of sardines, still his favourite fish.

Just how fierce the fighting at sea around the island must be was indicated by their first order from Admiral Cunningham: "Proceed in company with *Kashmir* and *Kipling* to assist *Kandahar* rescue survivors from *Fiji*." The *Fiji* was a large cruiser; so was the *Gloucester*, also reported sinking from bombing attacks.

The next signal, before they reached the scene, was even more ominous. The cruisers' survivors must be left to their fate. The destroyers were desperately needed to bombard Maleme airfield, which the Germans were fighting for, and to prevent reinforcements by sea. Now the *Kipling* suffered a steering fault which would take hours to correct. "We will go ahead and bombard ourselves," Mountbatten radioed Cunningham (a signal that later led to some ribbing from the c.-in-c.: "Please instruct me how it is done." Mountbatten was not amused).

That night no one got any sleep. The two destroyers poured a barrage of 4.7-inch shells onto the German positions, then turned their guns onto Greek fishing vessels loaded with supplies and German troops, sinking two of them. Already thousands of German soldiers had been drowned, and it is to the eternal credit of the Royal Navy that in spite of fearful losses, until the island fell not one German soldier arrived by sea of the thousands despatched recklessly from the Greek mainland.

But now the invaders did not need to come by sea. They came by air. It was air power alone that led to the capture of Crete and the destruction of so many British ships—among them, the next morning, the *Kelly*.

The date was 23 May 1941. Tomorrow would be his father's birthday, an anniversary Mountbatten never forgot. Due to a signalling error, Admiral Cunningham had been incorrectly informed that two of his most powerful units, the battleships *Warspite* and *Valiant*, were running short of anti-aircraft ammunition. For this reason, all naval forces were ordered to withdraw from Crete during the night to refuel and replenish in Egypt. And it was because of the same mistake that Mountbatten's destroyers were fated to confront the full might of Luftwaffe dive bombers without the support of the battleships' gunfire which would otherwise almost certainly have been available to them. It was a sad reflection that the one officer who had striven to perfect the signalling efficiency of the Mediterranean Fleet for so many years should now have to suffer catastrophe through a signal error.

The first bombers came in at six o'clock out of a cloudless dawn sky. According to Mountbatten: "The Stukas came in at eight, a couple of hours later. We knew they would come, as day follows night, but we had hoped there wouldn't be quite as many. Twenty-four we counted. And they split up between the two of us, coming down on different bearings to split our fire."

The great accuracy of the Ju-87 Stuka derived from its near-vertical angle of dive, the extendable brakes slowing it down and giving the bomb-aimer time to steady the pilot's aim. But off Namsos a year before, Mountbatten had recognized that this advantage could be turned into a powerful disadvantage by swift reaction on a destroyer's helm and speed: "As a dive-bomber pilot, you will know that if you could tempt the pilot into too steep a dive, and then a bit more, by sudden acceleration or deceleration, you might force him beyond the vertical. I was able to do this twice. The Stukas just went straight in, saving us a lot of ammunition. But as the Japanese and Americans later discovered in the Pacific—especially the Americans with the kamikazes—there's a limit to the amount of dodging if the numbers are too great."

Each Stuka carried a single 500-kg bomb under its belly, but after the first ones had dropped, the enemy came in again to confuse the defences, machine-gunning all the way down. For ten minutes of incessant screaming and gunfire, with the bomb sprays spouting up high to break the twisting patterns of the two destroyers' wakes, the *Kelly* and *Kashmir* evaded every bomb. Then the *Kashmir* took one dead amidships. She sank in two minutes, but before she went under, Mountbatten saw one of her gunners continuing to fire as the seas swept over him, destroying a Stuka with his last rounds.

"We got two and probably a third with our guns," said Mountbatten. "We were on full starboard rudder when we were hit. I saw the bomb falling from the Stuka's belly, and watched it all the way down. It was just like that torpedo a year earlier, except this time I knew we weren't going to survive. It hit square on X gun deck, killing the 4.7 crew immediately, and exploded just abaft the engine room.

"I gave the order 'Midships' when the sound of the explosion had died, and then 'Hard a-port.' But it was no good, and we listed over more heavily than ever. So I gave the order 'Stop engines.' "

It was like telling a dead man not to try so hard. In seconds—as before—the doom-laden words were shouted up the voice-pipe by the coxswain: "Ship won't answer the helm, sir. No reply to the engine room telegraphs."

The Stukas were still coming in. "Keep all guns firing!" Mountbatten shouted. He could have saved his voice, which no one could hear, anyway, for the shattering crackle of the machine guns, Oerlikons and pom-poms. Then, as the *Kelly* began to roll over, still travelling at 30 knots, one by one the gun crews were torn from the weapons.

Mountbatten was telling himself, "I must stay with the ship. Whatever happens, I must stay with her as long as I can—must be the last to leave . . ."

Mountbatten remembered it as a great heavy blanket being pulled up over him, bringing suffocating darkness. He held on for what seemed a long time, clutching the gyro-compass pedestal until he was torn from that grip, and feeling the pressure on his lungs and the desperate need to breathe, put one hand over his mouth, another over his nose.

"I came up in the end," he said, "though it seemed an awfully long time. The first thing I saw was the stern of the ship no more than a dozen yards away, travelling fast, propellers still rotating. Lieutenant Butler-Bowden, the navigator, was near me, and I shouted at him, 'Swim like hell!' A nasty end, being chewed up. The ship just missed us, still travelling fast. When I paused for breath and looked around, an oil-stained head popped up beside me. It was a stoker petty officer, and he said at once, 'Funny how the scum always comes to the top, sir.'

"All we had was one Carley raft someone had managed to release in those last seconds, and I shouted at the top of my voice, 'Swim to the raft!' Unfortunately, there were quite a lot who couldn't. I realized I was still wearing my tin helmet, and I thought that was crazy. So I took it off and it sank, and the next second the Stukas came in again, machine-gunning us like hell, and I wished I hadn't."

They put the wounded inside the Carley raft, and the others who had reached it clung to the side. The Stukas came in again and again. The survivors could see the pilot in his cockpit, goggles up for clearer visibility, as he pressed the button to spray them with bullets. A lot of them were killed, and the worst part was dragging out the dead from the centre of the raft and pushing them into the sea.

"The sea was beautifully warm and dead calm, just the sort of sea people look forward to when they go to the Mediterranean for a holiday. But now we all needed cheering up, so I called for a song or two. We began with 'Roll Out the Barrel.'

"The *Kelly* wasn't far off, bottom up, but she was going, so I called out, 'Three cheers for the old ship!' And then down she went." In fact, she only turned turtle and remained half awash for some time, true to her motto "Keep On" to the end.

The *Kipling*'s steering-gear trouble indirectly saved their lives. If she had been with her consorts, she would have gone to the bottom, too. But the Stukas never saw her. Commander St. Clair Ford, her captain, brought the destroyers alongside the Carley raft, and lowered scrambling nets.

Helped by the *Kipling*'s sailors, who eased them out of the water and helped them up onto deck, the survivors were slowly dragged on board. Then the *Kipling* turned to the *Kashmir*'s survivors. There were more of them, five Carley rafts scattered widely. There was a far distant booming sound, increasing in volume. They looked up and saw, high above, the big formation of bombers staining the bright blue sky, peeling off towards them—the ripest target in the whole Mediterranean. They were big twin-engine Ju-88s this time, armed with 550–kg bombs and MG 131 and 81 machine guns, which were used to spray without mercy the men in the rafts and the water and those who were clambering, oil-soaked and exhausted, up the netting.

Rudyard Kipling himself would have been proud of the destroyer that carried his name. For an hour Commander Ford manoeuvred his ship like a speedboat to evade the bombs, returning in the brief lulls between attacks to collect more survivors. Every time the sky was temporarily clear of their tormentors, Mountbatten had to make the decision: Should they leave now, with a better chance of reaching Alexandria, or pick up a few more and increase still further the risk to those already on board? Each time, they came back to the same oil-stained patch of ocean, with its few remaining struggling figures and many drifting, burned corpses.

Once the *Kipling* grazed the submerged wreck of the *Kelly*. Even in death, the old ship continued to bring bad luck, tearing a hole in the side of her sister ship, releasing oil that was not only precious but that would mark her passage with a trail no plane could miss.

In the long, dramatic ordeal, there were many small tragedies. One man said, "I'm all right—I'm fine." And the next second he whispered "Ave Maria!" and died. A figure floated past, covered in oil, sitting in a beer crate like a baby in its pram. One of the *Kelly*'s officers who had just escaped from drowning was killed in the confusion of lowering the *Kipling*'s motorboat. He was Lord Hugh Beresford, a close friend of Mountbatten's. His great-uncle had led the attacks against Prince Louis which had driven him from office.

It went on like that to the end. Someone in the *Kipling* logged forty attacks from Ju-88s, and they were still coming in when Mountbatten ordered the ship to leave. There were, it seemed, only corpses and an empty boat left. But as she steamed away, with a list and capable of only 20 knots now, several of those on board saw a figure rise from the bottom of the boat, stand at attention and salute. He was still standing when he faded from sight.

The torment was not yet over. It was four hundred miles to Egypt, and the bombers came back, time and again. "She must have had a charmed life," said Mountbatten. "But somehow we missed them all. Not that I saw many of the bombs fall. I spent most of the time with my wounded, taking down messages for their next of kin. Some of them couldn't talk, and I couldn't recognize their faces. So I had to rely on their identity discs. And for some of them I was too late. We lost a lot of good men from burns and shock in the first hour or two after we sailed."

The *Kipling* had used up the last of her fuel before the Egyptian coast lifted above the horizon, and for some time she lay wallowing in the swell. Fortunately they were beyond the range of the bombers now, and before long the 2,900-ton target tower H.M.S. *Protector* came alongside and replenished the destroyer's tanks.

As they went through the boom defence at Alexandria, there were thousands on shore and lining the rails of the ships in the harbour, caps raised and cheering the battered destroyer with her decks packed with sailors still oil-stained and carrying the scars of their fight. Mountbatten was wearier than he had ever been in his life, his throat still sore from the oil fuel he had swallowed, what was left of his uniform stained and torn. No one had ever seen him come ashore from his ship other than spruce and valeted, least of all his nephew Philip, who was on the jetty awaiting him.

Midshipman Prince Philip already had much service behind him, including the Battle of Matapan back in March, in which for his part the Prince had been mentioned in despatches. Now he glanced in astonishment at his battle-weary uncle.

Mountbatten, though delighted and relieved to see his nephew, for once did not feel that there was much to laugh about. The Royal Navy had been thrashed by the Luftwaffe; there could be no denying it. Many hundreds of British and Commonwealth sailors had died in the seas around Crete. More than half the *Kelly*'s company had been killed outright, or drowned or burned to death, and many more were suffering from appalling wounds. It had been a bad way to celebrate his father's birthday.

In Alexandria, Mountbatten gathered the uninjured survivors of the *Kelly* together for the last time. There were scarcely forty of them. "I have always tried to crack a joke or two before," he told them. "But today I'm afraid I have run out of jokes." He spoke then of their dead comrades. "If they had to die, what a grand way to go, for now they lie all together with the ship we loved, and they are in very good company. We have lost her, but they are still with her."

Now the survivors would be going to other ships. "And the next time you are in action, remember the *Kelly*. As you ram each shell home into the gun, shout '*Kelly!*' and so her spirit will go on inspiring us until victory is won." Then he concluded, "I should like to add that there isn't one of you that I wouldn't be proud and honoured to serve with again. Good-bye, good luck, and thank you all from the bottom of my heart."

It is a measure of the special morale of the *Kelly* that today, forty years since she went to the bottom, the Reunion Association is as active as ever, the only one of its kind run by the survivors of a destroyed ship's company. This is perhaps the greatest tribute of all to Mountbatten's leadership.

A few days later a Fleet Air Arm airman at a Fleet Requirement Unit outside Alexandria was detailed to fly an officer to Cairo in his Blackburn Skua. The officer arrived, right on time, dressed in civilian clothes as if he had walked straight out of Savile Row. The airman at once recognized Mountbatten, whose exploits with the *Kelly* were already legendary throughout the fleet. He was, reported the airman later, off to Cairo to complain about the total lack of air cover during the Crete operations, which had cost him his ship and the lives of 9 of his officers and 121 of his men.

"When I offered him his parachute harness, he declined to wear it," reported this airman, "saying with his usual charm, 'I'm sure if anything goes wrong, you will show me what to do.' The Skua was not the most reliable of planes and I was somewhat dubious as to what my reactions would have been if put to the test."[8]

Later another plane flew Mountbatten to London. Within a short time he was in America and then at Pearl Harbor as a guest of the United States Navy and Admiral Harold P. Stark, Chief of Naval Operations. As an officer who had witnessed tragically and at first hand the terrible power of the bomber against naval vessels unprotected by fighter aircraft, Mountbatten was appalled at the lack of preparedness in Hawaii. But when he saw Stark again in Washington on his way back to London and gave him his opinion, Stark did not take it as seriously as Mountbatten had hoped. "I'm afraid putting some of your recommendations into effect is going to make your visit out there an expensive one for the Navy," he commented with a laugh.

It was just ninety days before the Japanese attack.

*W*hile H.M.S. *Kelly* was being completed on the Tyne in the summer of 1939, Mountbatten had been one of the royal party who visited Dartmouth Naval College in H.M.Y. *Victoria and Albert*. The guests, George VI and Queen Elizabeth and the two princesses, Elizabeth and Margaret Rose, were making an informal visit to join the cadets for morning service. Mountbatten was acting in the capacity of A.D.C. to the King. He was also anxious to see how his nephew was getting on.

Unlike Mountbatten, and to Mountbatten's delight, Prince Philip had shone from the beginning as a cadet, winning the Eardley-Howard-Crockett prize as the best cadet of the year. For this occasion, he had been told to entertain the princesses. Royal reporters, biographers and gossip columnists have, for forty years, pinned down this royal visit as the occasion when romance first sparked between the eighteen-year-old Prince and thirteen-year-old Princess. In fact, they had met several times already, as members of the same family do. Another seven years—and the war—were to pass before he and Princess Elizabeth began to talk seriously about marriage.

When Mountbatten told his mother that Prince Philip was likely to marry Princess Elizabeth, she approved but made no comment. In her long life, she had seen so many royal matches, so many unions of dynasties. Besides, engagements in themselves were of no interest to her. "Like her grandmother [Queen Victoria], love affairs bored her," recalled Mountbatten's daughter Lady Pamela Hicks. "She never gossiped and she never discussed love affairs. Either you were married, or not married, and anything in between was a bore."[1]

In fact, Mountbatten's role in the match was mainly passive, but the question of what Philip's name and title were to be was something close to his heart. With his strong sense of family pride, Mountbatten was determined that this surrogate son would carry on his name.

When the suggested, and fairly obvious, name Mountbatten was first put to Prince Philip he was not, as he said, "madly in favour." By this time, 1947, his uncle was a world hero in war and peace, and Prince Philip has always attempted to guard his own individuality as strongly as his own achievements. He had no wish to be linked with "a legend in his own time," no matter how much he loved and admired his uncle. (The general public learned, but did not necessarily believe, that the name Mountbatten had been approved by George VI at the suggestion of the Home Secretary.)

"But in the end I was persuaded," said Prince Philip, "and anyway, I couldn't think of a reasonable alternative."[2] Royal arrangements, and royal nomenclature, were as usual working out exactly and precisely as Mountbatten wished.

The debate, or even struggle, over the future name of the royal family was not yet over. When Mountbatten had accepted with seeming casualness the loss of his family's name Battenberg in 1917, and the assumption by the King of the name Windsor, he could have no idea of the dynastic complexities and conflicts that lay just thirty years ahead. When any reference to the royal surname controversy was omitted in the manuscript of the biography of Mountbatten's parents, Mountbatten made an urgent plea for it to be included (it was not), and in the capacity of president of the Society of Genealogists, drafted a long and complex statement which made it clear that for the first two months of her reign, the Queen had ruled as a Mountbatten, and not as a Windsor at all. Prince Charles and Princess Anne had the surname Mountbatten. "Thus the House of Mountbatten ruled for two months."

The first setback came in April 1952 when the Queen commanded by Order in Council that she had taken the name Windsor for herself and her children. Some seven years later Mountbatten countered by reaching a compromise. Charles and Anne and the Queen's yet-to-be-born children (Prince Andrew and Prince Edward) were given the surname Mountbatten-Windsor. But the legal wording was so ambiguous that the Queen's wishes, claimed Mountbatten, were not clearly established until the marriage of Princess Anne on 14 November 1973, when, in the marriage register, she was described as Anne Mountbatten-Windsor.

Mountbatten seized on this as a great family vindication. Now the Queen's four children and their descendants would bear the surname Mountbatten-Windsor, and "surely this gives the satisfaction of publicly linking the two family names in the Prince of Wales and his mother and their descendants." For those who are not obsessed with genealogy, Mountbatten's part in the marriage of the Queen and Prince Philip, and his concern for the perpetuation of his own name in the royal family, may be less important than his work in helping to shape the character, style and bearing first of Prince Philip when he was virtually an orphan, and then of Prince Charles, with whom his relationship was equally close and important.

Midshipman Prince Philip remained briefly in Egypt when Mountbatten flew home at the end of May, and returned more humbly and circuitously by troopship via the Cape, Puerto Rico and Canada, and it was some time before they met again.

The Mountbattens had bought a modest house at 15 Chester Street, which was to remain their London headquarters for the rest of the war, the greater part of Broadlands being now converted into a hospital. At their first dinner party, after Mountbatten's return, their old friend Noël Coward was present. Coward had known them both since the early 1920s and more intimately since his rise to fame in the 1930s, when he was a frequent visitor to the penthouse. Coward had worked closely with Mountbatten in the formation of the Naval Film Corporation, and Mountbatten had seen to it that his friend and collaborator was offered the honorary rank of Lieutenant-Commander R.N. Coward reluctantly turned it down as unwarranted and invidious.

After dinner, Coward extracted from Mountbatten the full story of the sinking of the *Kelly*, and later wrote: "He told it without apparent emotion, but the emotion was there, poignantly behind every word he uttered." Coward had always been deeply attached to the Navy, and in Mountbatten's account he recognized "all the true sentiment, the comedy, the tragedy, the casual valiance, the unvaunted heroism, the sad-

ness without tears and the pride without end."[3] Coward returned to the
Savoy Hotel, and on that night was conceived *In Which We Serve*.

Two days after the Noël Coward dinner, Mountbatten had lunch at
10 Downing Street with Churchill and Lord Beaverbrook. All through
the 1920s and 1930s, relations between Beaverbrook and the Mountbattens had been mainly cordial, with some quite violent unevenness.
A. J. P. Taylor, Beaverbrook's biographer, has suggested that "something about Mountbatten touched Beaverbrook on a raw nerve."[4] This
"something" was made up of a mixture of irritation and envy. Newspapermen by instinct and training do not care for, and deeply mistrust,
anyone or anything that is too good to be true. Beaverbrook was frequently exasperated at his failure to find anything wrong with the
golden boy of the 1920s. It went against his professional instincts.

Nevertheless, the two men had much in common. They were both
passionately patriotic, pro-Empire and royalist. Even Mountbatten's
quirky socialism sparked off something in the Canadian. They both
liked power, and they both liked to be surrounded by pretty women or
by men who admired them rather than competed with them.

They both had unlimited charm and wealth. But Beaverbrook had
had to work for his riches and title. Mountbatten's had been presented
to him. Mountbatten was extremely handsome, Beaverbrook the reverse. Mountbatten appeared to Beaverbrook (and to many others) as
an easy winner. Victories came hard to Beaverbrook.

Taylor has written that "Beaverbrook's relations with Mountbatten,
as with other men, went up and down." But with no other men did
they seesaw so violently. The first deep dip occurred soon after the
Mountbatten wedding. In 1923 a close friend of Edwina's was a prominent and extremely attractive debutante. She married and then very
quickly fell out with her husband, although there was no separation.
One evening Edwina arranged a small dinner party which included
Beaverbrook and her friend. To the Mountbattens' astonishment, this
led to an affair. But because of Edwina's friendship with the woman,
they continued to see a lot of Beaverbrook. "Then suddenly Max conceived the fantastic notion that I was having an affair with her, too,"
said Mountbatten. "This was quite crazy and I told him so. But he
didn't believe me, and we fell out." This odd non-event was, in due
course, forgotten, and during the early months of the war, he and
Beaverbrook were, in Mountbatten's words, "great buddies." Now

Beaverbrook, after doing a much-praised job as Minister of Aircraft Production during and after the Battle of Britain, had recently become fed up with the post. "We now have more aircraft than the Air Ministry can use," he had announced with justifiable self-satisfaction, and after a certain amount of coquettish side-play, accepted the appointment of Minister of State. "What that means is anybody's guess," he and his editor, Michael Foot of the *Evening Standard*, wrote in a lead article. In fact, it turned out to be considerable, and that is why, a month or so later, he was at No. 10 with the Prime Minister and Mountbatten.

Churchill was late, and for a while the two men were alone. "Max practically kissed me," said Mountbatten. " 'Here is the hero of the *Kelly*—well, Dickie, it is swell to see you alive . . .' "

Then Churchill arrived and apologized. "I bring grave news," he said. "We now know that Hitler in about three days will invade Russia. This completely transforms the war. They will suffer a grave defeat."

Beaverbrook agreed. "They will be overrun in two or three weeks."

"No, it will be six or seven weeks," said Churchill. "The Americans agree with you, Max, and say it will be three or four weeks. So does the J.I.C. [Joint Intelligence Committee]. My belief is that it will be six or seven." Then, turning to Mountbatten, Churchill said, "My dear Dickie, tell us about your experiences in Crete and the sinking of the *Kelly*."

Mountbatten, for the first and last time in his life, brushed aside the sinking of the *Kelly*. Instead he asked if he could express a view about the latest news. "Max and you are quite wrong," he said. "So is the J.I.C., and the Americans are crazy. I don't believe that the Germans will be able to fold up the Russians in *any* number of weeks. I think this news is important for quite different reasons. This is the end of the war. The Russians will certainly win."

Mountbatten's belief was not based upon any military considerations. He had thought about the problem in terms which he understood better than most authorities: in every country the Nazis had invaded previously, there had been a fifth column preparing the ground for them; in Russia, any potential fifth column had long since been liquidated. The old tsarist officers were all dead, or had joined the Germans. "The Russians defeated the Allied intervention in 1919," said Mountbatten to the politician who had so strongly supported it, "because they had something to fight for. Their creed and their objective today are much stronger. They have a country to save, as they did in 1812 when they rolled back Napoleon. The German army will become enmeshed in Russia just like the French army. Only it will be worse."

Churchill listened tolerantly and then said, "My dear Dickie, it's nice to hear young people speaking their minds."

Mountbatten replied, "All right. But do one thing for me. Just remember that I am the only person who has apparently told you this."

While Mountbatten was being proved wrong (or so it seemed in the summer and early autumn of 1941), and Churchill right, plans for the film *In Which We Serve* went ahead, at first stumblingly and with many obstacles to overcome, then more swiftly. Coward soon convinced Mountbatten that he had no intention of basing his film "too exactly" on the career of the *Kelly*, or her commanding officer at all closely on Mountbatten. Coward wrote: "Mountbatten is definitely one of the most outstanding men of our time . . . My Captain (D) was a simpler character altogether, far less gifted than he, far less complicated, but in no way, I hope, less gallant."[5]

Once satisfied that this was to be no personal accolade, Mountbatten got busy cutting through red tape and using all his powerful influence to get total Admiralty co-operation. But however convinced Mountbatten himself might be about Coward's motives, a number of senior officers suspected that they were being pushed into helping one friend to present a fat tribute to another, who had received quite a number already. At one point the Ministry of Information threatened to ban the screening of the film outside the country, as it was bad propaganda to show one of H.M. ships being sunk. Coward sent an S O S to Mountbatten, and together they went to the Ministry of Information, to be received by the minister himself, Brendan Bracken. They made their complaint together, and Bracken sent for the official responsible for the threat.

"Dickie went off like a time bomb," Coward recalled, "and it was one of the most startling and satisfactory scenes I have ever witnessed. I actually felt a pang of compassion for the wretched official, who wilted under the tirade like a tallow candle before a strong fire."[6]

The film opened at the Gaumont cinema in September 1942. Unfortunately it led to a vendetta with Beaverbrook that lasted (with only the smallest letup) until Beaverbrook's death, and caused as much pain to Mountbatten as any other event in his life. The scene to which Beaverbrook took such violent objection was the one showing in close-up a copy of the *Daily Express* floating in oil-stained water, carrying the headline that there would be no war this year. For Beaverbrook, this was an affront to his political responsibility, to his power as a seer and prophet, and to his beloved newspaper. And this became the tinder that set off a deep-seated feud.

Almost twenty years after they had crossed the Atlantic together on their honeymoon for their first visit to the United States, Mountbatten and Edwina began another American tour. The contrast between the jazzy, lavish celebrations of 1922 and the stern, purposeful round of visits of September and October 1941 was significant. The Atlantic Charter had just been signed, Lend-Lease was in full swing, the United States was training RAF personnel as well as supplying the aircraft for them to fly in action. The nation was at peace, but there was an uneasy feeling everywhere that this state of neutrality could not be held for much longer.

In New York, the Mountbattens saw many of their old friends and then went their separate ways. Edwina's task was to tour the country on behalf of the British Red Cross and the St. John Ambulance Association to thank those who had contributed over £5 million during the first two years of war. Mountbatten's first duties lay at the United States Navy Yard in Norfolk, Virginia. Here the carrier *Illustrious*, whose command he was to take over, was undergoing repairs after being hit by six heavy bombs in January in the Mediterranean. He also again saw Antoine Gazda, who was manufacturing Oerlikons for the U.S. Navy and had designed a 60-knot E-boat hunter, which aroused Mountbatten's enthusiasm.

Then came the flight to Pearl Harbor, which gave him much concern. While he was in Los Angeles on his way back from Honolulu a cable arrived from Churchill: "We want you home here at once for something which you will find of the highest interest." The date was 10 October 1941.

The invitation to stay at the White House on the way home had to be refused ("We want Mountbatten here for a very active and urgent job," Churchill told Harry Hopkins) and Mountbatten had time only to give his warning to Stark before taking the Clipper across the Atlantic and reporting at once to Downing Street.

Less than two weeks after the evacuation from Dunkirk in June 1940, when in the eyes of the world Britain became a beleaguered island awaiting German invasion, a small group of British troops made a series of raids on the German-held French coast near Boulogne. Two Germans were killed, and a British colonel took a bullet through his ear. The world did not hear about it. But it was the first raid of Combined Operations Command, an organization that was to become associated with some of the most effective and daredevil operations of the war, and whose work would eventually culminate in the D-Day landings of 1944, and victory. "We have got to get out of our minds the idea that the Channel ports and all the country between them are enemy territory," wrote Churchill in June 1940. "How wonderful it would be if the Germans could be made to wonder where they were going to be struck next, instead of forcing us to try to wall in the island and roof it over."[7]

One of the most hazardous and renowned raids of the 1914–18 war had been made on the German U-boat base at Zeebrugge, on St. George's Day, 1918. It had been carried out under the command of Roger Keyes, a vice-admiral with a fine record already behind him, and a straight-talker. Churchill had made Keyes chief of Combined Operations, with fifty American "Tommy guns" and a handful of staff. The command developed fast, but not fast enough for the admiral, who was bursting with ambition and ideas but did not fully comprehend the art of political infighting. Time and again he was deprived of promised supplies and support. By the summer of 1941 he was scarcely on speaking terms with Churchill, and later told Mountbatten that "the Chiefs of Staff are the greatest cowards I have ever met."

"A new and young figure [at Combined Ops] . . . would be in the public interest," Churchill wrote at this time. And decided on Mountbatten.

What caused Churchill to single out Mountbatten, a junior captain, age forty-one, from the great wealth of talent available to him to fill this highly important command? He had been attracted to him from the earliest days, even if he did forget his extra sardine at Osborne. He had admired and worked well with his father, had recognized Mountbatten's special qualities when he was at Cambridge. His admiration for Edwina has already been mentioned. He judged her mind to be at least the equal of Mountbatten's own, and more important, saw that she kept her husband's wits fine-edged.

Churchill regarded them as among the most brilliant couples in the land. Martin Gilbert, Churchill's biographer, considers Edwina's emotional appeal to Churchill very strong, and has published Churchill's moving letter to her on the death of her grandfather. Gilbert has also written of Churchill's dislike of what he used to call the "instinct for the negative," which he recognized in leaders like Admirals Jellicoe and Dudley North and General Auchinleck, and the "instinct for the positive," which he saw so clearly in men like Beatty, Montgomery and Mountbatten.[8]

Brains and positivism were the two qualities that led to Mountbatten's selection, and to the crucial turning point in his career. And, once again, the royal connection was no handicap. From this time, Edwina and those who knew him well recognized a new authority in Mountbatten's stance and style. "Dickie much grown in stature since he took up his highly important, indeed vital, command," noted the observant diarist Sir Henry ("Chips") Channon.[9]

Admiral of the Fleet Lord Keyes, age sixty-eight, handed over his command to the officer twenty-seven years his junior whom he had once refused to have in his flagship and then come to admire. "He was very friendly about the turnover," Mountbatten said later. " 'The trouble is that the British have lost the will to fight,' Keyes told me. I could see *he* hadn't, but I didn't agree with him. Winston had told me what he wanted, and now it was up to me to carry it out."

Beaverbrook ordered his editors to condemn the appointment in the strongest terms. Mountbatten's mother, remembering how deeply press attacks had wounded her husband, wrote reassuringly to him that "luckily the general public is not much perturbed by the *Daily Express*' outcries and scandal sniffing."[10]

Mountbatten defined his task as "a two-fold job. The first was to continue the raids, so splendidly begun by Keyes, in order to keep the offensive spirit boiling and harass the enemy. Second, to prepare for the invasion of Europe, without which we could never win the war. 'I want you,' Winston had added, 'to turn the south coast of England from a bastion of defence into a springboard of attack.' "

The Russian armies were falling back all along their enormous front, the German armies had taken one major Russian city after another and were almost in the suburbs of Moscow. It had been a terrible year in the Mediterranean and North Africa; the Japanese were becoming more and more threatening in the Far East. It took enormous courage and optimism to talk of a springboard for the destruction of Germany in the autumn of 1941, especially when Churchill's dire predictions of June about the fate of the Russian armies seemed about to be fulfilled. But after the attack on Pearl Harbor, when Mountbatten's prophecy was fulfilled all too fearsomely, Churchill was able to note: "So we have won after all!"

It was the end of Mountbatten's fighting war and the beginning of his command war. He had inherited an uneasy and unloved organization that was neither fish, flesh nor fowl, and it was distasteful to lovers of all three. If the Combined Ops dish had not yet gone bad, it was widely regarded as "going off."

A command that is widely regarded as a *corps d'élite* will, by its nature and comparatively small numbers, always attract enemies among the majority, who fear they will lose both their best men and a degree of their own status to it. Furthermore, straight-talking Keyes had made numerous enemies. That notable Commando leader, Bernard Fergusson, has written of the "formidable inheritance of feuds"[11] Mountbatten had to cope with the moment he entered the Combined Operations H.Q. situated on a single floor in Richmond Terrace, Whitehall, London. The staff, including messengers and typists, numbered around twenty, and most of the officers were superannuated. Mountbatten was appalled, and amazed that anything at all had been accomplished. He inspected the setup for a single whirlwind month and reported back to the Chiefs of Staff. His suggestions were accepted without question, and he began his appointments, expansion and reorganization.

Judgements on Mountbatten's powers of administration and organization are as mixed as they are on everything else about the man. The reason for this is simple: he was brilliantly good at some things and less good, even quite bad, at others. Some of his appointments were masterly, others were weak. Some of the good appointments lasted too short a time, some of the poor ones lasted far too long.

Mountbatten in high command needed, looked for and nearly always found brains and smart, dedicated organizers who could prepare the briefs he needed. But he also needed charmers and sycophants with a ready sense of humour who would say what Mountbatten wanted to hear; as one of his senior staff put it, "handsome social chaps who could always be relied upon to say, 'The champagne's over here, Dickie.' " This second group was recruited mostly from his own service, and one or two admirals with "not much on top" lasted to the end of Mountbatten's serving career. But their presence made Mountbatten comfortable, they tended to be good on the public relations side, and their contribution cannot be entirely written off.

Captain John ("Jock") Hughes Hallett, who became the Naval Force Commander on Combined Ops' biggest raid, had a fine, original mind and was utterly courageous. His brother Charles could be indirectly classed as one of Mountbatten's "brains," since his division in the Admiralty was responsible for dealing with Combined Operations' day-to-day naval needs. This division was also responsible for the strategic disposition of landing craft. It was the Admiralty that mostly staffed him in those early days," he said, "and some of the people they put in were not first-class. And Mountbatten did not realize how bad some of them were."[12]

Mickey Hodges, an old friend who had served with him in the Mediterranean, became Mountbatten's Chief Signals Officer. Halsey was made his personal assistant, his "winger." Captain "Ronnie" Brockman was later lured from the First Sea Lord's office and remained at Mountbatten's elbow, or just behind it, for twenty-two years as his secretary.

Then there was Peter Murphy, a somewhat grey figure in Mountbatten's life, whose functions were not immediately clear but who, from the early 1920s to the 1940s, always seemed to be around, or near. Little has been made public about him, or his role. Ludovic Kennedy describes him as a left-wing ex-Guards Officer whose friendship with Mountbatten was long and important.

Mountbatten once spoke briefly of him to this writer, with obvious reluctance, referring to him as a very left-wing family friend for many years whom he had met at Cambridge after World War I, in which he had been severely wounded. Then we catch a glimpse of this ubiquitous man through the eyes of the American journalist Ray Murphy, who in

1945 wrote an unofficial but officially assisted biography of Mountbatten called *Last Viceroy*.

Ray Murphy was in Mountbatten's flat in Singapore, awaiting an interview with the Admiral when Peter Murphy ambled in, "a tanned, rather heavy man, clad in corduroy trousers and a checked sports shirt . . . as bald as a bust of Caesar," who referred to Mountbatten as "the old boy" and asked the journalist whether *Cannery Row* by John Steinbeck would be a good "plane read" for Mountbatten on his imminent flight to Delhi, and then joined them both for dinner.

Mountbatten's enjoyment of simple "salts" who charmed and admired him was balanced by his appreciation for eccentrics, which was one of his greatest assets. It showed most brightly at this difficult time when his pitiably small organization had, in the broadest and most literal sense, to prepare to beat Germany in Europe. The German armies could be beaten only by a successful preliminary invasion of the mainland. And this was what Combined Ops was ultimately preparing for.

Mountbatten needed planners and visionaries with minds as broad as the Channel, which would one day have to be crossed in force. In the end he obtained three, who all in some degree resembled the popular idea of the mad inventor, but whose genius mercifully stopped far short of insanity: Geoffrey Pyke, Professor J. D. Bernal of London University, and Professor Solly Zuckerman, then an anatomist and authority on apes who was soon known throughout Combined Ops as "the monkey man" and by Mountbatten as "my witch doctor." Zuckerman became Mountbatten's lifelong friend whose contribution to his achievements was immeasurable in its weight and extent.

One more figure among so many recruited during these early months was Mountbatten's relative Sir Harold Wernher, the ex-soldier and immensely successful businessman, who had special talents as liaison and co-ordinating officer. When Mountbatten grabbed him, Churchill (no slouch at nepotism himself) raised an eyebrow. "Some relation of yours?" he is said to have asked bleakly. "Not as close a one as Duncan Sandys!" retorted Mountbatten, referring to Churchill's son-in-law, who had recently been catapulted to Financial Secretary to the War Office.

If, by the end of 1941, Mountbatten's Combined Ops team was a mixed one, it was complete, its comparatively small number of really brilliant appointments more than outweighed the larger number of weak appointments. Above all, it was established and stabilized and recognized. This was entirely due to Mountbatten's energy, charm and ruthlessness—and to his priceless asset of access. He could talk on equal terms to George VI *and* his Prime Minister *and* his Foreign Secretary. He had the ear of anyone whom he wished to complain to, acquire something from, or praise.

The First Sea Lord, the crusty, able (and already sick) Admiral Sir Dudley Pound, had some grave reservations about Mountbatten's style and character. But Mountbatten was the only officer below flag rank who could raise the telephone (as he often did) and speak to him personally at any time. Poor old Keyes had scarcely been on speaking terms with anybody at the Admiralty.

This reformed and enlarged command could now begin its creative work, and plan and carry out its first raids under the new regime. There were to be ten raids of varying sizes in the first six months of 1942.

The first of note, but on a very small scale, was on a cliff top in northern France. A reconnaissance plane had photographed an unusual radar station, which Allied scientists clearly wished to examine. Combined Ops laid on a brilliantly conceived and executed raid on the night of 27 February 1942, with paratroopers dropping behind the site at Bruneval, and Commandos with a radio mechanic landing on a nearby beach. In the face of intensive fire, the necessary vital parts of the radar set were dismantled and brought safely home. The findings were of an immeasurable importance, especially to the future air offensive.

A second raid a month later was of equal value to the Royal Navy. One of Germany's mighty battleships, the *Bismarck*, larger and more formidable than any possessed by Britain, had been sunk in May 1941 after a dramatic chase and at the cost of the Royal Navy's biggest man o' war. The *Bismarck*'s sister ship, the *Tirpitz*, was now complete and such a threat to the Atlantic supply lines that she was distorting the whole structure of Allied naval strategy. Her destructive powers could be greatly reduced, however, if she could be deprived of the only dockyard on the French Atlantic seaboard big enough to accommodate her.

This was at St. Nazaire. The idea of destroying this dock was

broached to Mountbatten by one of his oldest naval friends and con-
tempories, Captain Charles Lambe, Director of Plans. The operation
was carried out with complete success on the night of 27–28 March
1942, and involved the ramming of the lock gates by an old and expendable U.S. Navy destroyer, with delayed charges on board.

This second triumph by Combined Ops confirmed Churchill in the
wisdom of his choice of leader, and ensured once and for all that
Mountbatten was henceforth to take his part at the very top for the
remainder of the war. A few days later Churchill wrote to Roosevelt:

> Dickie's show at St Nazaire, though small in scale, was very bracing. For your
> personal and secret eye, I made him Vice-Admiral, Lieutenant-General, and Air
> Marshal some few weeks ago, and have put him on the Chiefs of Staff Committee
> as Chief of Combined Operations. He is an equal member, attending whenever
> either his own affairs or the general conduct of the war are under consideration.
> He will be in the centre of what you mention about the joint attack on Europe.[13]

"I was now an Admiral at forty-one, two years younger than Nelson," Mountbatten recalled later, "and with the other honorary ranks,
I was the first serving officer to hold all three ranks in all three services.
To save Keyes's feelings, my official position up until then had been
Chief Adviser to Combined Operations, although, of course, I was still
the boss. Now Winston felt able to call me 'the boss' properly, and I
was one of only four members of the British Chiefs of Staff Committee.

"But all that was nothing compared with the fact that I now had the
power to get what I wanted. There were still a lot of people about who
saw nothing virtuous in combining the work of the three services. They
were no use to me, but they had been a pain in the neck in the past.
Now, not only did I not have to use them, I could overrule them. And
did so. The people I was working with now were the heads of the
services, all of them a lot senior to me in age, of course. The one nearest
to me was 'Peter' Portal [Air Chief Marshal Sir Charles Portal, Chief of
Air Staff]—he was only seven years older. And I got on specially well
with him, and we became great friends.

"Dudley Pound was now much more helpful, too. He had been
pretty sticky sometimes in the past, and he explained to me why he had
not always been helpful towards Combined Ops. It was, he said, because the Navy had to give all its attention to winning the Battle of the
Atlantic. If we lost that, we lost the war."

Increasingly during 1942, "Combined Operations" came to mean not only combined services but combined Anglo-American. America entered the war with the agreed commitment that the first priority was to defeat Germany, the second to defeat Japan. This led to immediate and close liaison and constant Atlantic traffic as American participation rapidly increased and the miracle of American war production altered the strategic and tactical concepts on every front.

In April 1942 Roosevelt sent his personal adviser, Harry Hopkins, and his Chief of Staff, General George C. Marshall, to London to formulate plans, long-term and short-term. One of their first visits was to Combined Ops headquarters. Whatever conflicts and abrasive relationships there may have been—and sometimes still were—between British and American commands, none of these occurred when Mountbatten was involved, or else were soon smoothed over. Mountbatten's love for America, added to his natural tact and charm, led to valuable harmony in war.

"The most important man in the American military machine throughout the war was George Marshall," Mountbatten once claimed unequivocally. "We got on marvellously from the start. He was a terrific personality. There was absolutely no nonsense about him, and you always knew where you were with him.

"When he came to Richmond Terrace he was amazed to see the three services working side by side as if there were no barriers—as there weren't, of course. Marshall said, 'This is amazing—it's inspiring. How did you do it?'

"I said, 'It's quite simple, sir. They all speak English, you see.' He didn't understand what I was getting at, at first; then he laughed, and I took advantage of the moment to make a suggestion. 'General, I believe you speak English, too, in America. So why don't you send over some soldiers and airmen and sailors and join us here at headquarters?' And so, quite early on, we got the first integrated Allied Headquarters operating in London."

This worked like a dream. Not only staff officers but American Rangers (the equivalent of British Commandos) were soon training alongside British and Commonwealth troops. And on the next big raid, Rangers served in strength and suffered heavily.

Fundamental political attitudes were more difficult to resolve. In the simplest definition, the American high command found in the British attitude to the war a certain caution and weariness—pessimism even. The Americans had all the fresh eagerness for battle but not the hard statistics nor the experience. For their part, the British attitude could be patronizing to the Americans. There was a very serious conflict of temperament and character between those who had been fighting alone, vastly outnumbered, for more than two years and the newcomers to the battlefield, all eagerness, inexperience, smart uniforms and medals before they had even begun, or so it seemed. In the lower echelons, the mutual wisecracking was not always comradely, and the British definition of American troops in England as "overpaid, oversexed and over here" had an edge to it.

Only the bigger minds could rise above these conflicting attitudes and see that co-operation was all-essential. One of Mountbatten's greatest contributions to victory was to help to bring about a fundamental change in attitude on the part of the two Allies. His visit to Washington in the early summer of 1942 was notable in the wartime history of Anglo-American relations.

The most serious conflict arose about the date of "the return to Europe"—the invasion and liberation of the enslaved nations. The American Chiefs of Staff in early 1942 believed that an invasion of France was possible later in that year (Operation Round-Up); and if not, then certainly in 1943 (Operation Sledgehammer).

"The British Chiefs of Staff paid me the compliment of suggesting that I was the only person capable of convincing them that Round-Up was quite impractical," said Mountbatten. "My task in Washington was probably the most important job I had to do in the war. I had to persuade Roosevelt and his advisers that American strategy and expectations needed rethinking."

"Dickie will explain to you the difficulties of 1942," Churchill told Roosevelt on 28 May. Mountbatten arrived to begin this formidable task on 3 June. On that same day the Battle of Midway was fought, the Pacific naval engagement that proved to be the turning point in the war against Japan. The Americans were jubilant; they had sunk four carriers, destroyed 250 enemy planes and broken the back of the Japanese air arm, which had everywhere been triumphant.

In a sense, this worked against Mountbatten, especially as the war in North Africa was going badly and Tobruk was soon to fall to the Germans. American senior officers of all services saw these events as confirmation of American strength and superiority and British weakness and defeatism. No one could have won over some of the hard-core prejudiced senior service officers in Washington. It was a measure of the success of Mountbatten's mission that he brought around a number of men of power and influence to the British view. He left behind him an impression of resolution and good will, and a President, according to Bernard Fergusson, "who was fast coming to share the British conviction that Sledgehammer was impossible, and Round-Up in 1943 rash."

For his part, Mountbatten returned with one of the most able American admirals, H. Kent Hewitt, commander of the newly formed "AmphibLant" in Norfolk, Virginia. He had been selected by Admiral Ernest J. King, Chief of Naval Operations, to be an observer at Combined Ops H.Q. in London for a period.

Churchill flew off to Washington a few days after Mountbatten had reported on his meetings and conclusions. It was an appropriate time for Admiral Hewitt to be in London. He had no idea that Churchill would be discussing with the President the subject code-named "Tube Alloys"—the atomic bomb—but he was well aware that a fundamental switch in strategy and priorities was on the agenda for the White House talks, and that preparations for an imminent landing in France were likely to be altered to preparations for a landing in French North Africa that year. He was therefore a witness to the planning in Richmond Terrace of Operation Torch, and of another, much smaller operation, though the biggest of all raids, which was even more imminent.

A great deal has been written about the Dieppe raid of 19 August 1942, and a great deal of it is rubbish. The most lunatic judgement on it was (not surprisingly) provided by the enemy. The Germans, for propaganda purposes, claimed that the raid was a full-scale invasion, which they had easily and bloodily repulsed. They then began to believe their own lie, which did their cause considerable damage.

Dieppe was, in the simplest definition, a raid in unusual strength to test German defences, absorb lessons for the real invasion nearly two years later, capture some troops and invasion barges in the harbour, give the Russians proof of Allied intentions, and at the same time prove British resolution to doubters at home and across the Atlantic and lift the flagging morale of the idle Canadian troops in England, who were to be the chief participants. Its motive, then, was about four-fifths political, one-fifth military.

Dieppe is particularly fascinating in the context of Mountbatten's life and war record because it was widely regarded as ill conceived, poorly and expensively carried out, dubious in its lessons, and very much Mountbatten's "show." To the end of his life, "Dieppe" was engraved upon Mountbatten's heart, and the name would always raise an instant defensive response, almost as if he were protesting too much.

It was while Hopkins and Marshall were in Britain that the first plans were formulated for a major raid on Hitler's Atlantic Wall. The most suitable target was clearly Dieppe, and Jock Hughes Hallett and his team devised a scheme for a pincers attack from the east and west, avoiding a head-on assault. The town, port and airfield would be held briefly, and the force re-embarked on the same day.

There were certain objections to this plan which favoured the frontal approach. Mountbatten remained convinced throughout that the "pincer" idea was better. Then came his Washington visit in June 1942. In his absence, General Bernard Montgomery, C.-in-C. South-Eastern Army, pressed for a frontal assault after a heavy bombardment. Churchill refused to allow bombers to carry this out because of the French casualties and anti-British feeling that this would cause. Dudley Pound had already refused to allow battleships to be used for a bombardment in case they, in turn, might be bombed by the Germans. A staff assessment at Combined Ops showed that any sort of bombardment would fill the streets with so much rubble that the tanks would be stalled and become sitting ducks.

The problem was still unresolved when Montgomery conveniently departed for North Africa to win his spurs at El Alamein. No one knows to this day whether anyone tried to explain the problem to him before he left. But everyone agreed later that there was a lack of communication between Southern Command and Combined Ops H.Q., and for this Mountbatten must finally be held responsible.

The date of the attack, conditioned by moon and tides, was postponed twice and finally fixed, in spite of security risks, for the night of 18–19 August. By this time Mountbatten had been back at H.Q. for weeks, knew that the operation was to be conducted in a manner quite different from that devised by his own planning staff and approved by him, but did nothing to halt it. "He should have cancelled or bombarded," is Charles Hughes Hallett's view today."[14]

As the world learned very quickly, the assault was a bloody fiasco. There were local successes, examples of great heroism, further valuable radar secrets were unearthed, but in all its prime military objectives, the raid failed, and the frontal assault was repulsed on the beach and promenades of the town.

The statistics of losses, when they first came in, appeared alarming. Of the 5,000 Canadians engaged, nearly 1,000 were killed, 2,000 captured (many of them wounded), and of the 2,000 who got back, 25 percent were wounded. A destroyer and 33 landing craft were sunk, 106 RAF aircraft were shot down in the biggest fighter battle of the air war. There were over 1,000 futher casualties above the Canadians' figure. The Germans suffered 591 casualties and won a considerable propaganda victory.

Aside from those who even today call out "Disaster!," there are still many historians who consider that the lessons of Dieppe could have been learned less expensively. They may be right, or simply wise after the event. In the count of war, one dead soldier can be defined as a disaster. But the Dieppe casualties must be seen in terms of 1941–42, when, for example, the shelling of H.M.S. *Hood* killed many more sailors than all the soldiers at Dieppe; when the RAF was losing many times that number every month; when a small-scale raid on a quiet afternoon outside Stalingrad could result in ten times as many casualties; when the Japanese would not bother to count 1,000 dead defending a minor beachhead on a Pacific island. The scale of casualties at Dieppe in terms of World War II were tragic and infinitesimal. Yet they were large enough for their shock to have a salutary effect and for the lessons learned to be taken much more seriously than if the operation had been a walkover. The price paid, the benefit gained are as incalculable as the numerical reckoning. But to talk of Canadian lives being "thrown away" on the beaches of Dieppe is far from the truth. Never were more lifesaving lessons learned on one operation than at Dieppe. Among them was that an attack on a defended coast required many times more powerful bombardment than that provided by destroyers. From this stemmed the multiple-rocket (a thousand at a time) bombardment ship.

Dieppe also taught that tank obstacles must be breached before tanks were landed; that landing craft needed very skilful piloting; that a higher degree of training was required for beach assault parties. Above all, Dieppe provided confirmation beyond doubt that an assault on a port must result in the total destruction of that port. Therefore, invaders must either capture ports intact, *or bring their own harbours with them.*

Mountbatten afterwards claimed that he had already reached this conclusion. He also claimed that Churchill took all the credit for Mulberry, the famous floating artificial harbour of the 1944 Normandy invasion. He would imitate Churchill's voice—"You must have great piers that rise and fall with the tide . . ."—raising and lowering his hands as he did so, with a mischievous smile on his lips.

"The truth is this," Mountbatten said. "I knew we would have to make artificial harbours. I knew we would have to bombard any port to such an extent that it would destroy the facilities. We had to have them because of the weather and the vast supplies we would have to put ashore immediately. No one person invented Mulberry. The knowledge that we had to have this floating harbour slowly *grew.*

"But no one outside Combined Ops believed in it. So I went to Winston and asked him to write a minute to show that he liked the idea, and he said yes. And he wrote it, and it was very powerful, and it is now used as evidence that he thought the whole thing up. I am not complaining for myself. I couldn't care less. But Winston long ago (it was the same in my father's time) got this habit of picking up people's ideas without their permission. His claim later that he thought of ideas that really belonged to others was the price you had to pay to get them through."

Actually, Churchill makes no such claim in his war memoirs. According to Churchill, the prime originator of Mulberry, which made a successful invasion possible, was Jock Hughes Hallett.

Zuckerman, Pyke and the other "boffins" (the slang name for scientists then much in vogue) busied themselves with finding answers to the lessons of Dieppe during the autumn and winter of 1942. However, Dieppe post-mortems continued far beyond this time, and for long after the war was won. When Mountbatten was Fourth Sea Lord in 1951, he was shown the draft of the Confidential Staff History covering the Dieppe raid. The whole operation had been examined in immense detail, and the conclusion was that it failed operationally because of the last-minute interference of General Montgomery, who insisted on the frontal assault. No direct cause of failure was ascribed to Mountbatten.

Yet when the draft reached Mountbatten's desk he telephoned Lieu-tenant-Commander Peter Kemp, the head of the branch responsible for Staff Histories. "He wanted it withdrawn," Kemp recalls. When Mountbatten found that this was hardly possible, he asked, " 'Well can you rewrite this bit saying it was an operational failure?' And I replied, 'Frankly, sir, no. We are merely repeating what the official records say.'

"He walked up and down his office. He seemed more hurt than cross. Then he said, 'Now, about these figures of casualties. I'm sure they're exaggerated.' 'No, sir, we have seen all the returns, the prisoner-of-war lists, and so on. They are as written.'

"In the end he persuaded us to do a little tinkering, dividing the casualties into those wounded, taken prisoner and dead, which was fair enough. But it is quite interesting because it shows how badly he felt about Dieppe."[5]

Dieppe was a recurring sore for Mountbatten because it was seen by some as *his* failure. It was not a failure because the price was high. It was not a failure at all, by some interpretations. But like Boulogne to Nelson, the name Dieppe hurt Mountbatten for the rest of his life.

One of the strongest reasons that Mountbatten used for not permit-ting an authorized biography to be written in his lifetime was that he believed he had never made a single mistake in his life. "It is a curious thing, but a fact, that I have been right in everything I have done and said in my life," Mountbatten said many times. "No one would believe a biographer who made this claim while I was still alive because read-ers would conclude that I had caused it to be written, that I was leaning over the author's shoulder."

It was, then, to be left to posterity. Posterity would correct the rec-ord. Posthumously, the public was more likely to recognize the truth that his official biographer was certain to write: the truth that he had never made a single mistake in his life. Dieppe was a threat to this clean record; and there was one man who never allowed him to forget it, Lord Beaverbrook, who had not yet seen *In Which We Serve*.

"In spite of his violent attacks on me later, Max Beaverbrook always claimed that I was made head of Combined Ops and then promoted and made one of the four running the war on the Chiefs of Staff Com-mittee on his advice to Winston," said Mountbatten. " 'This is a very important position I've got for you,' Max would say. 'Preparing for the invasion.'

"Max had been using his newspapers for some time to agitate for an invasion—'Second Front Now!' It was one of his great wartime campaigns. He really believed that we could successfully invade Europe long before we had the men and the arms and equipment—just like some of the Americans.

"Now, having—as he tried to convince me—got me onto the Chiefs of Staff Committee and made a vice-admiral, he expected me to support *his* cause. He saw me as the young man who would make Winston change his mind about the date of the invasion. It was a sort of exchange arrangement. 'The Chiefs of Staff need my help, and you as a young man can let me know what you hear.' Several times he said, 'Stick to me!' Of course I could do nothing of the kind, and told Max so. And—well, 'Hell hath no fury . . .' "

Two events occurred in quick succession, which between them set the seal on a most notorious public vendetta. The first was Dieppe. Not only was this not the invasion for which Beaverbrook had been agitating, it was an ill-judged gamble in which Mountbatten had laid down the chips—and the chips were thousands of Beaverbrook's countrymen. They were lost, squandered. They were wasted by military folly. Just to prove the hollowness of Beaverbrook's campaign for a full invasion *now*.

Then a month later, on 17 September 1942, came the premiere of *In Which We Serve*, the work, in Beaverbrook's judgement, of an effete "pansy" and war slacker. Noël Coward had often been the target of the Beaverbrook newspapers in the past. Now he had produced a film which made a mockery of the *Daily Express*, purported to show Coward as a naval hero, when the whole world knew that it was Mountbatten— Mountbatten, who had broken his trust with the man who really put him in a position of power, and had then thrown away Canadian lives in a futile exercise . . .

The extent of Beaverbrook's anger, which might have warned Mountbatten that this time it would be a lifelong vendetta, became evident a short time later, on 21 October 1942. It was Trafalgar Day, and Averell Harriman gave a large dinner party to celebrate the occasion.

"Max was there, and he got very drunk," Mountbatten remembered. "Afterwards he came up to me and said very loudly, 'You and I were once good friends, but now I'm through with you.' Suddenly there was great attention concentrated on us, but Max went on, 'You attacked me in that film of yours—you changed the real events to attack me. *You're* responsible for linking that film with me. That was a very unfriendly thing to do, Dickie.' I was stunned. He hadn't finished yet. 'And then what about Dieppe? You murdered my countrymen. So, you look out—your career's finished.'

"I tried to soothe him down and make the peace, but it was no good—he was beside himself and much too drunk."

The next operation for which Mountbatten's H.Q. prepared all the plans put the controversial Dieppe raid in its proper scale as a small but important signpost pointing towards victory over Germany: Operation Torch, the invasion of North Africa, to be followed by the invasion of Italy. "So much of my time when I was serving in the Mediterranean had been spent in preparing for war against Italy," said Mountbatten, "that it was a particular satisfaction for me that my H.Q. prepared the plans for its defeat."

Mountbatten's term as Chief of Combined Operations was nearing its end. Soon he was to be called to even higher responsibilities. But there were still two occasions that show the variety and weight of his activities during this time. New weapons and instruments of war of all kinds, from rocket-launching bombardment craft to giant floating platforms made from a frozen compound (called Pykerete, after its inventor) of sea water and sawdust, were one of the chief preoccupations of Combined Ops H.Q. Mountbatten, with his ingenious, curious, technical, inventive and ever-open mind, followed all proposals and experiments with enthusiasm. Nothing was beyond consideration; it was a characteristic that he shared with Churchill, and a factor in Churchill's decision to give him this job.

At one stage, new underwater craft were high on the agenda at H.Q., and Mountbatten turned up at a joint Chiefs of Staff meeting, somewhat damp and dishevelled, from an examination of a new craft. Churchill looked at him in dismay. He had never before seen Mountbatten improperly turned out. "What have you been up to, Dickie?" he asked.

"I have been trying out a new one-man submarine," Mountbatten replied.

"What on earth for?"

"Well, I think it might be useful for Commando raids, or fixing limpet mines and that sort of thing."

Churchill glanced up and down at the figure again. "How did you get so wet?"

"I tried it."

Churchill, aghast, demanded, "You don't mean to say you went down by yourself?"

"It's a one-man submarine, so only one man can go down in it."

Churchill bellowed at him like a sergeant-major on the parade ground. "This is the most irresponsible thing I've ever heard! I give you an important job in the conduct of the war and you go and try to kill yourself. If you do it again, I shall fire you."

At about the same time, August 1942, there came another, gentler rocket, from another quarter. The Duke of Kent, serving in the RAF, was killed in a flying accident along with all the crew. He and Mountbatten had been good friends as well as cousins, and Mountbatten was deeply shocked. Shortly after the news came through, he went to see the King at Buckingham Palace. George VI was heartbroken. "I'm also very proud, Dickie," he said, "that one of the family has given his life. I know David took many risks in the Great War, but this is the first member of the British royal family to lose his life in a war for a very long time."

The question of the funeral and other matters were discussed, among them the fact that there were no brothers left to take over from Kent the voluntary societies of which he had been grand president, etc.

"I'd like you to take them on, Dickie," George VI said.

Mountbatten replied that he was greatly flattered at the suggestion but that he did in fact have a pretty full-time job on his hands already.

"But there's no one to take over the Royal Societies," the King persisted. "Surely you could manage them. You need only keep formal contact until after the war." Mountbatten reluctantly agreed, and that was why, from this time on, increasing numbers of lines in *Who's Who* were devoted to his presidency and patronage of Royal Societies and others. It was not until the last years of his life that he began to shed some of these responsibilities.

Throughout his period at Combined Ops, Mountbatten insisted on keeping in direct touch with the men, confident in his belief that his presence alone could lift their morale and fill them with greater vigour and courage. At the end of an inspection, and talks to many of the individuals present, he would give a general talk.

The routine was invariable and became known to tens of thousands of men during the remainder of the war. He would call for a box—anything to stand on, which always happened to be immediately available. Then he would get up on it, and if an overassiduous officer had provided his stand with a pulpitlike rest, he would have the stand reversed, or more often turn it around himself so that there was nothing between him and his audience. He was usually without his hat, and if it was warm, he would be without his jacket, too, informality being the essence of his style.

Often he would start off with a joke appropriate to the men's circumstances. Before a raid he would often tell the assembled Commandos, weary from training, "Well, you have done it here, now you've got to do it over there. It reminds me of a sailor who had a girl friend at home and then was posted overseas. He wrote to her for a while, then stopped. Her letters remained unanswered. Eventually, in desperation she wrote: 'I am sure you have found another girl, but I can't understand what she has got that I haven't!' To this he replied: 'She hasn't got anything that you haven't got. You've got everything that she's got, but she's got it here!' "

It never failed, any more than the inspection that preceded it could fail. "We were lined up," wrote one lieutenant preparing crews for tank landing craft, "and each member of the staff was presented to him. I shall never forget the manner in which he looked at me—I have never been looked at so 'squarely in the face' in my life—his eyes seemed to be reading my thoughts! It was a wonderful experience and, by his questions, he obviously had a great knowledge of the work we were doing.

"He spoke to each of the officers in turn, and all of us were astounded by those penetrating eyes. He ended with an encouraging remark, and a smile. It was an experience of a lifetime."[16] It also, inevitably, became known as "the Mountbatten touch."

By the summer of 1943, with Africa cleared of the enemy, Italy vanquished (though not yet liberated) and the plans and men and weapons and equipment for the invasion of France almost complete, Mountbatten felt that he had done all that he could for his command.

Like his father, the longer an appointment rooted him ashore, the more his longing to return to sea increased. He did not care how many temporary ranks he dropped: he wanted to feel the throb of turbines beneath steel decks and the salt air in his face. He got both. But not as he expected or wished. The ship in which he sailed down the river Clyde on 4 August 1943, twenty-nine years to the day since he had dined with his father in Mall House on the night the country went to war, was the *Queen Mary*. He was a mere passenger. His fellow passengers included his boss, Winston Churchill, his fellow Chiefs of Staff and almost two hundred more staff officers and advisers in every field of warfare.

It was a pleasant enough voyage, with much interesting talk and the usual amount of heavy drinking in Churchill's cabin. Mountbatten remained restless, however. Here, on board this liner and lacking the distractions of Whitehall, was the time and place to cultivate the First Sea Lord, Dudley Pound, the one man who could "fix" a sea appointment for him.

"I followed him like a shadow," Mountbatten recalled, "pacing the decks for exercise, or up on the bridge. He always seemed to be talking to someone. It never occurred to me that he might be avoiding me. Then one day I did catch Pound alone.

" 'I've about finished my work at Combined Operations,' I said, 'and I think it's about time I went back to sea.' He did not seem to take any interest at all. 'Look, sir,' I persisted, 'I'd very much like to go back to the *Illustrious*.' 'Yes, yes,' he said—or I thought he said. But it was more a mumble, and then someone came and interrupted us."

A few days later Mountbatten discovered why the First Sea Lord was even more uncommunicative than usual.

"SUPREMO" I

he *Queen Mary* docked at Halifax five days after clearing the Clyde. Even Churchill the gourmet commented that the menu was up to peacetime standards. He had been looking forward to a short period of rest; instead, every waking minute had been fully occupied, so unrelenting was the pressure of conducting the war.

Shortly before leaving London, Churchill had discussed the possible creation of a new command in South-East Asia, where the land war had grown stale and unsatisfactory and the morale of the troops was known to be low—"This lethargic and stagnant Indian scene," as he defined it. He had asked Clement Attlee, the Deputy Prime Minister, and the Foreign Secretary, for their views on his suggested candidate for the job of running the command. Churchill referred to this matter again in the first report he telegraphed to George VI, mentioning for the first time Mountbatten by name. "I am increasingly inclined to suggest this solution to the [American] president," he added.[1]

In fact, the die was cast. Churchill knew that the King would welcome the new and dramatic promotion of his cousin, and that Roosevelt, already an ardent admirer, would also approve of his choice. Among those of his fellow passengers on the voyage with whom Churchill discussed the appointment were Dudley Pound; his Senior Assistant Secretary of the War Cabinet, General Leslie Hollis; and General Sir Ian Jacob, member of the War Cabinet Secretariat.

Jacob recalled later that Churchill had teased them by asking who they thought would make a good Supreme Commander. "It was rather an important question, but we suggested some names," said Jacob.

"Then he, with a look like a naughty schoolboy, produced Mountbatten's name and asked what we thought of that. I said I thought it a splendid idea, and one which would appeal to the Americans."[2]

The Quebec Conference of August 1943 took place in the Citadel—"in every way delightful, and ideally suited to the purpose," Churchill pronounced. On the agenda for discussion were such items as the invasion of Italy now that both the island of Sicily and Mussolini had fallen; and Operation Overlord (the invasion of France) the following spring.

But, according to Churchill, "the greater part of it concerned operations in Burma and the Indian Ocean . . ."[3] No discussions could take place until the choice of Supreme Commander had been approved by all concerned, and Mountbatten remained in ignorance of his nomination until several days after their arrival in Quebec.

"Winston asked me to take a walk along the battlements overlooking the Heights of Abraham," Mountbatten recalled. "He asked me about my health, as he knew that I had been badly overworking and had been feeling the strain. I said I thought it was pretty good, and he asked me next, 'Do you feel up to anything?' and I said 'Yes.'

"Then he asked me what I thought of the situation in South-East Asia. 'It's a pretty good mess,' I said, and he said, rather surprisingly, 'Do you think you could put it right?' I thought about this for a moment. It would mean a lot of paperwork and I had a lot on my hands already without another assessment for the Chiefs of Staff. 'Isn't that a thing for Pug Ismay?' I said. [He was referring to Churchill's Chief of Staff, General Hastings Ismay].

" 'Pug Ismay?' Winston exclaimed. 'You don't understand what I'm offering you. I am offering you to go out there and do the job!' I still didn't understand. I thought he meant that I should make a trip out there before doing my assessment.

" 'A trip!' This time it was an explosion. 'I'm offering you the job of Supreme Allied Commander of South-East Asia. What do you think of that?' "

Mountbatten said, after a pause to digest this astonishing proposal, that he would like twenty-four hours to think it over. Churchill provocatively asked him if he was afraid he couldn't do the job. "Not at all," said Mountbatten. "I have a congenital weakness for feeling certain I can do anything, but I do want to ask the British and U.S. Chiefs of Staff to satisfy myself that they agree with your choice wholeheartedly and will back me to the full."

Churchill assured him that he had the support of the President. "He's as keen as I am, but you can talk to the Chiefs."

Mountbatten always claimed that he satisfied himself in his own unique way and with his usual destroyerlike speed, starting with Lieutenant-General Alan Brooke, who assured him that all the Chiefs thought he was the right man for the job. "If I don't like your generals out there, can I sack them?" Mountbatten asked.

"We can consider it," said Brooke.

"That's not the point," Mountbatten insisted. "Do you trust me enough—can I send you a signal saying I am sending So-and-so home?"

Brooke agreed; and Mountbatten next pinned down the Chief of the Air Staff. Portal not only agreed at once but added, "If you like we can go through the list and shift some of them around now."

A day or two earlier, Mountbatten had by chance literally saved the First Sea Lord's life when he stumbled on the edge of a ravine during a sightseeing trip—further confirmation that Dudley Pound's health was failing. There had been no further opportunity of discussing a seagoing appointment. Now the old admiral enthusiastically welcomed Mountbatten's appointment. "This is absolutely splendid, Dickie, to have the Navy getting this job. Now you understand why I couldn't let you talk about going back to sea."

Mountbatten thanked him, and followed up smartly with the question, "Can I sack anybody—including James Somerville?" Somerville was c.-in-c. of the Eastern Fleet and had already been a post-captain when Mountbatten was a sub-lieutenant, twenty-three years his junior.

Pound replied, "Well, no, Dickie, obviously you can't. We can't have a young chap like you going out and sacking all the admirals."

At once Mountbatten said, "Thank you very much, sir. I don't want the job. You know I want to go back to sea, and this lets me out."

Pound said he did not understand, and Mountbatten continued, "You don't think I'd go out there with the authority to sack generals and air marshals and not officers of my own service?"

"Have you really had this permission from the others?"

Mountbatten confirmed that he indeed had, and Pound reluctantly agreed. "Well, yes, I suppose so. But you mustn't abuse it."

"No," said Mountbatten, "I won't abuse it, but I shall certainly hold you to that."

Mountbatten recounted this episode many times, and it has frequently been printed. But, at best, it is an oversimplified account of what happened at Quebec. Field-Marshal Lord Alanbrooke and Marshal of the RAF Lord Portal both denied that Mountbatten had been given this authority when questioned about it after the war.[4] And Dudley Pound's successor as First Sea Lord confirmed that only Churchill, or the minister concerned, had the power to sack a c.-in-c., so that these Chiefs of Staff were not even in a position to grant Mountbatten the power he insisted they gave him as a condition of his acceptance of the appointment.

No doubt Mountbatten sought, and was granted, unusually strong independent power to appoint and sack without reference to his Chiefs, but certainly not the dictatorial power he claimed. But this story of his, like so many others, is more dramatic.

Having now, as he claimed, "cleared the British team," Mountbatten said that he went after the American Chiefs of Staff. There was, it seems, no serious trouble with any of them. George Marshall said, "Sure—sack anyone you like so long as the President confirms you have the authority." General H. H. ("Hap") Arnold said the same thing, and Ernie King (now an old friend) not only agreed but offered Mountbatten one of his biggest aircraft carriers, the *Saratoga*. As Britain had flatly refused to lend the U.S. Navy a carrier in the desperate post–Pearl Harbor days, this was particularly magnanimous.

"After that, I went to see the President," said Mountbatten. "And he gave me a little lecture. He said, 'Now, don't forget that you're an *Allied* commander. Ike is loyal to your King, and you've got to be loyal to me. It's a matter of trust. I trust you to act not from the point of view of your country but from the point of view of the war effort—the Allied cause.'

"I agreed with all that and asked, 'Can I fire your generals if I think it's essential?'

"And Roosevelt replied, 'With pleasure. But don't fire them directly. Send me a personal telegram saying "Please remove this officer." It can be Stilwell [Lieutenant General J. W. "Vinegar Joe" Stilwell, already in China, and Mountbatten's nominated deputy.] But don't say "You're fired!" I'll do that.'

"I said, 'Thank you very much,' and went back to Winston. 'All right,' I said. 'All six say yes, and the President agrees, so I'm prepared to go.' "

Mountbatten returned to his quarters at the Château Frontenac. "I drew up a chair, sat down, took a blank sheet of paper and began to write down all the things I would have to do. Before I had even finished, there was a knock on the door. It was Bill Donovan, head of the OSS. 'Let me be the first to congratulate you on being appointed Supreme Allied Commander South-East Asia.'

"I was appalled. It was still white-hot secret. 'I don't know what you're talking about. Why do you come barging in here talking complete nonsense? Anyway, I'm much too young—halfway down the captains' list.'

" 'You can't fool me,' he said. 'Why do you think we're here? I've got spies everywhere. I know that the P.M. and the President have offered you the job.'

" 'Well, supposing you're right, why do you come and worry me about it?'

"Quick as a shot, Bill replied, 'Because I want your permission to operate in South-East Asia.'

"I told him Joe Stilwell was already there so why didn't he ask him. 'That bastard won't let me operate with him. He's a prejudiced old son of a bitch. But you've been working with SIS and SOE, so you know what we're all about.'

" 'Are you any good?' I asked him.

" 'You bet we're good.'

" 'Then I'm going to test you.' The test was to get me two of the best seats for *Oklahoma!* when I was due to stay in New York for a couple of nights with my flag-lieutenant.

"He nearly exploded. 'Goddamn it, that's impossible! There are absolutely *no* seats for six months. How do you expect me . . .?'

" 'No seats for *Oklahoma!*, no operations in South-East Asia.' Then I threw him out.

"A few days later he met us in New York. He had two of the best seats and two of the prettiest girls in New York for the evening. After the show, we all went to a night club. On the way out, in the foyer there were a couple of photographers. By this time Bill thought he was in. But I said, 'If those photographs are published, not only are you out, but I'll probably be out, too.' And in a flash, two toughs suddenly appeared and marched off with the photographers."

Immediately after receiving Mountbatten's agreement, Churchill sent telegrams to all those closely concerned with the most important outcome of the Quebec Conference. To the Viceroy of India, Lord Linlithgow, who would be most affected by the decision, Churchill wrote:

> We have now formed and set up the South-East Asia Command, separate from the command in India . . . We have had some discussions with the Americans in the weeks that have passed upon the person of the commander. After a great deal of consideration I decided to propose Lord Mountbatten for this very important post. Mountbatten has unique qualifications, in that he is intimately acquainted with all three branches of the Services, and also with amphibious operations. He . . . knows the whole of our war story from the centre. I regard this as of great importance on account of the extremely varied character of the South-East Asia front by land and sea. Mountbatten is a fine organizer and a man of great energy and daring.[5]

On the following day, 25 August 1943, the appointment was made public officially. Many Americans and a number of powerful politicians were incensed when they learned that this new command was to be led by a British officer—and a young, recently elevated naval officer at that. It was one thing to be popular as a royal playboy in peacetime and the hero of the *Kelly* (and *In Which We Serve*) in wartime. But this appointment was seen as a snub to General Douglas MacArthur. "It would be a tragic thing," wrote one columnist, "if MacArthur were to be shorn of his authority while a London glamour boy is elevated."[6]

The anti-Mountbatten lobby in the U.S. Senate was led by H. Styles Bridges, a Republican from New Hampshire and a member of the Senate Military Affairs Committee. Letters were "planted" in newspapers all over the United States. "A wave of anger will sweep this nation," ran one, if it should turn out that "America's No. 1 hero MacArthur is to play a subordinate role to ex-playboy Mountbatten . . ."

In the end, Churchill protested to Roosevelt. Mountbatten, he told the President, "has been affected by accounts telegraphed here describing him as 'the British princeling and glamour boy who has ousted the proved veteran . . .' "[7] The campaign simmered, died down in the press of events, was briefly revived, and then finally ended some eight months later.

In the last weeks of 1941 and the early months of 1942, the free world had watched in wonder and fear the spread of Japanese power across the globe. Few observers had recognized the eventual disaster that must overwhelm Japan as a result of the attack on the American fleet at Pearl Harbor; and only a few far-sighted members of the Japanese high command recognized that if Japan did not force America to agree to surrender terms swiftly, the imperial Japanese empire must eventually be doomed.

At one time American defeat seemed very close, when the Japanese navy controlled most of the Pacific and Indian oceans, and the Japanese armies were at the doorstep of India, had conquered huge areas of French, British and Dutch territory, the Philippines and vast numbers of Pacific islands, and had penetrated deep into China. The tide had been turned at Midway by a handful of U.S. Navy fliers, but the Japanese were even more tenacious on the defensive than they had been swift and successful on the offensive. The war was clearly going to be long and arduous.

In August 1943 Japanese arms were opposed by hundreds of millions of Chinese, a great part of the rapidly growing American military machine, a substantial Indian Army, and British, Commonwealth, French, Dutch, Burmese, Gurkha, and East and West African troops. This ring around Japan comprised four commands, headed by Admiral Chester A. Nimitz in the Central Pacific; General Douglas MacArthur in the South-West Pacific; Generalissimo Chiang Kai-shek in China; and now, despite widespread American apathy, Mountbatten in South-East Asia. Of these, the two American commands were doing best. Chiang Kai-shek was fighting a desperate battle, depending wholly on the Americans for supplies. The British command was in a sorry mess.

It was this deplorable and humiliating situation that was to occupy all the creative energies, the inspiration, tact and diplomacy which Mountbatten could muster for the next two years—twenty-four epochal months of unprecedented strain and achievement in a life of eighty years.

.   .   .

After his two nights in New York, Mountbatten proceeded to Washington to pay what he called his "official respects" to the President and the Chiefs of Staff. "They couldn't have been better or kinder," he said.

"I was wearing a khaki uniform, and I called on Ernie King for the last time. We chatted for a while and then I said—eying his uniform— 'Admiral, I have a great favour to ask you. I want to ask you for something of yours which must be very precious to you.'

"He looked at me doubtfully. 'Carriers?' he asked. 'More carriers?'

"No, not carriers. I just want one of your buttons. Will you cut that button from your coat and give it to me?'

" 'What in hell's name—?'

" 'Look, Ernie,' I said, 'I'm going to have a button of yours, and one from George Marshall, one from Hap Arnold—Brookie's going to give me one, and so is Peter Portal. Just five buttons, that's all I ask.'

"Ernie laughed for a long time, then took a pair of scissors and cut it off. I got all the others, too, and had them sewn onto a coat. I still wear it sometimes."

When Mountbatten left the American continent at the end of August, it was as if he were following that old appeal of Kipling, whom he so admired, and in careful truth and steadfastness was taking over "the yoke in youth." For Dudley Pound was dying at the time when his young protégé, representing his beloved Royal Navy, took up his new command. He had been looking very ill when Mountbatten last saw him and had suffered the first of several strokes on his arrival in Washington. Pound eventually made it back to England, dying on 21 October—Trafalgar Day—1943.

Churchill, suddenly in poor health himself and increasingly concerned about his First Sea Lord, was now worried about the decision that most of what he called his "war machine" was returning to England by air without him. Without the navigational aids and the engine reliability we take for granted today, these long-distance flights posed many natural hazards in addition to the very real risk of interception by the enemy. The Duke of Kent, Admiral Yamamoto, General Gott (en route to take over the Eighth Army), Air Marshal Leigh Mallory, the bandleader Glenn Miller, were only a few of the many who were killed flying on wartime duties.

Alan Brooke, Eden, Portal, Jacob, Mountbatten and others were due to take off in a flying boat from the St. Lawrence River below Quebec on the morning of 28 August for the direct flight home. "Splashing about his bath," as Eden described him shortly before their departure, and agreeing to take a long rest, Churchill in maudlin mood told him, "I don't know what I should do if I lost you all. I'd have to cut my throat. It isn't just love, though there is much of that in it, but that you are my war machine. Brookie, Portal, you and Dickie. I simply couldn't replace you."[8]

By any reasonable law of averages, a man with an accident-prone record, who had experienced two serious train crashes should have had at least one serious—if not fatal—air crash in the course of his wartime flying, hundreds of thousands of miles of it. In his new command Mountbatten flew in single-engine "spotter" machines of doubtful reliability, bombers of all kinds, countless C-47 Dakotas (very reliable, unlike the weather conditions and landing strips), and flying boats.

In the course of his morale-boosting tours, he once flew six hundred miles southwest of Ceylon to Addu Atoll. On arrival, he told his audience, "I am the Supremo and as such I have come to see you all. As I am 'important,' many precautions are taken for my safety, so the Navy despatched several ships on the route here in case my aircraft ditched. Additionally, the RAF sent a Sunderland flying boat out ahead in case it was needed to rescue me. I flew in here in an American Mitchell B-25 bomber fitted with extra tanks.

"On the way the radio operator sitting next to me stubbed out his cigarette on a metal can, so I said, 'What's inside?' and he said, 'Gas!' So much for saving the Supremo."[9]

On takeoff for the return flight, the pilot left the autopilot on "engaged" and the Mitchell nearly crashed. So Mountbatten returned in the reserve Sunderland. The pilot warned, "It'll mean a night flight and I haven't flown one of these at night for a year or so."

Not only was it pitch dark but a thunderstorm was raging when they reached Ceylon. The great flying boat got down all right, however, and the pilot said, "My passenger was completely calm throughout. He even left me a note thanking me for the trip."[10]

It was in another flying boat, a Clipper, that Churchill's "war machine" returned before Mountbatten took up his command eighteen months earlier. The nineteen-hour flight went off without a hitch, and the great Boeing touched down in Poole harbour, Dorset, to the utmost relief of the British War Cabinet as well as the American General Staff. Mountbatten hastened with the others to London. Edwina and George VI were among the first people to greet him.

Mountbatten had just one month to prepare himself and his staff and to learn all that he could about the state of the war with Japan and those fighting it. From that single sheet of paper which he had begun to fill in at the Château Frontenac, he swiftly built up the structure of his command:

"I chose Al Wedemeyer as Deputy Chief of Staff—an American, one of Marshall's smartest staff officers—a tricky customer but very loyal to me. As Chief of Staff, I chose an Englishman, Pownall, a very good mediator. Marshall had recommended to me 'Specs' Wheeler, who was already out there, and I took him on as Allied Principal Administrative Officer.*

"Winston had told me he wanted me to take on [General Orde] Wingate, for what he was worth. He was a great hero, and Winston liked heroes. Wingate's Chindits were famous for their deep penetrations behind the Japanese lines, but they suffered dreadful casualties, mainly due to lack of air support of their own. I got them this, through Hap Arnold, and we called it 'No. 1 Air Commando.' I hoped now that there would be no more of this leaving behind of the wounded with a revolver, six shots and some rations, which I thought was very bad."

The setup Mountbatten was inheriting consisted, on the ground, of Eastern Army under General Sir George Giffard; an Eastern Fleet, consisting of a single ancient battleship, an escort carrier, seven cruisers and a handful of destroyers, submarines and auxiliary craft under Somerville; and a relatively much more modern and numerous air force, Eastern Air Command, under Air Chief Marshal Sir Richard Peirse.

Mountbatten's relations with all three commanders lacked mutual trust from the start. With Somerville the difficulties were compounded by a daft directive that Mountbatten had no control of his fleet when it was operating in the western end of its area of responsibility. In his characteristic way, Mountbatten wasted no time complaining about

*General Raymond A. Wheeler. Others mentioned here are General Albert C. Wedemeyer and Lieutenant-General Sir Henry Pownall, C.-in-C. Persia-Iraq.

this and other anomalies, pitfalls and hazards. His business was to get on with things.

Before he had been rudely interrupted by Bill Donovan, Mountbatten had got as far as putting down his own initial *M* three times on his piece of paper. He already knew a good deal about what was going on in Burma, for Combined Ops had eventually to be involved on every fighting front, and about the only way of defeating the Japanese finally in that terrible terrain of jungle, swamp and mountains was by landings along the coast in amphibious operations, just as the landing at Salerno (a week after Mountbatten returned from Quebec) was intended to cut off the Germans in Italy.

Now Mountbatten completed in London the private exercise he had begun in Quebec, and under the first *M* he put "Morale." "It hardly existed," he said. "It had sunk so low because defeatism was rampant and so many of the troops were being cut off by the Japs. I put down three means of correcting this state of low morale.

"First, I'd try and pick the right generals. Second, I'd go round stumping on a soapbox, much as I had done at Combined Ops. Third, I'd start a paper, call it *SEAC*, and I thought of two men at once who should be involved—one was Charles Eade of the *Sunday Despatch*, another was Frank Owen, who had edited the *Evening Standard* so brilliantly for Max before the war, and among the others was Ian Coster.

"I wanted this paper to be closely linked with the British press so that the families at home would feel proud of their chaps out there—who had absolutely no chance of home leave for years on end—and they would feel in touch with what was happening at home."

The second *M* that Mountbatten put down, firmly and irrevocably, was "Monsoon." He had learned to his astonishment that for five months in every year the British army did not fight, due to the monsoon. It was just like the British Grand Fleet in the Great War, which did not fight at night because it had not practised, which was one reason why the German fleet escaped at Jutland. "I saw no reason why we shouldn't fight right through the monsoon. It would probably give us a tremendous advantage to do so."

Then there was *M* for "Malaria." "I can't remember the exact figures which I had put down in Quebec, but as far as I recall, one hundred and thirty percent of the Eastern Army got malaria every year. That is, on average, everyone got it once, and a third of them for a second time. Scrub typhus was another menace, and the ratio of battle casualties to disease casualties was something like one to a hundred. For a start, I persuaded Winston to let me have a Medical Adviser in Chief to head a Medical Advisory Division.

"With the help of that old German invention, DDT, Paludrine and other drugs, mosquito repellant, orders to wear long sleeves and long trousers, the ratio soon started to tumble, until we seriously considered making malaria a disciplinary offence. We never did, but COs were told that if they reported more than two or three cases, they'd be sacked.

"This gave us a huge advantage because the Japs had been suffering as badly as we and went on doing so, fighting nature instead of us."

Finally, *M* for "Movement"—an additional item. No longer must units be surrounded and cut off from supplies, their morale slumping to zero so that everything seemed to confirm that the Japs were unbeatable. There must be mobility on the ground at all times, and where necessary, supplies must be flown in. Constant movement on the ground and in the air and at sea to keep the Japs on the run, never knowing where the next attack would come from.

To fly in supplies—the Chinese were now being supplied exclusively—meant aircraft in great numbers, and that brought Mountbatten up against the hard fact that as far as war matériel was concerned, his new command might have been the most important item on the Quebec agenda, but was at the bottom when it came to priorities.

"We were worse than at the bottom," said Mountbatten, "because we often had to send back stuff that we had managed to squeeze out of the Chiefs of Staff—like some 5.5-inch ammunition, for example, a calibre of shell that was the only answer to the Japanese foxhole. And landing craft . . ."

Under the "Morale" heading, sub-heading "Sense of Identity," one of the decisions that could be made in the few weeks remaining in London was the design of a badge for Mountbatten's new army. Mountbatten's abiding interest in heraldry and genealogy gave him a head start, and he rather fancied himself a designer and letterer. Shortly before his death he recast for the publisher the jacket design of his parents' dual biography, much to its advantage, in about one minute flat. By 1943, Mountbatten had already designed the insignia for Edwina's St. John Ambulance uniform, and the flash for Combined

Ops, which consisted of RAF wings, an infantryman's rifle and a naval anchor, all in blue and gold.

For his new command, Mountbatten sketched out a circle of red on white, representing the enemy, with a blue sword cutting a slice. It was warmly approved all around, and an order for a million was despatched to America. Then, by chance, it was seen by an Oriental authority at the Foreign Office who, in horror, protested that any prisoner wearing this blatant insult to the sacred emblem of Japan would certainly be tortured to death instantly.

So that was scrapped, to Mountbatten's chagrin, and later someone came up with the idea of a phoenix, which became, as one wag put it, "the burning question of the day." Someone else, who happened to have a first edition of *Lady Chatterley's Lover*, recommended the phoenix used as a device on all D. H. Lawrence's books. "Lady Chatterley's Plover!" was Mountbatten's disgusted comment; and he got to work himself again. "I was still working on it during my last night in England," he recalled. He was very proud of his phoenix. When one of his staff was asked what it meant, the man explained that "it represents the transition from the futile fumblings of the past into the flaming fantasy of the future." But the facetious comment was not made within the hearing of Mountbatten, who took this sort of thing seriously.

Mountbatten took off with his staff on 4 October 1943 in a Douglas C-47 lent to him by Churchill and named by Mountbatten *Marco Polo*, signalling both his enthusiasm for the game and the fact that he was going out East. Like all his subsequent planes, it was fitted with every luxury he could lay his hands on, and among his considerable luggage was a box of chocolate for the eight-year-old King of Iraq to be presented en route.

His arrival in New Delhi was received with mixed feelings. There was plenty of the old hostility and suspicion which had greeted him in the past when he came on board a new ship. There was also a deep sense of relief among many of the senior officers of all services. In spite of Dieppe, still regarded as a black mark by most people, his work at Combined Ops could not be denied him; and the glittering image of the carefree playboy, spoiled by wealth and royal connections, had faded into the dark reality of four years of war.

General Giffard entertained the gravest doubts and thought Mountbatten far too young and inexperienced. The Air Force usually tended to be more sympathetic than the Army to Mountbatten, a youthful service's fellow feeling for youth perhaps. The outgoing Viceroy, Lord Linlithgow, was to be replaced within a few days by Mountbatten's old friend Field-Marshal Archibald Wavell, who referred to Mountbatten as "the boy champion" and was not the only one to predict that he was in for some rude shocks and a shattering of his optimism.

SEAC did not formally come into being, and Acting (now full) Admiral Lord Louis Mountbatten become its Supreme Commander, until midnight 15-16 November 1943. But he was in action at once, expressing a wish to continue his flight, with scarcely a pause, to Chungking to see Chiang Kai-shek. Mountbatten sensed that the Generalissimo was going to be his own equivalent of Churchill's De Gaulle—the worst cross he had to bear, and he was absolutely right. He wanted to leave immediately but at the last minute he was warned that it would be a more than usually dangerous trip.

"I was almost ready to take off," said Mountbatten, "when the Chinese Foreign Minister, who was also the Generalissimo's brother-in-law, T. V. Soong, arrived on the scene. 'Please don't fly out now,' he pleaded with me urgently. 'The Japs are lying in wait for you on the Hump, they know you are coming and will shoot you down.'

"This was just an occupational risk which I had to take, and I told him I had to disregard the warning. Then Soong tried another tack. 'I must be there before you. The Generalissimo wants to talk to me before you come.'

"This was confirmed by the American general Bill Somerville, who had been sent out by Roosevelt to explain to Chiang Kai-shek about the new SEAC. So I put off my flight.

"But the Japs had a complete sweep and shot down a record number of sixteen aircraft on the day I was to fly. When I did get over the Hump and arrived in Chungking, the reception was sticky all round. In fact, there wasn't any from the Generalissimo. I didn't see him for three days."

General "Vinegar Joe" Stilwell was a man of complex character in an almost impossibly complicated position. He was already Chief of Staff to Chiang Kai-shek and commander of the Americans in the

China theatre when he was given the additional task of Mountbatten's deputy in his new command. He was therefore now responsible through Mountbatten to the Allied Combined Chiefs of Staff, through General Marshall to the American Joint Chiefs of Staff, and to the Generalissimo himself.

Stilwell shared the general American view that the British were fighting for the sole purpose of recovering the large chunks of their colonial empire the Japanese had taken from them, all the way to Singapore and Hong Kong. He was therefore set to give Mountbatten almost as unwelcoming a reception as those Japanese Zero fighters had intended for him. But a curious thing happened, which had quite unintended repercussions. Before Mountbatten's plane landed, Chiang Kai-shek sacked Stilwell. If Mountbatten had been puzzled by Soong's concern for his safety, and his own need to reach Chungking first, all now was clear. Soong brought with him Roosevelt's approval of Stilwell's dismissal—if the Generalissimo insisted.

Chiang Kai-shek did insist. The Generalissimo had lost face as a result of Stilwell's efforts to reform the corrupt and reluctant Chinese army. He had had enough of the American's criticisms. Mountbatten learned of the loss of his deputy as soon as he landed. "It was a disaster. Stilwell was a fine fighting soldier, and he was the only man who could get the Chinese to behave. I went straight to his H.Q., and he confirmed that he had been thrown out. I took him by the arm and led him outside where there were a lot of photographers and reporters waiting to record our meeting."

Stilwell appeared uncharacteristically reluctant to meet them. "Don't be seen shaking hands with me," he told Mountbatten, "or you'll be finished too." Mountbatten insisted, however, and the two men shook hands and smiled at each other.

Then Mountbatten said, "Do you want this job back?"

Stilwell said, "You bet."

"Well, I'll give it back to you."

"You can't," said Stilwell. "He's made his decision, it's a matter of 'face.' "

"I can give it back very easily. You see."

Mountbatten went to Soong. "Tell the Generalissimo that I've no Chinese armies. Not one Chinese soldier will be moved one yard nearer to the enemy except on the orders of General Stilwell. They can rot as far as I'm concerned. You tell him that. And if he doesn't believe me, he's making the biggest mistake of his life. Tell him I'm one of those curious people who mean what they say. Tell him his ruddy Chinese are right out of the fighting from now on."

As Mountbatten controlled every plane supplying Chiang Kai-shek and transporting every one of his soldiers, the Generalissimo had to either reinstate the American or accept the greater loss of face of taking no part in the new SEAC's future campaigns. Stilwell got his job back.

According to "Vinegar Joe's" biographer, Stilwell's first reaction to Mountbatten's defence of his office was to say that Mountbatten was only "burned up because he'll have to work with a new man. Wants me to wait over and break him in."[11] But later Mountbatten's straight manner, ease, authority and tact made its usual impression. Mountbatten, Stilwell decided, had not only saved his job at a tricky time; he was "a good egg, energetic and willing to do anything to make it go."

Henceforth, the two men got on brilliantly. "He thought I was wonderful," said Mountbatten. "So wonderful that he came to stay with me in Delhi, and we became great personal friends. But just to show how difficult he could be, and how well we got on, he once made the unanswerable remark, 'Admiral, I like working with you. You're the only limey I've known that wants to fight.' A very curious fellow. He hated the British, was rude and prejudiced, didn't like staff work. But he could train the Chinese and could lead them in battle. And that made him pretty valuable."

Even Chiang Kai-shek succumbed to the Mountbatten touch, and when the two men parted they had developed a working relationship. "But he was always a problem," said Mountbatten. "He didn't speak a word of English and didn't want to. He didn't care twopence for our problems or the logistics of getting supplies to him. He just wanted more and more of everything. He was also extremely rude and didn't think much of our fighting capacity. He was really my worst headache."

An old acquaintance from the Norwegian campaign, a man whose life Mountbatten had probably saved at Namsos, now did a great deal to ease relations between Mountbatten's SEAC and its giant, difficult neighbour across the mountains, casting his single beady eye in turn on the Supremo and the Generalissimo, willing them to remain on speaking terms.

General Carton de Wiart had succeeded in remaining in the fighting line after Norway; he had been captured, but managed to escape from his Italian prisoner-of-war camp. Churchill decreed that he should have a quieter time for a while, and sent him out East as his personal liaison officer with Chiang Kai-shek. It was a curious choice, as the general was mainly noted for his fighting prowess, but it worked out very well, and he became Mountbatten's ambassador, too.

The other prominent and effective ambassador at Chungking was another general, the Frenchman Petchkoff, who became a great friend of De Wiart's. As they both had one arm, one eye, and a great number of medals, the Chinese may have got a curious idea of the qualifications in the West for a diplomatic career.

Although De Wiart always referred to Mountbatten behind his back as "Archduke Charles," he had a high regard for him, and later recounted this anecdote: "Dickie Mountbatten is a curious mixture of royal democracy; he can mix equally well on a high or low level and be exactly right in each. He was inspecting some American posts, and it was obvious that the Americans had been well primed beforehand as to their behaviour. All went swimmingly until Mountbatten came up to a certain sentry who immediately stretched out his hand and said: 'I'm Brown from Texas.' Mountbatten, not the least taken aback, shook the outstretched hand and answered, 'There are a lot of you Texans out here.' Whereupon the soldier replied, 'Yes, that's why the war's going so well.' "[12]

During the early months of his command, Mountbatten's first offensive had to be directed against apathy, defeatism, and morale as deep as the Chindwin River. Moreover, it had to be fought at every level, and a new spirit, a new philosophy of fighting, an entirely new attitude of mind, instilled.

It was easiest to effect this revolution of will and mind with the troops, and Mountbatten was always at his best with them. He made so many morale-boosting visits to so many units—a mere platoon sometimes, within grenade distance of the enemy, or a massed battalion on a barrack square—that he worked out an act as carefully scripted and timed as any put on by the ENSA professional performers whom he was, at the same time, persuading to come out to entertain the forces.

In the early days the script, delivered as always from the conveniently available box, invariably began, "Gather round so you can all hear me . . . Right. Now, I understand people think you're the Forgotten Army. I understand you all talk about yourselves as the Forgotten Army on the Forgotten Front. I've come here to tell you you're quite wrong. You're not the Forgotten Army on the Forgotten Front. No, make no mistake about it. Nobody's ever *heard* of you!"

This always caught their attention. He had his audience with him, and he went on from there. "Now the picture's changing. People are hearing about us, and they're going to hear more. From now on they'll be hearing about our victories. If the Japs try their old dodge of infiltrating behind you and cutting your lines of supplies and communications, you're going to stay put. There's going to be no more retreating, and you'll be supplied from the air, and that's my job."

Then he would talk about the enemy. "Who started this story of the Jap superman? I've seen them at work in Japan. Most of them are unintelligent slum people, with no factory laws, no freedom, no trade unions. They've got nothing that we take for granted—nothing at all except an ignorant, fanatical idea that their Emperor is God . . ."

Short, sharp, confidently delivered, confidence-inspiring, so gripping and memorable that, nearly forty years later, many of those who listened then can remember every word today. Sikhs, West Africans, Americans, Hindu and Moslem Indians, French and Dutch, Burmese, an English corporal from Tyneside who hadn't heard from his wife for three months, a Belfast Irishman with septic blisters, and a Glaswegian sergeant still hoarse from morning drill—all of them in their khaki drill, upturned faces shining with sweat, listened and felt comfort and inspiration.

Major R. A. Cooper, in command of B Company, 9th Battalion Border Regiment, remembered when he was in the Chin Hills, nine thousand feet up. Mountbatten had driven two hundred miles over mud tracks in his jeep with just two members of his staff. He had come to make himself known to widely scattered companies, including these twenty men, to give them encouragement in a very trying, very dangerous outpost. The major, with an injured hand, had just returned from an arduous patrol, successfully ambushing a Japanese column.

"He stood on his well-known soapbox, dressed in a bush jacket like us, and began talking, telling us our position absolutely straight, without frills. He seemed to have a complete understanding of what we were up to, and how we felt. It was a marvellous tonic. We could feel our spirits revive as he talked, and felt we had some place in the general scheme of things. Then he enquired about our needs and promised to get what he could for us . . ."[13]

Mountbatten worked out a quite different technique to deal with officers at big-scale inspections. "I would get an A.D.C. to write down every officer's name above the rank of captain [Army] upwards, adding anything special about them, professionally or domestically, any special awards and so on," said Mountbatten. "You could call it calculated, but it worked." Then he would have the officers fall in at double intervals to allow privacy, for he had the same two questions for every one and did not want to be overheard: "How long have you been out here?" And, "Where do you come from?" In most cases he knew the place and talked about it briefly before moving on.

The sergeants next, and the same formula would be followed, before he called them to gather round for his speech, at the end of which he would usually introduce some topic or future event that he gave the impression was confidential, although it was really nothing of the kind, but it encouraged further a sense of solidarity and sympathy.

Meanwhile, the senior officers' names were all noted and filed, and the office system was organized so that if anything important happened to them, or they were killed or got a bravery award, a letter would automatically be typed out and would land on Mountbatten's desk. "Dear Major So-and-so, I congratulate you on your well-deserved M.C. [Military Cross]. I well remember discussing Bodiham Castle near your home on . . ." Or, "Dear Mrs. So-and-so, Your loss, I fear, is a terrible one, and I would like you to accept my condolences . . . When I last talked to your husband . . . He was a very brave officer, and it was a privilege . . ." He signed them by the score without even glancing at them. A grandson of one of Queen Mary's old ladies-in-waiting received one of these letters after he had been wounded. "After the war," Mountbatten recalled, "Queen Mary asked me how I had time, with all that was going on, to keep in personal touch with him. 'He was your slave for life!' she told me . . ."

Two interesting things, which reflected the new and the old spirit of the Burma war, happened at one of Mountbatten's earliest visits. It was in Calcutta on the way back to Delhi from Chungking, at the H.Q. of the Third Tactical Air Force. Air Marshal Sir John Baldwin was the commander. "A great man," said Mountbatten. "I was asked if I'd like to meet the senior officers, and I said yes. They were all lined up, over a hundred of them, colonels American and British, group captains and the rest. I said my usual piece, fighting through the monsoon, fighting tropical diseases, and so on.

"Afterwards a chap came up to me, a brigadier of about my age. I'd played polo with him before the war. And he said, 'Dickie, why don't you take a tip from an old friend? What you've just been telling us, it won't wash, you know—all this march on, fly on, fight on. You don't yet know what it's like out here. And for God's sake, don't put the troops in these disease-ridden places—they'll die like flies.' I listened but didn't say anything. He had plenty more to say, all about competing with the terrain, which is what I had told them we had to do. He ended up by saying, and he was very friendly about it, 'I'm afraid your speech went down rather badly, Dickie.' So I said, 'Oh, I'm sorry about that.' I really was surprised because I thought it had gone down rather well.

"But something else, more important and more encouraging than this, happened too. I met the Fifteenth Corps Commander. He was called Bill Slim, and he was very tough-looking. I took the most violent liking to him at once, and I said, 'Would you like to be the Army C.-in-C.?' He said he would. He also said, 'Let's change this ghastly name "Eastern Army." Let's just get a number.' "

And that was how one of the most effective partnerships of the war was sealed, and how the Fourteenth Army got its name.

George Giffard, the overall Army c.-in-c., was, according to Mountbatten, "a dear old fellow, and as obstinate as hell." He represented everything non-Japanese that Mountbatten had come out to fight. He was reactionary, defeatist, inflexible. He was also, unfortunately, a sort of living caricature of Stilwell's idea of a British general. It was not surprising that they could not get along at all and "Vinegar Joe" refused to serve under him. Mountbatten recounted a skirmish with Giffard at a staff meeting some time after his arrival at H.Q.

"I want some divisions to fight in the monsoon," Mountbatten said.

"I've none to spare," replied the c.-in-c.

"All right, then I'll have to ask you for a list of all the divisions in South-East Asia and India, what they're doing and which, in order of priority, can't be spared."

Later Giffard approached Mountbatten and said, "Supremo, as I understand it, your job is to tell me to produce the troops, and I then produce the troops. Is that right?"

Mountbatten confirmed that that was so.

"I tell you, Supremo, there are no troops available. Can't you spare the time to come and check for yourself? Then you'll see I'm telling the truth."

"If I don't get the troops from you, then there'll be no fighting during the monsoon."

Giffard pounced on that. "That's just what we shouldn't be doing."

Mountbatten told him that it was the Supreme Commander's decision whether or not there was to be fighting during the monsoon, and he had decided that there was to be.

Giffard said, "If I don't make any troops available, does that mean you've lost confidence in me?"

"If you don't help me—then, yes."

Later Mountbatten had to ask Pownall to demand a relief. The moment it was known he was going, Giffard let him have as many troops as he wanted. "I'm no longer responsible," he said in explanation of this sudden change.

The early days at Delhi were chaotic. If he had been starting from scratch, it would have been comparatively simple. Mountbatten was trying to put together an entirely new command out of the sorry, disillusioned mess of an old command that had become discredited in its own eyes and was made up of numerous nationalities, many of them in full scale departmental war with one another. No one trusted anyone else, and *everything* was in short, sometimes desperately short, supply: transport, weapons, clothes, medicines, ammunition, fuel . . .

"There were just a few of us to get things started, and we worked from day to day, supported by the certain truth that every day things *must* get better if only because they couldn't get worse," Mountbatten remembered. "The first thing was to make contact, make friends. It wasn't the men who were wrong—Slim had been there for a long time, after all—it was the leadership and the spirit.

"It's quite a big thing to set up an Allied H.Q. to deal with a war and over a million men with nothing to start with and no one willing to help. If Chiang Kai-shek was my first difficulty in China, Auchinleck was my first difficulty at home. He had had a very rough going-over from Winston, been kicked out of North Africa by him and was C.-in-C. Indian Army. He was supposed to be training my troops, and my H.Q. was actually in his area. So that was very tricky. He was touchy as hell and it took me about six weeks to break him down. However, things gradually began to get into shape."

There was not much time. A high-level conference scheduled to take place in Cairo at the end of November at which the Allied Chiefs were due to sort out their priorities and difficulties before the Big Three (Roosevelt, Churchill and Stalin) met in Teheran later in the month. Mountbatten was to present his plans for the defeat of Japan in South-East Asia, and Chiang Kai-shek and Stilwell would be among those flying in from the East.

It was a reassuring and enjoyable get-together for friends and those who understood one another, especially Churchill and Roosevelt, Marshall, Mountbatten and Brooke. But there was a great deal of fighting, too; much of it so fierce that the word "Allies" took on a new reversed meaning.

Amid searchlight beams of curiosity, the Chinese delegation made its first appearance, Chiang Kai-shek taking offence straight away, even at the airport, because his arrival was top-secret and there could be no one of equal standing to receive him. From then on, the Generalissimo and Madame Chiang made every meeting they attended hell by their implacable insistence on having everything they wanted, by their deafness to any sort of reason, and by frequently going back on what they had earlier agreed to. Churchill could not understand why Roosevelt was so sympathetic to the Chinese cause, and Mountbatten was brought in to use his charm and powers of simple explanation to the Chinese. It worked, as always, but, like a winter tan, its effect quickly faded.

The Americans thought the British were ducking out of Operation Overlord, the invasion of northern France, and that Churchill was still preoccupied with an attack on Europe from the south through the

Balkans, the "soft underbelly." Through all this unseemly international bickering, Mountbatten presented his promised plan. An amphibious fleet was to assault and conquer the Andaman Islands off the coast of Burma, Operation Buccaneer. At the same time, on land there were to be assaults down the Arakan and across the Chindwin; and to the north there were to be three related thrusts to open up a direct route to China, and a major attack by Wingate's Long-Range Penetration Force—seven offensives in all.

Churchill's orders to Mountbatten on his appointment to his new command had included this clear-cut directive:

> Your first duty is to engage the enemy as closely and continuously as possible, so that his forces may be worn down and consumed by attrition, and to establish our superiority to the extent of forcing a diversion of his forces from the Pacific theatre.

Mountbatten's plan, which had been prepared during the first hectic weeks at Delhi, was expressly designed to meet these requirements. It certainly went some way towards easing Chinese and American doubts about British willingness to fight in South-East Asia. But Churchill's reception of the proposal was cool, and worse was to come.

Mountbatten returned to Delhi with his staff, leaving the leaders (minus Chiang Kai-shek) to join Stalin at Teheran. He was in a buoyant mood. His great offensive was due to open in March. He had the necessary equipment, or it had been promised to him; detailed plans for the land campaigns were well advanced; training for the amphibious landings was going ahead speedily. He was utterly confident that he could break the Japanese in Burma and occupy Rangoon, the capital, by the middle of 1944 at the latest.

Within a week or two of Mountbatten's return to Delhi, Churchill and Roosevelt were jointly drawing up a message to Stalin which was to dash all hopes of launching SEAC's great offensive. At Teheran, Stalin—truculent, resentful, censorious and implacably demanding—had got his way with the Americans and the British. Roosevelt, in his innocence, had come to Teheran in the dual role of a solid ally to Britain and a peacemaker between Stalin and Churchill who—from the other side of the Atlantic—appeared to be at loggerheads over almost everything. Roosevelt appeared to be, at best, a prophet and arbitrator; at worst, a Western toady bent on encouraging a Russian view that the U.S.S.R. and the U.S.A. were the two great powers with so much in common: forward-looking, egalitarian and above all anti-colonialist. The implications of Operation "Grovel" (as some cynical observer named it) was that the arch-imperialist Churchill must, by joint effort, be gently nursed into accepting the right priorities.

In spite of every protestation by Churchill and Brooke, the Americans and Russians both believed that the British were still stalling on the invasion of France, from the north and south. Stalin also strongly opposed Churchill's eastern Mediterranean "soft underbelly" plans, which might thwart Russia's well-laid plans for Romania, Greece, Bulgaria, Hungary, Yugoslavia, Albania, etc.

Not all the American generals considered their remarks very carefully, the exception being Marshall. Eisenhower, for instance, at one point suggested that the Italian campaign, where Britain was heavily committed and the American contribution had not been wholly successful, should be slowed down in favour of the southern French invasion. Stalin thought this was a wonderful idea. Churchill thought it madness, and got his way.

As to the East, Stalin refused to enter the war against Japan until Germany was defeated. He had no interest in Chiang Kai-shek's war; Burma was a sideshow, a skirmish unworthy of comment had it not been for SEAC's ambitious amphibious plans for 1944, which involved a great number of landing craft. To Stalin, landing craft meant only one thing: the means for an earlier invasion of France by his allies, which would draw off German troops from the Russian front and allow the Russian armies to storm into Eastern Europe: Prague, Budapest, Berlin . . .

Roosevelt and Churchill returned to Cairo to unravel, as compatibly and neatly as possible, the criss-cross pattern of national demands that would shape the postwar world; and despatched their message to Stalin with their conclusions. It included this paragraph: "We have reduced the scale of operations scheduled for March in the Bay of Bengal to permit the reinforcement of amphibious craft for the operation against southern France."[14] The consequences for Mountbatten and SEAC were much more fundamental than this reassurance to Stalin suggested. Churchill had, in fact, persuaded Roosevelt very reluctantly to accept that the whole Buccaneer operation should be abandoned, and that virtually all the landing craft assigned to it and prepared by Mountbatten for the amphibious operations should be returned. Roosevelt was in favour of the invasion of the south of France but strongly against letting down Chiang Kai-shek and Mountbatten.

On 9 December 1943 Churchill confirmed to Mountbatten that Buccaneer was off. "This arises from the decisions at Teheran to concentrate everything on Overlord and a simultaneous operation against the south of France." He then did a very characteristic thing, showing that the schoolboy in him was never far beneath the skin while his eye on history's verdict upon him was as keen as in the time of Mountbatten's father. Anticipating the justifiable protests, he drowned them in a great shout of abuse.

> Everyone here has been unpleasantly affected by your request to use 50,000 British and Imperial troops . . . against 5,000 Japanese. I was astounded to hear of such a requirement, and I cannot feel sure you are getting competent military advice . . . while such standards as those you have accepted for the Andamans prevail there is not much hope of making any form of amphibious war.[15]

Mountbatten was as outraged at the loss of his landing craft as at the accusation that he had been extravagant and poorly advised militarily. It was the greatest rebuke of his active career, and he never forgot it. What he did not know was that the Combined Chiefs of Staff had said that they would resign in a body if Buccaneer was not cancelled.

Mountbatten regarded Churchill's jealousy and vanity as only marginally less than Max Beaverbrook's, and his eye on posterity infinitely keener. Churchill had sent Mountbatten out to South-East Asia to win the war against the Japanese in that theatre. But Mountbatten harboured the gravest suspicions that the speed of his preparations had taken Churchill by surprise and that he did not want the thunder of the invasion in the West to be stolen by victory drumbeats in the East: drums beaten by someone who could so easily and truthfully claim that he had, first, laid the foundations for the successful invasion of Europe, and then gone East to avenge the greatest humiliations the British Empire had ever suffered. No one adored a hero more than Churchill. But megalomania had seized him in a tight grip, as Mountbatten saw it, and he could not allow anyone's stature to overshadow his own. Forever after, Mountbatten suspected that Churchill feared for his own exclusive position in the annals of history as the man who had saved the free world, and had "put him down" by cancelling Buccaneer and making it impossible to implement, for a long time, the instructions he had given Mountbatten only seven weeks earlier.

Churchill had written of "amphibious descents" with the "necessary transports, assault ships and landing craft" made available to him. Now he had taken them away. Churchill had also instructed Mountbatten to make his superiority tell and force "the Japanese enemy to divert his forces from the Pacific theatre." Instead, Mountbatten had been deprived of that superiority so that the German enemy would be forced to divert his forces from the Russian front. It was an odd turnabout. As Mountbatten saw it, Churchill at a stroke had done more by this deed to appease Stalin than all Roosevelt's petty flirtations had succeeded in achieving.

"I was completely horrified by this sudden cancellation," said Mountbatten. "It was unjust and unwarranted. We weren't asking for a thing. We had everything for the operations, our men were training hard, our morale was rocketing. Winston had sent me out primarily to conduct amphibious operations to beat the Japs quickly. And now we seemed fated to slog our way through the Burmese jungle and the worst terrain in the world.

"As to the accusations of extravagance, this was absolute rot and Winston knew it, and the rap over the knuckles was purely political. The Americans, with all their experience and terrific resources in the Pacific, were using a six-to-one superiority when air cover was only from carriers—which was always much riskier and more limited than from land-based planes." Allowing for the fact that a third of Mountbatten's force was noncombatant, the ratio of superiority for Buccaneer had been no higher.

Mountbatten feared that the repercussions in Chungking would be disastrous, and he was right. "The Generalissimo broke entirely with us, and wouldn't make his armies available under any circumstances." Only Mountbatten's innermost circle learned of the depth of his bitterness and disappointment at Churchill's policy reversal and what he called "the complete lack of support of the Combined Chiefs of Staff."

At no time during the war did Mountbatten's youthful resilience prove more valuable. "Well," he said, "the Japs were still there, the war was still going on, and we had to adapt ourselves and keep our peckers up. Frankie Festing [Major-General F. W. Festing commanding 36th Division] and George Giffard said the the news would be disastrous for morale and we would never be able to do anything again. The whole of Thirty-three Corps had been trained for the amphibious landing, and somebody had to tell them.

" 'I'm not going to do that,' they both said.

" 'You mean you want me to do it?' I asked. 'Don't you mind my coming and doing your work?'

"They both said no, they didn't. So I went down and spent three nights with each divisional corps. I knew I had to follow my old principle of turning bad news to good, but this was going to be tough. What I did say was something like this:

" 'I've come down here personally to bring you some very exciting news. You all know that you'll not be able to get home to see your wives and families until the war is over—and that means when Germany is beaten as well as Japan. Now, when I left England the war against Germany was going very slowly. But things are better now. I've just heard some highly confidential news. The invasion of Europe will take place sooner than we all expected—in fact, this very spring. I know this because they have taken away for the time being our splendid landing craft. Now, this is splendid because it means that the Germans will soon be crushed, we'll get all and more of our landing craft back, and we'll have a very quick victory.'

"This was received with loud cheers."

Mountbatten always retained the firm conviction that fate was on his side and setbacks merely temporary. A month before his aborted operations were due to begin, the Japanese opened a major offensive against two divisions of XV Corps, relying on past experience that the British would retreat, leaving behind them, as before, massive supplies on which the Japanese would sustain themselves. This time it did not quite work out that way. Under Brigadier Geoffrey Evans, the troops did not retreat. It was as if Mountbatten's spirit had infused them with a special sense of pride and purpose—just like the *Kelly*'s company and the Commandos who had gone out with blackened faces and knives on those earlier raids. They held on for eighteen days, and when it seemed as if their supplies must be exhausted, the planes came in as Mountbatten had promised, and then the relief columns arrived, and the Japanese were forced to retreat. They lost half their men—and their record of unbroken victory.

It was called "The Battle of the Admin. Box" by Slim, who considered it the turning point of the war in Burma. Meanwhile Wingate's long-range penetrations had some spectacular successes—again thanks to supplies from the air. During these early months of 1944, the Burma war became the first major campaign in history to be supplied almost exclusively from the air.

A month later the Japanese struck again, at Imphal, and the toughest battle of the campaign began. The Japanese infantryman was a superb jungle fighter, but his first asset was his relentless determination and disregard for setbacks and the desperate rigours of living and fighting in the jungle. At one time Imphal and Kohima, eighty miles to the north, were surrounded by Japanese forces, and it appeared as if both towns must fall. High fighting morale and the tireless courage of the transport aircrews turned the tide. Against express instructions from Roosevelt, Mountbatten borrowed large numbers of the American planes that were flying supplies to China over the Hump. He liked to relate this incident as if it were one of great daring, with apologies afterwards to the President, who was so forbearing because he was such a "big" man and understood Mountbatten and the nature of the emergency. But in fact the thirty C-47s were taken off the China run with Churchill's encouragement and a guarantee that he would square things with F.D.R. if there was any trouble.

Another story of this time, on a lighter level, which Mountbatten enjoyed concerned Major-General F. W. Messervy, who commanded the 7th Indian Division when it was overrun by the Japanese, half his force being outside the Admin. Box. To keep open some form of communication was as essential as the burning of all code books. All the general retained to keep in touch with the part of his force from which he was separated was one radiotelephone.

"Messervy recognized that it was of the utmost importance," Mountbatten recounted, "that the Japs, who were known to be listening in on their wavelength, shouldn't be able to understand the messages. An absolutely unbreakable new code was required. The general had an inspiration. At each end of the line he put an ex–public school English subaltern, and they were instructed to talk only French. Not even the

French knew what they were saying, and the French-talking Japanese thought it was gibberish."

Now at last things really did seem to be going better. Churchill, in a more benign mood, signalled: "I am so glad this measure of success has attended [the fighting]. It is a sign of the new spirit in your forces, and will, I trust, urge everyone to keep closer to the enemy."[16] (Churchill loved the Nelsonian phrase "keep closer to the enemy" and used it frequently.)

The three *M*s were proving their worth, contradicting every pessimistic prediction by those who "knew." The Fourteenth Army held the Japanese, who hoped now to build up supplies during the monsoon before another, final onslaught which would lead them to India. Instead, to their amazement, the British and their allies continued to fight—through drenching rain, through cloying mud; and the planes, at high risk and with considerable losses, continued to fly, thanks to the indefatigable work of the ground crews, and the unflinching courage of the aircrews. Once again, Mountbatten's early choice of signals (in the broadest sense) as a specialist branch, proved its value. From the beginning as Supreme Commander, Mountbatten had taken a special interest in signals intelligence. Ultra, the then highly secret but now popularly known intelligence project, was already established at the Wireless Experimental Centre, analyzing Japanese army and air force formations.

"Our unit was just beginning to produce useful short-term inferences on Japanese intentions and reactions," wrote an Indian Army officer in signals intelligence. "Japanese security was in some respects very lax and our very well trained intercept-operators, British, Indian and African, laid the foundations for the extraction of much accurate and timely intelligence from the Japanese networks.

"I recall that Mountbatten, having found his own 'baby' flourishing in the unexpected environment of the Indian Army, overspent his time in his inspection of our sub-unit. He met everyone involved and went through the minutest details of their work with them. We were intrigued to have a Supreme Commander who had an intimate grasp of the technical details of the work. Later I heard that Mountbatten had made it a high priority to ascertain that signals intelligence was in good working order in his command. His relaxed and confident manner and his assessment of the value of our team were very great morale-raisers."

Backed by greatly superior intelligence, the Fourteenth Army was fighting through the monsoon, malaria was comparatively negligible, morale was high—and the army was continuing to move. The Japanese, stricken with fever, did not. And the C-47 Dakotas roared overhead, over the most dangerous terrain and through the most dangerous weather in the world. The sturdy twin-engine American transport, mainly American-crewed, was the jungle war's real winning weapon.

By the end of the monsoon, the Fourteenth Army had by no means won the war or driven the Japanese out of Burma, but it had broken the spell of Japanese invincibility, gained valuable ground, shaken the Japanese high command, and was bursting with pride and self-confidence. "The Forgotten Army" was ready for the last offensive and was feeling that it might be remembered, after all.

At the height of the battle for the Imphal plain, Mountbatten was struck down by one of those silly mishaps to which he had always been so prone. Although highly competent drivers were, of course, always available, he often chose to drive himself. On 7 March 1944 he was driving his jeep, fast and leaning out over the left side and, no doubt, with his mind on other things, as usual, when a bamboo stump over which he had just driven sprang up and struck him hard in the eye. He was rushed, in great pain, to the nearest field hospital, an American one. Here he remained for a week, with both eyes bandaged, and for a time the doctors feared for his sight. The accident could not have happened at a worse time. The Japanese had attacked strongly on 8 March and were within an ace of cutting off IV Corps. The military situation was fluid and dangerous. With Pownall's aid, Mountbatten kept in touch with Slim and with the day-to-day situation.

On the fourteenth, after Mountbatten had persuaded the doctors to remove his eye bandage and discharge him, he flew straight back to Delhi for consultations with Slim and Baldwin. Ten weeks later, with his eye completely recovered and the battle for Imphal and Kohima now transformed into a pursuit of the enemy, he was further cheered by a message from the Joint Chiefs of Staff.

"It was dated June tenth, and was about the nicest telegram I ever received during the war. The invasion of northern France had occurred four days earlier, and I had already had news that the Allied armies had secured a toehold on the Normandy coast and that things were

going pretty well. I learned later that Marshall had composed the
message to me while at dinner with Brookie, Winston, Ernie King,
Smuts and Hap Arnold. He had handed it to the others, and they had
all signed in turn:

> "Today we visited the British and American armies on the soil of France. We
> sailed through vast fleets of ships, with landing craft of many types pouring more
> and more men, vehicles and stores ashore . . . We wish to tell you at this moment
> in your arduous campaign that we realize that much of this remarkable tech-
> nique, and therefore the success of the venture, has its origin in developments
> effected by you and your staff of Combined Operations."

The most willing signatory to this message was Field-Marshal Jan
Smuts, the South African statesman whose judgement was so sought
after by the British War Cabinet and by Churchill himself. Smuts had
a very high regard for Mountbatten and told Churchill (27 September
1944) that he thought he had had "a raw deal" over Operation Buccaneer, and was glad that he would "get his chance in Burma and Malaya."[7] The far-seeing Smuts was referring to the amphibious operations that would clear out and finally defeat the Japanese in South-East
Asia. These would be on a scale that would make Buccaneer appear
like a minor skirmish. The landings on the Malaysian peninsula in
1945 would be Mountbatten's own Overlord, the relief of Singapore the
equivalent to the Allied liberation of Paris, the final vengeance for
Japanese infamy and British humiliation.

8

"SUPREMO" II

The situation in China remained unsettled and unsatisfactory, the only predictable factor being its complexity. It was becoming increasingly clear that the Generalissimo was as concerned with his future war with the powerful Communist elements in his own country as he was with the occupying Japanese. The Allies, and more particularly the Americans, were investing vast sums in supplying and supporting the Generalissimo's armies, constructing air bases for bombing the Japanese mainland and building a road from Burma (a million dollars a mile, and up to heights of 16,000 feet).

Chiang Kai-shek procrastinated, lied, dodged decisions, issued orders behind his generals' backs. The "war lords" in the south-east were on the point of revolt; the Communists in the north-west refused to accept orders from Chungking while they laid plans for the civil war they would one day win. Mountbatten viewed the picture with an anxious and increasingly cynical eye. Roosevelt again sent a personal representative, Major General P. J. Hurley, and at the same time promoted Stilwell to full general to increase his prestige in the Generalissimo's eyes.

But the end, which Mountbatten had deferred in 1943, was near for "Vinegar Joe," and the one general who had attempted to lend direction and will to the Chinese for so long, had to be recalled by Roosevelt (at Chiang Kai-shek's insistence) on 18 October 1944.

With Mountbatten's consent, the American Chiefs of Staff took Wedemeyer from SEAC to replace Stilwell and divided the American China-Burma-India theatre into two, with General D. L. Sultan commanding the Burma portion and Wedemeyer the China portion, the latter also acting as the Generalissimo's Chief of Staff.

It was hoped at Mountbatten's H.Q. that Wedemeyer would behave at Chungking with the needs of his old command in mind. But within weeks, the Japanese were overwhelming one Chinese-American air base after another and even threatening Chungking and the vital Hump air terminal—an advance of 300 miles. With China out of the war, some four million Japanese troops could be released for operations in defence of their homeland.

Wedemeyer promptly advised his new master that he should demand the withdrawal from Mountbatten's Burma front of two American-trained Chinese divisions and five cargo and troop-carrying squadrons of planes. Mountbatten, hoping to forestall even greater demands, complied. But he felt extremely bitter about it, and the man he had once admired for his loyalty as well, for it meant a further postponement of his plans. Now it seemed that commitments were being broken from East as well as West.

Mountbatten had decided sometime earlier to move his H.Q. from Delhi, where the heat was as stifling as the infighting, and set up a base well removed from the intrigue and politicking of the capital—a place he could call his own and from which he could more suitably control the final stages of the war in Burma and the eventual invasion of the Malay peninsula. To the surprise of everyone but his closest staff, and the disapproval of the Delhi "brass" he left thankfully behind, he chose Peredynia, a little place high in the mountains of Ceylon near the town of Kandy. Here the climate was healthy, the scenery exotically beautiful, the gardens paradisical. A royal residence had been built here many years earlier for Mountbatten's godmother in the event of Queen Victoria's visiting the island. She never had, and the palacelike building had been used instead as a summer residence for the governor. It now housed Mountbatten in the very considerable splendour he always relished.

"Supremo's palace" was surrounded by informally laid out buildings linked by roads named Fleet Street and Ludgate Circus, Times Square and Broadway, to give a home-away-from-home as well as an Anglo-American style to the H.Q. The various messes and clubhouses, thatched living quarters and canteens, were situated on the banks of a river.

On first arrival, men and women who had become hardened to soulless barrack life thought they were dreaming. Surely the war was over and they were trespassing on some country club! But if Kandy came closer to Mountbatten's Valhalla than any H.Q. he ever created, including the very prettiest servicewomen in their trim uniforms, it was also very Mountbatten in its odd mix of weak and strong, experienced and inexperienced. He had been sent or had chosen some first-rate "brains" and brilliant soldiers. But the amount of "deadwood" at Kandy, recognizable within a few days of arrival to a discerning eye, was also considerable and revealed that Mountbatten was as often obtuse in his selection of staff as he was occasionally brilliant. His instinct was never reliable. All that you could be sure of was that the numbers would rapidly grow like any self-multiplying bureaucracy that is not run with a tight rein. The numbers at Kandy eventually grew to over seven thousand, which appalled Churchill and a great many others in London when they heard about it.

One brigadier recalls being given the task of arranging for cut-up landing craft to be flown into Burma and finding that this was technically impossible with the aircraft available. At every stage up the hierarchy his case was either shrugged off or he was told of the dire consequences for himself if he ever reached the top. At length he got to Kandy, where he forced his way on to Mountbatten himself. The brigadier spread out the drawings which proved his case. Mountbatten saw the problem at once, pushed aside the papers and with a sigh said, "Why doesn't my staff *tell* me these things?"[1]

On the other hand, Kandy's cumbersome, overstaffed machine could also work very speedily and efficiently, thanks to the driving force of the "Supremo" and the ablest of his lieutenants. Mountbatten would claim that Kandy was unsurpassedly efficient in every respect and that this was partly due to the creature comforts provided and not in spite of them; just as, long before, the *Daring* had hot and cold water for the commander, and the *Kelly* had a covered bridge.

Before Stilwell was relieved of his command, and while Mountbatten was briefly absent in London, the American general took over at Kandy. It was like putting John Wayne's sheriff's office in the Palace of

Versailles. Stilwell used Mountbatten's magnificent Cadillac to send his cook out for groceries, drove around in a scruffy jeep himself and was completely at sea in the Supreme Commander's daily meetings, which he soon cancelled. He never could bear conferences.

For reasons which many thought at the time to be reasonable, Giffard and Peirse both refused point-blank to move their H.Q. to Kandy, which they regarded as too remote from the Burma fighting areas. Both were relieved of their command in October and November 1944. It is no reflection on these commanders that the Burma campaign prospered after their departure. The build-up of reinforcements and of supplies, the growing experience and winning spirit, all played their part in the Fourteenth Army. In continuous and intense fighting, that once-forgotten army increasingly got the measure of the enemy—and its share of the headlines at last.

The great Irrawaddy River was crossed by means of giant teak barges, made on the spot and powered by small marine engines which had been flown in. Slim, by a series of feints and bluffs as cunning as anything the Japanese could have contrived, completely outwitted his opposing generals, one of whom later described them as "the masterstroke of Allied strategy." Mandalay fell on 9 March 1945; Rangoon itself capitulated two months later, just as the monsoon broke.

"Heartfelt congratulations" arrived from Churchill, regretting that landing craft and shipping had "had to be retained in the decisive European theatre. . . . In spite of this diminution and disappointment, you and your men have done all and more than your directive required. Pray convey to everyone under your command or associated with you the sense of admiration and gratitude felt by all at home at the splendid close of the Burma campaign."[2]

So perhaps Mountbatten had been getting "competent military advice," after all. Certainly this message served to offset the damaging earlier one concerning Buccaneer.

Churchill concluded by telling Mountbatten of George VI's command that a special decoration, the Burma Star, be struck. The ribbons would be flown out shortly. No campaign ribbon was worn with greater pride than this star, by the men who had fought through swamp and jungle, in suffocating monsoon rain and heat, over precipitous mountains, across raging torrents, against a ruthless and formidable enemy.

"Looking back now," said Mountbatten nearly thirty years later, "there seemed to have been more events in the spring and summer of 1945 than in all the interwar years together. Certainly I had to make more important decisions than at any other time in my life."

The saddest event in April was the death of Roosevelt. "Every time I met him it was a thrill, and I had a terrific admiration for him—long before the war. I thought his New Deal was a master-stroke. He was a compassionate as well as a very brave man. Like Churchill and everyone else in Britain, I was thankful for his moral and material support when we were alone. We became personal friends in 1942 when I stayed at the White House. And later, when I was offered South-East Asia, I promised him I would be a good American. 'You stand in a very special relationship with me, Dickie,' he said. And that was one of the nicest things anyone said to me. When he died, I knew that I had lost a very good friend. He knew that victory was just ahead, but it would have been nice if he had seen it, for it was the war that killed him, of course."

One of the arguments that Roosevelt had used against placing SEAC under MacArthur during the period of American sniping at Mountbatten was that the two commands were thousands of miles apart. But now, as the four-pronged pincers squeezed Japan tighter with every day that passed, this distance diminished and the need to formulate joint policies increased. A month before the fall of Rangoon, MacArthur's forces had stormed the island of Okinawa, and already Mountbatten was preparing Operation Zipper, the amphibious assault on Malaya.

"I thought I ought to go and see MacArthur at Manila, and flew off," said Mountbatten. "I had heard much about his presence and his powers, that he was an outstanding figure. When we met, I wasn't disappointed. He was a terrific man. He simply oozed personality. He was also—unlike me—a complete autocrat. We got on marvellously, and our talks were terribly useful. I would have liked to stay longer, but I was needed back in England."

The reason for this had now become a commonplace in Mountbatten's command. During his last night at dinner with MacArthur two things had been agreed upon. The first was that the boundaries of SEAC should be further expanded so that MacArthur would be able to concentrate his resources more fully on the eventual invasion of the Japanese mainland. The Dutch East Indies, French Indochina, Portuguese Timor and Borneo would all come within Mountbatten's scope—another few million people, another few thousand square miles!

The other point of agreement between the two commanders was that Mountbatten had had a raw deal in the line-up for supplies. "I didn't raise the subject," said Mountbatten. "It was MacArthur. It was at the end of dinner. He was smoking that pipe of his, looking like a caricature of himself, and he had given me a very good cigar. Suddenly he said, 'I am the best person in the world to judge how difficult it is to run a command when you are low on the priority scale. I have had a terrible time, while Ike got everything he asked for. I also know that you have had an even worse time. Sometime in the future, history will prove what a wonderful job you have done, all without priorities.'

"I thanked him. It was a nice thing to say, and I gave him some compliments, too. It was a very satisfactory meeting. But with these huge new responsibilities, I knew I should have to go to London to get some reinforcements—and this time without any double-crossing."

Mountbatten had decided to stop off in Paris to pay his respects to De Gaulle in his newly liberated capital. He got no farther than Cairo. During the refuelling stop there, an urgent telegram arrived from Churchill. The Big Three—the new American President, Stalin and Churchill—were meeting in the ruins of Berlin, at Potsdam, following the defeat of Germany. And Mountbatten was summoned to join them.

Everyone there was in a buoyant mood. Mountbatten dined privately with Churchill the first evening. Even before the first drink "Winston, after checking the doors and windows, said to me in a low voice, 'I have something highly confidential and very important to tell you. You are going to revise your plans.' I thought, Oh no, not again—not more cuts—I've had enough . . . ! But before I could speak, Winston said, 'The war with Japan will be over in less than a month. We are going to use a new bomb, an atomic bomb, against the cities of Japan, and the Emperor will be forced to capitulate. Of course, you are not to mention this to a soul. You'll have to tell your people without explaining how or why . . .' How could I? It was an impossible situation."

The next day, at lunch with the Chiefs of Staff, Brooke looked around the room cautiously before saying in a hushed voice, "Dickie, I have something highly . . . ' Then he met the new American President. "I liked Truman very much. He was very precise and businesslike. After a while, it was *his* turn. 'I have something highly confidential . . . ' The funny thing is he never told MacArthur, so I was a lap ahead of him there."

Then there was Stalin, an almost fabulous figure, a dictator, the most powerful man on earth, who had smashed Hitler's dreams and the most efficient military machine ever conceived. It was more than thirty years since Mountbatten had confronted a ruler of Russia. Then it had been the Tsar, his own kindly uncle, and Mountbatten had been met by a laugh, an exclamation of wonder at his cadet's uniform and how he had grown, and an embrace, with Uncle Nicky's beard tickling his face, just as his father's always had.

In those faraway pre-revolutionary days, one passed between lines of cossacks, and the surroundings were the most glittering and extravagant of any monarch in the world. Now, in this desolate, tragic city, filled with the smell of death and dust, Mountbatten, in the uniform of full admiral, was escorted swiftly through ring after ring of ferocious-looking sentries and secret police, to Stalin's presence, with his brilliant interpreter, V. N. Pavlov, beside him.

"He was in a very benign mood," said Mountbatten, "as well he might be. His face was just like his caricatures, but I was struck by his clothes—a white doeskin tunic with nothing but a hammer and sickle in red on each shoulder, and dark-blue trousers tucked into calf-length boots. He didn't repeat yet again the 'confidential' news. He assumed I knew already and agreed that the war with Japan would very soon be over. He was very polite and correct."

Frontiers and areas of influence and areas of control, armaments and priorities, and a thousand other things that have affected the world ever since, were discussed and decided at Potsdam. On South-East Asia, the new areas of control for SEAC agreed upon at Manila with MacArthur were confirmed, and even more territory allotted to Mountbatten's command.

"There was a very interesting consequence to this," said Mountbatten (at the height of the Vietnam war). "Roosevelt had had this mad desire to suck up to Chiang Kai-shek, and I'm sure he had transmitted this to Truman. Truman also knew that there was a lot of jealousy and worry about the Generalissimo losing face in Chungking. But after I left it was decided that I should have only the South part. The Generalissimo was to take over the North. I asked, 'How far north?' 'At the sixteenth parallel,' I was ordered. 'You're to clear things up south of the sixteenth parallel and then hand over to the French.' I was forbidden to send a soldier, a plane or a ship north of that line.

"The Chinese sent in a second-rate lot under a second-rate commander, and they were swallowed up in Hanoi. I went in and rounded up the Japs, looked after and then got rid of the internees and prisoners of war, and got some sort of civil organization going. Much later, the French gave me a procession up the Champs Elysées for this, and Médaille Militaire and Légion d'Honneur.

"After things were going, I took away our troops and General Le Clerc came in. Later I handed over to Admiral Dargenlieu—everything south of the sixteenth parallel—and I remember him saying to me, 'Thank you very much, but I wish you could have given me everything because without the North there's always going to be trouble in the South.'

"So that's one of the results of Potsdam."

In the midst of the epochal international meeting in Berlin, Churchill returned to England with his daughter Mary to hear the result of the British general election, a remarkable event in the eyes of Stalin. To the surprise of the Americans, but not of the British, the Russian was also displeased when, as a result of the Labour Party's victory, Churchill was replaced as Prime Minister by Clement Attlee, who picked up the ferryboat in midstream and carried on, with Ernest Bevin as the new Foreign Secretary but with the rest of the crew as before.

"I had had a lot to do with Attlee and liked him very much," said Mountbatten. "Nor was I surprised that he won the election. I had seen plenty of signs among the troops out East of a likely turn against the Conservatives. I had meetings with him in London and told him how I proposed to deal with the liberated territories, and was delighted that I had his full backing."

Mountbatten had always believed that the Japanese had to be defeated in the field—demonstrably defeated—and was appalled at the nation being given a chance to surrender before this happened. They had to lose "face." Now, threatened with unprecedented bombing, the destruction of all their cities and the loss of millions of lives, they were offered unconditional surrender, and at once refused.

"My feelings about the dropping of the atomic bomb were mixed. On the one hand I was afraid that this would mean the end of the war *without* the defeat of their armies in the field, just as the Germans had claimed in 1918. Against this was the colossal saving of human lives. As many Japanese had been killed defending the small island of Okinawa as at Hiroshima. Imagine what the invasion of the Japanese mainland in 1946 would have led to! You didn't count Japanese casualties—you counted their *dead*. They would blow themselves up rather than surrender. Millions would have been killed—civilians and soldiers."

For Mountbatten, after his return from London, the last act remained to be played out: Operation Zipper. The attempt to set up this invasion of the Malay Peninsula had been as slow and obstacle-strewn and disheartening as every major offensive Mountbatten had attempted. Until the successful invasion and liberation of France, it was the European operations that had, time and again, deprived Mountbatten of resources. Now it was the invasion of Japan that demanded all the priorities. On 6 April 1945, the American Chiefs of Staff flatly rejected Zipper for this reason.

It was no use Mountbatten's arguing that the greater the delay, the stronger would be the enemy build-up, especially in Singapore, and the greater the suffering and mortality among civilian detainees and prisoners of war alike. Later there was an easing of the American attitude. Zipper could go ahead, but Mountbatten could not have the light fleet carriers he had already been promised. He would have to make do with escort carriers.

At every stage, in both London and Washington, Zipper continued to be regarded as something of a sideshow. With the war over in Europe, the Far East seemed farther away than ever. The lights were on again in London. In Washington, where they had never been turned off, everyone's eyes were on Nimitz and MacArthur and the cataclysmic closing stages of the Pacific war.

It is a measure of Mountbatten's dogged determination and implacability that he managed to assemble a very considerable force for his own final act. A preliminary bombardment would be provided by heavy bombers from the Cocos Islands and south Burma, and by two battleships, cruisers, destroyers and landing craft. He had managed to rustle up nine carriers, whose planes would provide air cover until landing strips ashore were completed within a week of the invasion.

In the first seven weeks from D-day 182,000 men, nearly 18,000 vehicles and 250,000 tons of stores were to be put ashore. Mountbatten reluctantly postponed D-day until 9 September; in June the command, which seemed set for SEAC's final effort, its first major assault, was struck a new and completely unexpected blow. The British involvement in the war in the East, already of nearly six years' duration, had led to troops being separated from their families for inordinately long periods—four years was common. An operation code-named Python had therefore been instituted, which permitted very long-serving men to return. This had been allowed for in all SEAC plans. Now, in June, with an election approaching, the Churchill government sought votes by announcing a radical reduction in this period, without any reference to Mountbatten or his staff.

"This wasn't just bad manners," said Mountbatten. "It was military insanity. Suddenly we faced having to recast all our plans, and even postpone Zipper yet again." He protested in the strongest terms. The Chiefs of Staff replied, in effect, that they were sorry he had been inconvenienced, but he should go ahead anyway, "with a weakened force of six divisions on the agreed date, regardless of the risk of failure should the opposition prove greater than estimated."

Zipper was launched on schedule. The great fleet put out to sea and headed for its beachheads on the Malayan coast. Meanwhile, Hiroshima and Nagasaki were both devastated by atomic bombs, and on 14 August 1945 Japan at last submitted to unconditional surrender.

"So our landings, when they took place, would meet no resistance," said Mountbatten. "The war was over. But we had to press on, of course. And then came the bombshell. MacArthur suddenly issued orders that no Japanese-held territory was to be reoccupied and there were to be no individual surrenders until the big formal surrender in Tokyo Bay. This was all very well, but it left us in a difficult situation." Mountbatten was concerned on two counts. First, many of his landing craft were already at sea and they could not turn back because they were not designed to head into a south-west monsoon and could easily sink. Most of them took shelter under the lee of the Nicobars, where they were refuelled and provisioned.

Then what about all the starving prisoners? For many of them, further delay could mean death. And the delay was almost three weeks.

Singapore was relieved on 5 September, and a week later the Council Chamber of the Municipal Buildings of Singapore City provided the scene of the formal surrender of the Japanese in South-East Asia. The ceremonial, the little touches, all were pure Mountbatten. With his American deputy, "Specs" Wheeler, at his side, Mountbatten was driven in an open limousine by a recently released prisoner of war through streets lined by sailors and Royal Marines, and was received at the Municipal Buildings by his c.-in-c.s. Four guards of honour, mounted by the Royal Navy, RAF, Australian paratroops and the Indian Army were lined up for inspection. Massed bands played "Rule Britannia," and a seventeen-gun salute was fired.

In the chamber two long tables, six feet apart, had been drawn up for the delegates of the victors and the vanquished. A large painting of the King and Queen, hidden during the occupation, had been reinstated on the wall. But internationalism was everywhere evident: armed guards standing at the pillars represented every country that had suffered under brutal Japanese occupation: French and Australians, Dutch and Chinese, Americans and Indians and British; and at the table sat the senior officers of these nations and the top brass of Mountbatten's staff, from old one-eyed De Wiart, who had won his Victoria Cross in another war, to little Major-General Feng Yee from Chungking, who had been fighting the Japanese for longer than anyone else present.

At the table facing them sat the seven Japanese admirals and generals, balding, impassive, expressionless, bespectacled. Behind them was a crowd of some four hundred, many of them released detainees and prisoners of war, pale, thin and hollow-cheeked from their years of suffering.

Mountbatten, sublimely resplendent in white tropical admiral's uniform, and looking thirty rather than forty-five, marched in, feet characteristically splayed wide. His expression, as always on ceremonial occasions of great moment, was one of solemn exaltation, like an archbishop about to grant his blessing to the universe. Staring straight ahead, he proceeded to the dais with its microphones and the thronelike chair. Behind him trailed four A.D.C.s; and the whole assembly arose in silence.

"I have come here today to receive the formal surrender of all the Japanese forces within the South-East Asia Command . . . " The voice already familiar to so many thousands within his command, consciously authoritative, patrician, slurred at the end of each sentence.

The Japanese field-marshal had sent a message of regret for his absence—he was indisposed. Mountbatten said that he had sent a doctor to confirm this claim, "but I have warned the field-marshal that I shall expect him to make his personal surrender to me as soon as he is fit enough." (He did, too, two and a half months later, surrendering his two swords, one sixteenth-century, the other thirteenth-century. Mountbatten gave one to George VI and kept the older sword for himself.)

Mountbatten also made clear that this was no negotiated surrender. "The Japanese are submitting to superior force, now massed here." A large fleet, 100,000 men already ashore . . .

So all the massive planning and execution of Zipper had not quite gone to waste, not quite dissolved in the mushroom cloud of Hiroshima. Zipper had brought Admiral Mountbatten to this dais before this international crowd of spectators, the world's press, the movie cameras, the flashbulbs.

The enemy was there, before him, General Itagaki of the 7th Area Army, placing his signature on the Instrument of Surrender. But afterwards, outside at the head of the steps reading out the Order of the Day, a Union Jack (concealed all these years in the notorious Changi jail) breaking out on the flagpole, there remained one absent note in the grand chorus of triumph on that day.

No one had fought more bravely against more fearful odds than the Fourteenth Army, no airmen in any theater of war had flown more intrepidly in such dreadful conditions; and between them they had cleared the enemy from Myitkyina and Mandalay, Meiktila, Imphal, Rangoon, and the whole of that mountain-and-jungle-wracked land of Burma. But there had been no great decisive and final battle, no Utah

or Juno beach, no Falaise Gap and pursuit to the Rhine, no Guadalca-
nal or Okinawa—no Agincourt for Mountbatten to be told by his herald, "The day is yours." At first forgotten and later denied supplies,
right to the last wickedly ironical denial while they were already at sea
for their own D-day, Mountbatten's command was also deprived of its
climactic last triumph. Even the unopposed landings had been bogged
down on unexpectedly difficult beaches, with dozens of vehicles sunk
without trace, and hundreds more stranded in the unforeseen drainage
ditches inland.

After the fighting was over, it was also well-nigh impossible for
Mountbatten to show himself as a great diplomat. During the closing
stages of the war in South-East Asia, and its aftermath, Mountbatten
found himself at the centre of a monsoonlike international storm, with
movements from a dozen different directions simultaneously. It is no
discredit to him or his political adviser, Esler Dening, that they never
really succeeded in plotting all the day-to-day changes of pressure ema-
nating from London, Paris, Moscow, Chungking, Washington, and
MacArthur's H.Q., as well as the Dutch government-in-exile, and later
back in The Hague.

American organizations identified by initials and often working in
grey areas, like the OSS, OWI and the F.E. Div. of the Department of
State; British bodies like PWJC (Political Warfare against Japan Committee) and the JIC and Foreign Office itself; numerous nationalist-
liberation groups and armies in Burma and Malaya and the old Dutch
colonies, some backing, some fighting the Japanese armies—all these
and more, many of them in conflict with one another, made a co-
ordinated policy on liberated territory a near impossibility.

The Foreign Office in London stated that the Americans were "virtually conducting political warfare" against Britain in the Far East,
playing up to the Indian Press. Mountbatten wrote in his diary
(15 June 1945): "It is horrifying to think that the American and Indian
press evidently still regard us as merely Imperial monsters, little better
than the Fascists or Nazis."[3]

Mountbatten believed that it was impossible to break the old American conviction that the British, when they did fight in the East, were
concerned only with reclaiming their former colonies in the face of
liberation movements. "The British game never varies," ran an edito-

rial in the Chicago *Tribune*; "what Britain has, she will hold." And there were frequent allegations that American lives were being squandered in order to rebuild the British Empire.

Mountbatten's old sparring partner at the Quebec Conference of 1943 despatched a series of reports from the OSS, many of them contradictory in their advice. Everywhere Donovan saw plots. The British, French and Dutch "have arrived at an agreement with regard to the future of Southeast Asia," ran one OSS message; and their strategy was, apparently, "to win back and control [that area], making the fullest possible use of American resources, but foreclosing the Americans from any voice in policy matters."[4]

But in the same month (April 1945) that the Chicago *Tribune* was blasting the British, the OSS was, in self-contradiction, sounding a note of caution about American policy and pressure directed towards the destruction of European colonialism in South-East Asia. As if discovering a bear under the bed, which Churchill among others had sniffed years before, the OSS reported to the White House that "the United States should realize also its interest in the maintenance of the British, French and Dutch colonial empires." The new regimes must be of a more liberal nature, of course, but they were important in order to check Soviet influence. "We have at present no interest in weakening or liquidating these empires."

As one historian has recently defined the situation: "Already, in other words, judgements were being expressed which were to lead the United States five years later to underwrite financially the French war in Indo-China, and to help bring about America's own military involvement, and defeat, in Vietnam."[5]

Mountbatten's policy—if it could be given that name—on Burma, Malaya and the Dutch ex-colonies, tended towards the more orthodox American view that liberation must be granted, and quickly. His socialist-liberal attitudes, inherited from his mother and nourished by his enlightened Hessian upbringing, were much closer to the White House and the State Department than Whitehall and the Foreign Office.

In spite of Churchill's loudly expressed and forlorn hope that "Mountbatten will not meddle in politics," and while the Foreign Office was casting anxious eyes in his direction, the "Supremo" was taking steps to back the Malayan Chinese Communists. They were, he considered, the only body that had put up serious opposition to the Japanese. In Burma, when the National Army, which had previously collaborated with the enemy, turned on the Japanese, Mountbatten strongly supported it. Certainly there were to be no reprisals, no persecution, of those who had worked with the Japanese in the past in the mistaken belief that this would hasten independence.

It was of the utmost importance, Mountbatten believed, that the world should witness the compassionate treatment of the first part of the British Empire to be liberated. "I wish the problem of Burma to be treated in a sensible manner," he wrote in his diary, "as we had done in South Africa after the Boer War." Then he added, with fateful reference to his own end: "We should not use a heavy hand which might result in disaster as it had in Ireland."

The depth and breadth of Mountbatten's responsibilities, and the strength of his prejudice in favour of nationalist forces, were seen also in Indonesia, where Dr. Achmed Sukarno had seized power before MacArthur accepted the Japanese surrender in Tokyo Bay and before the Dutch officials could return. Even the new British Foreign Secretary, the socialist Ernest Bevin, thought that Mountbatten was going too far in recognizing Sukarno, and thus damaging Anglo-Dutch relations; although in view of the eventual and inevitable fate of the Dutch in their ex-colonies, history now shows that Mountbatten was merely being realistic.

Among those on the balcony of the Municipal Buildings during the signing of the surrender in Singapore was Edwina, who found the ceremony "quite the most impressive and moving I have ever seen." Following in the train of the liberating armies in Europe, she had already accomplished a great deal visiting the sick and wounded, and comforting released prisoners of war. Edwina was a tireless and practical administrator, a great deal more efficient than her husband, and it was not her wealth or her name that had taken her to the rank of Superintendent-in-Chief of the St. John Ambulance organization. No one could discover the real condition of a hospital or rest camp as speedily and relentlessly as she could. She talked to everyone and missed nothing. Then she ruthlessly used her influence to correct faults and make good shortages of everything from bedpans to volunteer nurses. She was formidable but fair.

Edwina had already made one quick and effective tour of the SEAC area early in 1945, visiting Chungking as well on behalf of the Red Cross. With the end of the war in August, Mountbatten signalled an appeal for her to come out again. The moment she arrived in Kandy, looking svelte yet businesslike in her khaki uniform, eager as always for work, Mountbatten gave her a letter of authorization to go where she wished and apply for any help she needed in locating prisoners of war and internment camps and doing what she could for the inmates. The work was gruelling and harrowing, with travel that was primitive or—in the air—hazardous. The surrender ceremony was only a brief interlude in her hectic round from Borneo to Hong Kong, Sumatra to Malaya, from one camp to another, organizing relief, giving what comfort she could to the dying.

Edwina travelled 33,000 miles, making countless calls in sixteen countries, sustained by her will to give relief and her remarkable endurance and ability to go without sleep. When she next saw her husband, she told him of the almost unbelievable tortures prisoners had suffered—sadistic beatings were low on the horror list—of hospitals full of dying women and children. "Conditions indescribable" was all she could write on one report sheet after another, from Kranji to Adam Park, from Kakom Nayok (she found a young Cassel cousin here, his hair white) to Nakom Pathom.

When time allowed, Mountbatten visited camps, too. An officer who was one of six survivors of a party of twenty-six working on the notorious railroad tells of Mountbatten's arrival, greeted by the usual antagonism and suspicion, how he broke through by talking to them naturally, man to man, about the closing stages of the war and what would have happened if they had not pushed back the Japanese. He never uttered a single word of sympathy. At the end, they were all ready to do anything he asked, "even to going back to do a personal act of daring against the Japs."

The measure of what the Mountbattens did for the spirits and physical well-being of these starved, neglected and maltreated victims of Japanese cruelty was incalculable. This, their first contribution to the new era of peace, was certainly the greatest. But there was no trace of charity or forgiveness towards the Japanese in their personal reactions. Mountbatten especially was deeply and permanently affected by what he had seen, and by the accounts given to him by Edwina.

Above: The new Viceroy and Vicereine arrive at Delhi airport, 22 March 1947. Field Marshal and Lady Wavell left the next day.

Below left: 1947: The last Viceroy and Vicereine.

Below right: In full rig, India 1947.

With Mahatma Gandhi, 1947.

With Pandit Nehru at Delhi. Third in line to be greeted is Field Marshal Auchinleck.

Communal riots, Calcutta, 1947. Tear gas is used against rioters attempting to set fire to a Hindu temple.

The solemn acceptance of partition for India: Nehru, Ismay, Mountbatten, Jinnah.

The christening of Norton Knatchbull, Mountbatten's first grandson and future 2nd Earl Mountbatten of Burma. Patricia Brabourne, Prince Philip (godfather) and Mountbatten's sister, Louise, Queen of Sweden, November 1947.

Above: With his nephew, Prince Philip, October 1948.

Left: Second grandson, Michael John, June 1950. Edwina; Princess Elizabeth (acting as godmother); Mountbatten; Lord Brabourne; Norton Knatchbull; and Patricia, Lady Brabourne.

Commander-in-Chief Mediterranean Fleet 1951.

Grand Harbour, Malta. At the termination of his Mediterranean Fleet and NATO commands, Mountbatten is rowed in his barge by six of his admirals, December 1954.

Above left: With Edwina, Princess Anne and Prince Charles, Malta, April 1954.

Above right: The ultimate ambition fulfilled. Mountbatten as First Sea Lord, 1955, with Edwina at Broadlands.

Below: Edwina at her last London home, Wilton Crescent. The portrait is of the late Duke of Kent and the photograph of Princess Elizabeth and Prince Philip shows their arrival at Malta in 1949.

Edwina's bedroom at Wilton Crescent. The portraits are of her children.

Mountbatten's study at Wilton Crescent.

The Board of Admiralty, February 1959, with Mountbatten as First Sea Lord (*centre*) and the Earl of Selkirk as First Lord (*in the chair*). The Admirals around the table are (*left to right*) Sir Manley Power, Deputy Chief of Naval Staff; Sir Caspar John, Vice-Chief of Naval Staff; D. E. Holland-Martin, Second Sea Lord; Sir Peter Reid, Third Sea Lord and Controller; and N. A. Copeman, Fourth Sea Lord. Sir John Lang, Secretary, sits between Lord Selkirk and Admiral Holland-Martin. The portrait is of King William IV. Above the fireplace is the wind dial dating from the sailing navy.

The Suez Crisis, 1956. An anxious Mountbatten arrives at 10 Downing Street. He had already warned Eden in writing and by telephone that the operation would certainly lead to disaster.

Another family occasion. The wedding of the Mountbattens' second daughter, Pamela, in January 1960, to David Hicks. Among those present (*standing*) are Patricia (Lady Brabourne); Mountbatten; the Duke of Edinburgh; Edwina (who was to die a few weeks later); and Lord Brabourne; Princess Margaret; the Queen Mother; the Queen of Sweden (Mountbatten's sister Louise); the Duchess of Kent; and Princess Alexandra. Princess Anne and Prince Charles are in the front row (*right*).

Mountbatten kisses, then casts into the sea, a wreath of lilies after the burial of Edwina. Behind him is his eldest sister, Alice, Princess Andrew of Greece, Prince Philip's mother. Behind Prince Philip are Lord and Lady Brabourne.

With President John F. Kennedy and General Lyman L. Lemnitzer at the White House.

The last salute. Mountbatten on the day of his retirement as Chief of Defence Staff in 1965. Behind him are Field Marshal Sir Richard Hull and Admiral Sir David Luce.

With nephew and great-nephew. Mountbatten's love and guidance were of inestimable importance to Prince Philip and Prince Charles, as well as to the monarchy and the nation.

Retirement job: Mountbatten at Wormwood Scrubs during his ill-starred prison-security inquiry.

Above: Old friends since the 1920s: with Noël Coward.

Left: With Princess Anne in Vienna. The bride he holds is Princess Michael of Kent.

On 30 May 1979 Mountbatten paid his last visit to one of H.M. ships, the submarine *Superb*.

Above: At Broadlands, recently opened to the public, Mountbatten talks to the oldest member of the Burma Star Association, Jock Brown, in July 1979. Both men were dead within a few weeks.

Left: The regular August holiday at Classiebawn with his grandchildren—and in this picture, his great-great-niece, Tania George, whom he is leading.

Shadow V off Mullaghmore close to the spot where it was later blown up. With Mountbatten are his sons-in-law and grandchildren.

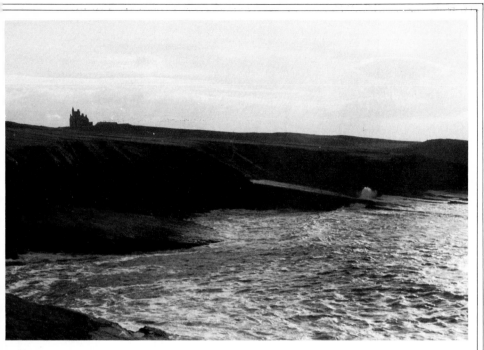

Author's photograph of Classiebawn Castle and the doom-laden Atlantic coast of County Sligo.

Westminster Abbey funeral procession, headed by the Queen and Prince Philip, the Queen Mother and Prince Charles, Prince Andrew and Prince Edward.

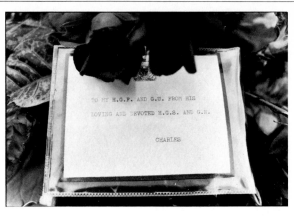

TO MY H.G.F. AND G.U. FROM HIS
LOVING AND DEVOTED H.G.S. AND G.N.

CHARLES

From Prince Charles, godson and great-nephew, who felt Mountbatten's loss so sorely.

Mountbatten wanted his funeral to be "a jolly occasion," but the sight of Dolly, with rider's boots reversed, caused more tears than the coffin she led.

"I had not liked the Japs when I had visited Japan in 1921. They seemed to me to be hard people with hard eyes," said Mountbatten. "Now I knew just how horrible they were after seeing such terrible things in Singapore and in the camps. It was the one thing during the war that seared my mind. There were no extenuating circumstances, and I could find no compassion for them at all. I loathed them. That was why I didn't go to the Tokyo Bay surrender—I just couldn't have stood the sight of them all there. My own ceremony at Singapore—well, duty obliged me to be there. But I didn't like it."

When the Japanese Emperor came over on a state visit to London in October 1971, Mountbatten at first refused to meet him. In the end the Queen commanded him—very gently—and he had to go, but he hated the whole thing and contrived not to shake the Emperor's hand. The Japanese, alone among the great nations, were pointedly omitted from the invitation list for the funeral which Mountbatten had so elaborately and meticulously prepared before his death. They were deeply wounded.

Mountbatten's unforgiveness towards his ex-enemy contrasted sharply with his humanity and compassion—over and above his realism—in his treatment of the Indian, Burmese and Siamese nationalists. In India, he made himself exceedingly unpopular with many people, especially the old colonial administrators and the bureaucrats of Delhi, but, as he said, whatever evil the Japanese brought to the lands they conquered, they also encouraged the growth of the demand for independence. In this he was strongly supported by Clement Attlee. "He impressed me greatly" was the socialist Prime Minister's typically economical way of describing Mountbatten.[6]

Over the following months, there were appalling difficulties to overcome in Indonesia and Singapore, Siam and Indochina. "This was something for which I had no previous experience," said Mountbatten. "Suddenly I was responsible for one and a half million square miles of territory and one hundred and twenty-eight million people, many of them starving, many more in some degree of political unrest. I had three quarters of a million Japanese prisoners of war to house and feed and employ until I could get them home, and one hundred and twenty-three thousand of *our* prisoners of war and internees to house and feed and get home. And there was the world's worst ever shortage of shipping."

Steadily, surely, progress was made to reconstruct the machinery of government and civil order. During these months of recovery and reorganization, Mountbatten met many of the future leaders of the liberated countries. One meeting especially was to prove of supreme importance. In March 1946 Jawaharlal Nehru, the most important politician in the Indian Interim Government, came to Singapore, Mountbatten's H.Q. since the surrender. Against the strong wishes of the local authorities, who wanted to pretend he was not there, Mountbatten had him to dinner and lent him a car for his tour through the streets to be greeted by the thousands of Indians and Indian troops in the city. Mountbatten prevailed upon Nehru not to lay a wreath at the Army Memorial to the Indian Nationals who had fought (not very effectively) with the Japanese. That was pushing things too far, Mountbatten judged. But both he and Edwina forged a close friendship with the brilliant, good-looking, highly articulate future Indian leader. And it was a relationship that was to pay heavy dividends little more than a year hence.

As soon as Pandit Nehru had left, the Mountbattens flew off to New Zealand and Australia, playing much the same part that the Prince of Wales had played after World War I—making a small gesture of gratitude to the Dominions for all the great achievements and sacrifices their people had made in the Allied cause during the war. Mountbatten had always got on well with Australians. One newspaper headlined Mountbatten's life story: "Australia Welcomes Mountbatten—Prince, Playboy and Paradox." And that was difficult to improve upon as a definition in three words.

Then, at last, it was home to Chester Street and Broadlands. First the honours, then the rest, and a happy family occasion. In June 1946 the Victory Parade, and, later, a special parade, too, for Edwina and himself with an open-carriage drive through the City of London to be presented with a Sword of Honour and the Freedom of the City. A viscountcy was bestowed on him, and other Freedoms and Degrees and foreign decorations, for which his appetite, as always, was insatiable.

Both the Mountbatten daughters had long since returned from their refuge in the United States. Patricia had served on her father's staff in Kandy during the last months of the war, but Pamela was still too young for war service. It was a great time for family reunions, and the Mountbattens' was as happy as any. Whatever difficulties there may have been in the past between the parents, the family always presented a united front.

Mountbatten enjoyed a special relationship with Patricia. He loved both girls, but he saw more of himself in her than in Pamela, whom he loved for her tenderness, understanding and creative abilities in the arts. Many years earlier, Victoria Milford Haven had likened the two girls to their cousins and friends, Princess Elizabeth and Princess Margaret Rose, and it was an interesting parallel. A sense of duty, industry and steadiness was to be seen in the elder girl of both families, while the younger tended towards the artistic, haphazard and forgetful.

Patricia—today the Countess Mountbatten of Burma—sits on numerous committees and is full of good works. Her father never failed to add "J.P." (Justice of the Peace) after her name when writing it. Pamela, with her dreaminess and restlessness and lack of organization, irritated both her parents, and in her middle age she continued to exasperate Mountbatten with her failure to keep appointments, or write letters, or confirm arrangements.

Patricia never gave any cause for anxiety, let alone exasperation. She grew up to be tidy and orderly and organized, like Princess Elizabeth, and both girls went into the services and, of course, performed their duties diligently. In due course Patricia met, in Kandy, John Ulick Knatchbull, 7th Baron Brabourne, and her father's A.D.C., and agreed to marry him. The groom's father had once been Governor of Bombay and Bengal, and temporary Viceroy of India in 1938. It was as satisfactory a match as Mountbatten could hope for.

Broadlands had been restored to its former domestic state, and from here, in October 1946, Patricia left with her father to be married in Romsey Abbey (where Mountbatten was to be buried thirty-three years later). It was a very grand, very Mountbatten social event. As at Mountbatten's own wedding, the King and Queen were there. For the first time, Prince Philip and Princess Elizabeth were photographed in each other's company publicly. The King was in the original photograph, too, but most of the newspapers printed only the young couple.

As the very satisfactory year of 1946 drew to a close, Mountbatten had one last wish to be fulfilled. He wanted to get back to sea again, and to set a steady compass course towards the real culmination of his career, the office of First Sea Lord.

VICEROY

ot long before he died, Mountbatten said, "You can divide my life into two. During the first part of my life I was an ordinary conventional naval officer, trying not to be different in the sense of being royal, trying not to show myself off as being rich and ostentatious—like always using a small car to drive to the dockyard instead of my Rolls-Royce.* Then we come to the period when I was pulled out and pushed one generation up. Dudley Pound, for instance, was twenty-four years older and was a Post-Captain while I was a two-striper. From that time everything was new for me, and most of it the first time for anyone.

"But my mother had prepared me for it. From the time we began liberating Burma and after the atomic bomb was dropped, I was out on a limb. None of my staff had anything to offer me except conventional nonsense about putting the clock back, suppressing national freedom movements, shooting traitors and all that. I decided not to go along with them, and I put the brake on—I didn't want things to go too quickly—and I think history proved me right.

"But this unconventional decision was largely due to my mother, who was always prepared to look at things unconventionally.

"I was the first inter-service officer, with a rank in each service. I was the only man who had ever been that. When I was Chief of Combined Operations, I was entirely inter-service. In South-East Asia I was not

*Not at first. This was something he learned, painfully.

only inter-service, I was inter-Allied. I was right out of the ordinary run from a military point of view. Then the war ended and I was the Supreme Commander with direct control over one hundred and twenty-eight million people. I had to get them food, see to their health, give them law and order, give them information, a broadcasting service. I had to offer them a policy, and I went ahead and did exactly what I thought was right. And in this connection, I always tried to imagine what these decisions would look like in history.

"My mother said, 'Don't worry about what people think now. Don't ever work for popularity. Above all, don't care what the newspapers say. What is important is that your decisions should be clear and stand up to history. So all you've got to think about is whether your children and grandchildren will think you've done well.'

"On that basis, I made my decisions about Burma, French Indochina, etc." He claimed that he was the first leader to liberate former colonial territories who really understood the historical implications of what he was doing, by contrast with MacArthur. "A lot of people today still think I gave away India, but . . ."

At forty-six, Mountbatten still looked ridiculously youthful, as he was the first to acknowledge. And now he was going back to his first love, in the more orthodox substantive rank of captain. But the Lords Commissioners decreed that he must remain an admiral. Mountbatten was furious. "It was the same old story. Already, straight away, I was being put again in a false position. My promotion was not due for months, but they insisted that I should carry the rank of rear-admiral immediately."

Mountbatten could see the progression of his service life clearly. He wanted to return to the Mediterranean, to command the 1st Cruiser Squadron, the closest parallel to his father's appointment as Rear-Admiral Commanding the 2nd Cruiser Squadron in 1905. Then he would be appointed Commander-in-Chief Mediterranean, the 1919 appointment of which his father had been robbed. Next he would come to the Admiralty as his father had done, and work his way up to First Sea Lord. Then, and only then, would his naval and family ambitions be fulfilled, and pride and order restored in the annals of Battenberg-Mountbatten achievement and duty.

As a start and refresher after his years of absence from the common round of naval practice, he went on a Senior Officers' Technical Course at Portsmouth. His attendance was brief. One morning he was interrupted with a message from Downing Street: "Please come and see me"—signed "Clement Attlee." It was not the first of its kind. Recently his advice had been sought on Burma and on "the mess caused there by the Governor," as Mountbatten himself expressed it.

This time India was the main item on the agenda. With Attlee was Sir Stafford Cripps, an expert on the subject: he had recently led a mission to Delhi which had very nearly pulled off an agreement for the transfer of power. "I had kept in touch with what was going on," said Mountbatten, "and I was able to produce reasonably intelligent answers. Suddenly I began to have suspicions. We were talking about Wavell, who was having a very difficult time. I said, 'You're not by any chance talking about me relieving him?' Attlee said, 'Yes,' and I said, 'Not on your life. And I'll give you my reasons. First, Wavell is a very honourable man. He may be taciturn but he's first-class, and if he can't succeed, no one can.'

"This, and all other reasons were swept away, so I started making conditions. I must choose my own staff, and there'd be a lot of them, and I'd want Wavell's too, and everyone must be allowed cars and to bring their wives. I wanted 'Pug' Ismay. I wanted complete control of the Honours List at the end, with no queries. I wanted my old York aircraft back, fitted out just as I liked it. I wanted . . ."

Was Mountbatten teasing them? Did he know that all the conditions he was likely to ask would be met? We can assume that he did. Then he tried two tough ones. First, he demanded that he could have his present appointment to the 1st Cruiser Squadron back again when he had finished in India as Viceroy (the highest appointment any British citizen could hold). Attlee said yes. But Mountbatten insisted on Admiralty approval, now. So the First Lord (Lord Hall) and the First Sea Lord (Admiral Sir John Cunningham) were called to No. 10.

Hall agreed at once. "Hey, not so fast!" said the admiral. "We had the gravest doubts about Dickie coming back after running SEAC, where he commanded fleets. It was only allowed after a lot of hesitation. But to come back after being Viceroy of India—absolutely out of the question."

There was a brief pause. Then Attlee spoke in his dry, sharp, even-toned voice. "I am not asking for your comments," he said to Cunningham. "I am giving you an order."

After they left, there was another pause before Cripps spoke: he would gladly go as Mountbatten's chief of staff if that would help. Mountbatten secretly thought this a terrible idea, that it would be read by the Indians as confirmation that Mountbatten was a mere regal figurehead. "It's very good of you, sir. But that is too great an honour," said Mountbatten.

Years later Mountbatten insisted that he was being relentlessly cornered. "I went on fighting." Next he brought up the King's name. He would have to discuss it with him. Attlee said he had already squared George VI, and that he thought it was a marvellous idea. But, argued Mountbatten, the King had not yet heard his arguments against his appointment. The meeting broke up with nothing decided except that Mountbatten would see the King at once.

Mountbatten reminded George VI that there were hundreds of princely and native states. The government had treaty relations with them, the King had a special responsibility towards them. Then, if there was civil war, terrible massacres, the royal family would be directly associated, perhaps even held responsible for them, through himself, even if he was only a minor member of the royal family.

Mountbatten reported George VI as saying that it was precisely because of his rank that he approved, that the royal family still had cachet in India, that Mountbatten should take a personal message from him to the princes.

Mountbatten: You do know that the job is almost impossible?
George VI: It *can* be done.
Mountbatten: Only by a miracle. And look how bad it will be for you and the family if I fail.
George VI: Ah, but look how good if you succeed!

"And that was that!" said Mountbatten. "I went back to Attlee and said I thought the King was quite wrong, and produced my trump card. I asked innocently if the Secretary of State for India was above the Viceroy, and was told yes, but that he was only a spokesman for the Cabinet.

"You mean I am going to have the Cabinet sitting on top of me all the time? This is ridiculous. The decisions must be mine and mine alone, on the spot."

Attlee replied, aghast, "But anything else would mean giving you plenipotentiary powers. We cannot possibly consider that."

Mountbatten rose from his chair. "For this relief much thanks," he said, smiling.

"You don't mean you're not going, Dickie?"

"I'm going, all right. I'm going back to the Navy."

With hardly a second's pause, Attlee said, "All right, you can have plenipotentiary powers."

According to Mountbatten, a week after he arrived in India, with a time limit of just fourteen months to hand over power, Nehru asked if by any chance he had managed to get some special dispensation. Mountbatten said, "Yes, as a matter of fact I did. Why do you ask?" Nehru said, "Because you act entirely differently than any other Viceroy. You talk as if *you* are making the decisions."

Between the time when the news of the appointment was made public and Mountbatten's departure, his enemies were inclined to say he had taken on the task for its grandeur and pomp, ceremonial and uniforms, and for the historical record: the great-grandson of Queen Victoria, proclaimed first Empress of India, giving away "the brightest jewel," a "socialist" viscount behaving traitoriously to his class.

His friends and relatives were concerned for quite different reasons. At best, he would be presiding over a great retreat. The man who had fought so hard to liberate and recover for the Crown vast areas of the Empire was now forced to hand back the sub-continent. At worst, he would go down in history as just one more whose reputation had been lost in the jungle of Indian politics.

A naval captain, R. C. Todhunter, who had been Mountbatten's Director of Combined Operations Material, invited him to lunch shortly before he left. "Why on earth," the host asked, "did you agree to take on such an absolutely impossible job when you were happily back at sea—where your heart has always been?"

"The whole thing appalls me," said Mountbatten. "If I could have turned it down, I would have done so. But what do you do if you are asked to do a job, first by the Prime Minister, and then by the King? How can you refuse?"[1]

Mountbatten's mother was horrified when she heard the news. She saw at once that her son was being made a scapegoat for the government's timorousness. He was going to soil his hands in politics—and look what the politicians had done to her Louis! It would be the end of Dickie's career, too.

"Politicians are incorrigible!" she exclaimed to him. He would be playing with fire. She was very passionate and almost incoherent with rage—not at him but at Attlee. "Damn! Damn! Damn!" was all she could say; and when her son apologized, that made it worse. They finally parted lovingly as ever, but Victoria's heart remained full of anxiety.

Attlee remained anxious, too, about the Mountbatten appointment, even though he was responsible for it (and was very proud of it), until he knew that it would be seen as approved by both parties. This would be revealed in the House of Commons debate on Indian policy in March, which would precede Mountbatten's departure.

Lord Butler recalls being summoned to the presence of the Prime Minister and finding him characteristically "sunk in the bottom of his chair." He was asked by Attlee if he would test the opposition Conservative Party to see if it would support or oppose the bill. "I don't speak to Winston on India," Attlee said. "I don't trust him. I would be glad if you would take some soundings over the next twenty-four hours and let me know."[2]

Butler agreed to do so. He had been Under-Secretary of State at the India Office for five years in the 1930s, and was a considerable expert on India. He was able to reassure Attlee. Butler had the gravest reservations about Churchill's India policy, anyway. "Winston's initial mistake over India," he says today, "was to lock up Nehru for the greater part of the war. Nehru was very pro-English, he was almost more English than the English, educated here and called to the bar, and so on. All he had to say to Nehru was, 'Japan is the great danger, you must see that. If they invade and conquer, they won't give you your freedom. But you know that we are only searching for ways to transfer power to you peacefully.' "

There was much criticism of Attlee's policy in the long debate, even though the Conservative Party did not vote against the bill. Butler himself, when he spoke, had some grave reservations—but not about Mountbatten. "It is true that Blake [Civil War colonel] became an admiral after the age of forty, and it is said that one of his commands to his ships was 'Right wheel,'" said Butler. "It is also said that this command, nevertheless, won a battle, and, so, it may well be that the distinguished admiral . . ., although his methods may be as unorthodox as Blake's, may yet be as successful in meeting the unsatisfactory complicated constitutional problems with which he will have to deal."[3]

One of Mountbatten's favourite stories about his Viceroyalty was that he had nearly been appointed four years earlier instead of being given the South-East Asia Command. Churchill had asked Leo Amery, Secretary of State for India, for a list of names for a successor to Lord Linlithgow, shortly to retire. Four names were produced, those of Eden, "Rab" Butler, Lord Salisbury and Mountbatten. Churchill favoured Eden, but the King turned him down because, for safety reasons, he had to have Churchill's successor at home. Butler was out, according to Lord Butler today, because, as Minister of Education, he was too busy and his work too important.

According to Mountbatten's story, that brought his own name to the top of the list. According to Leo Amery, he had put his name in as "an outsider," and at the bottom of the list. Churchill laughed at the suggestion. "No, no, much too young!" he said.[4] But Mountbatten maintained that he had not been given the job, and had been given SEAC instead, because Churchill feared he might be too swift and too successful in India.

Churchill certainly feared that Mountbatten would be too swift four years later in the debate in the House of Commons before his departure as last Viceroy. "Everyone knows that the fourteen months' time limit is fatal to any orderly transference of power," said Churchill, "and I am bound to say that the whole thing wears the aspect of an attempt by the Government to make use of brilliant war figures in order to cover up a melancholy and disastrous transaction."[5]

It could well be disastrous, according to Mountbatten, too. But the adjective "melancholy" was never spoken in Mountbatten's hearing and was never heard to cross his lips. The job of transferring power in India did, however, carry strong emotional overtones, and was one that would lay him open to criticism from all parties in India with whom he would have to negotiate.

The statistics were truly alarming. Mountbatten was charged with securing the political freedom within a unified state of some 400 million people (one in five of the earth's population), 250 million Hindus, 90 million Moslems, 6 million Sikhs, and the rest made up of numerous sects and Buddhists and Christians, and over 500 independent princes and maharajahs. They spoke 23 languages and 200 dialects and were divided into 3,000 castes, originating in racial, tribal, occupational and territorial differences. In the past few years, millions had died of hunger, and tens of thousands as a result of internecine riots. Some had fought against the Allies, many more had formed the main strength of Mountbatten's armies. Many princes and maharajahs did not welcome the end of British rule. The giant Congress Party, led by Nehru, wanted a united India within the Commonwealth. The Moslem leader, Mohammed Ali Jinnah, called out from the Moslem League for a separate Pakistan. The Moslems had been mainly loyal to Britain during the war, and had provided by far the greater number of troops. The Congress Party helped to widen the division of opposing the war, and Nehru, Gandhi and 60,000 of their followers were arrested. Nothing much seemed to have changed since 1921.

Mountbatten was taking on the political commitment of a socialist Prime Minister and would be recognized everywhere as the King's cousin and representative. Attlee himself "thought the odds were about six to four against success." Mountbatten's estimate of a thousand to one against seemed more realistic. It was a task that appeared even more difficult than that of liberating South-East Asia and bringing law and order, food and housing to that ethnic stew of creeds and colours of millions.

The record of past Viceroys was not encouraging. Wavell, a great soldier and with the best will in the world, had, in Attlee's judgement, been a disaster as Viceroy under the rapidly changing circumstances and the urgent need for a transfer of power. "He was a soldier and a singularly silent soldier" was Attlee's comment. "A great man in many ways, you know, but a curiously silent bird, and I don't think silent people get on very well with Indians, who are very loquacious. His mind wasn't supple enough."[6] Lord Linlithgow, and those before him, had also struggled unsuccessfully with the intractable problem.

There must be a time limit for the transfer of power. Mountbatten claimed it was his idea. This was not true. It was Cripps's, and Wavell had agreed that this was essential. But "Wavell was frankly defeatist by then," said Attlee; and "suddenly I had what I now think was an inspiration. I thought of Mountbatten."[7]

When all the official records and Mountbatten's own record in the Broadlands Archives are made available, they will probably add little to what has already been written about the transfer of power in India. It is not our aim here to recount yet again the full sequence of this remarkable contest of wits, of devious negotiation, of dashed hopes and final agreement thrashed and beaten out of the contestants for power in the two nations. The importance for this book is to examine the manner and style employed by Mountbatten *and his wife* in these negotiations, set against the main outline of events, to judge whether the high claims made for Mountbatten's achievements were justified.

The last days before the departure from London were marked by two massive social events: an evening reception at India House given by the High Commissioner, at which the press was quite uncontrolled and Mountbatten ("We live and learn") was driven nearly demented by Indian and British reporters and cameramen; and his own farewell party at the Royal Automobile Club, of which he was president. Members of the royal family, the Prime Minister, many senior politicians (mostly socialist) and many theatrical celebrities were there.

Noël Coward was among those who were very indignant about the corner into which his old friend had been forced. "The position having become impossible, they call on Dickie," he said. And when one of the few Tory M.P.s present inveighed against Attlee's government, Noël Coward turned on him and told him, "You're no better. Nicer manners perhaps, but no more talent."[8]

There were seven hundred guests altogether, and there can be no doubt that few of them gave Mountbatten much of a chance.

Mountbatten's York aircraft took off from Northolt Airport in northwest London at first light on 20 March 1947. Besides Rear-Admiral the Viscount and Viscountess Mountbatten and their daughter Pamela, there were on board their personal servants, Mountbatten's senior A.D.C., Lieutenant-Commander Peter Howes, who did so much of the hard work, and Captain "Ronnie" Brockman, his private secretary and for so many years before, and after, sharer of private jokes, whom Mountbatten always found congenial company for lighter moments.

46 YEARS

As usual when Mountbatten travelled, the luggage was prodigious in volume and quantity, and even Edwina, normally the lightest of light travellers, was obliged as Vicereine to bring a wide range of possessions and clothes. As on her honeymoon (and this year marked their silver anniversary), she brought with her much of her jewelry as well as a diamond tiara for the proclamation in Delhi. Then there were all the documents, and the two-page definition of the terms of Mountbatten's mission, signed by the Prime Minister.

Mountbatten had laid down a gruelling timetable for the flight, which set the tempo he was evidently intending to sustain throughout the mission. Most of the rest of his staff had left the previous day, preferring a more relaxed flight.

Wavell, the outgoing Viceroy, invited Mountbatten's staff members to lunch after their arrival. This straightforward, courageous military man, who enjoyed history and poetry and had struggled so long and patiently to bring about a settlement that would be acceptable to all parties (and was much admired by all Indians for his honesty and integrity), had accepted dismissal with the same dignity as he had shown when he responded to Churchill's telegram of dismissal at the height of the North African War. "I suppose they are right," he had muttered as he read the letter from Attlee. But after talking to Mountbatten's staff, he wrote without bitterness in his journal, and quite truthfully: "They do not seem really to know very much about it [India] or to have any very new or definite policy."9

Mountbatten's plane, because of its tight schedule, arrived only a few hours later, and the sixty-three-year-old field marshal greeted his forty-six-year-old naval successor. Their characters and styles were opposite in almost every respect, but the two men had always got on well. Wavell also knew all about Mountbatten's enjoyment of ritual and ceremonial. On his arrival, wrote Wavell, "the Bodyguard in full dress looked well, and he was very pleased with them."10

The two men then settled down to a two-and-a-half-hour talk. It was a partial success. With uncharacteristic lack of tact, Mountbatten let it be known that he had been asked to take on the job while Wavell was actually in London and while Wavell was being told by Attlee that all was well. "So that Attlee's assurances at that time and subsequent letters were completely insincere," wrote the field-marshal, now with unmistakable bitterness. "I am glad that I have finished with politics," he added as he flew out of Delhi.[11]

"Wavell was very helpful," said Mountbatten, "but I saw very little of him. He was anxious to quit as soon as possible so as not to be in the way and an embarrassment. We had dinner with him that first evening, and we talked a lot of politics but there was not very much new above what I knew already or had learned in London. I told him that I hoped to bring Gandhi and Jinnah together, and he looked at me rather inscrutably. He was probably thinking, Here comes the new smart boy who thinks he knows everything, but just let him wait! "

The next morning, Mountbatten and Edwina saw the Wavells off from the airport, an unusual and appreciated gesture, and returned to work. On 24 March, two years after Mountbatten had taken Mandalay, he and Edwina were sworn in as Viceroy and Vicereine, a function as grand as any Swearing-In Ceremony, but for this last time with the single purpose of granting political freedom to 400 million people instead of ruling them.

It was the nearest thing to a coronation, though mercifully briefer: trumpets sounding the prelude, the A.D.C.s leading the Mountbattens, he solemn and noble in the pale-blue robe of the Grand Master of the Star of India over the full-dress admiral's uniform and wearing the dark-blue ribbon of the Garter above the dazzling array of Grand Crosses, orders and decorations; Edwina in gold brocade, her splendid tiara and more modest display of decorations.

They moved to their thrones, cunningly lit red and gold with scarlet velvet hangings, and Sir Patrick Spens, the Lord Chief Justice of India, administered the oath: "I, Francis Albert Victor Nicholas Mountbatten . . ." Then, with the prior knowledge of only a few members of his staff, Mountbatten delivered a brief address, an unprecedented step. "This is not a normal Viceroyalty on which I am embarking," Mountbatten began. "His Majesty's Government are resolved to transfer power by June 1948 . . . I am under no illusion about the difficulty of my task, I shall need the greatest good will of the greatest possible number, and I am asking India today for that good will . . ."

June 1948—fourteen months. For thirty years a means acceptable to all parties had been searched for, and now this young admiral told them the transfer would take place in fourteen months. The shock when the Indians first heard could have been more electric only if he had added that he had promised his family that he would be home in a year. But even his staff did not know that.

He had spoken of good will, and it was the search for that good will that occupied Mountbatten's earliest days. "Everything, absolutely everything, was going to depend on personal relationships," said Mountbatten. "This I had known from the beginning. I knew Nehru, and there was plenty of good will there. We liked each other, and Nehru had always been one for rank and titles—a great snob and pro-English even if the English had put him in jail so often. He was marvellous to look at—wonderful eyes, very tall and handsome. Above all, he and Edwina got on marvellously, too. That was a great help."

In a country not at that time noted for the political influence of its women, the wives of those involved in the transfer negotiations played a strong part; and the leading role was, of course, played by Edwina herself, her leading man Jawaharlal Nehru, now widowed and lonely and needing a woman in his life.

Edwina charmed all the Indian leaders, and every Indian she met, for that matter, and they numbered thousands. Her blend of grace and authority, transparent kindness and interest in everyone she spoke to, her evident love of India and the people, played quite as big a part in the negotiations as Mountbatten himself in one formal and informal meeting after another. Whether in some riot-and-strife-torn town, with bodies lying rotting in the streets amid smashed glass and wrecked rickshaws and the litter of looting, with the temperature in the 110s and her hair soaking with sweat as she grieved or gave comfort, or in Viceroy House, surrounded by the glitter and riches of imperial power, two hundred servants at her bidding, acting with ease and charm as hostess to her guests, the Vicereine was indeed the graceful empress of the last months of British power. Nothing was too much trouble for her; her patience and energy were inexhaustible, whether at home or on the numerous social occasions, from maharajah's banquets to minor luncheon parties, to which they would fly to all parts of India.

At one of these, in south India, British residents—almost all tea planters—assembled with their wives. The host, who had served in the 14th Army, received the Mountbattens and Pamela. "Lady Mountbatten, as usual, had done her homework," the host remembers, "in respect to the people she was to meet and, on being introduced to my wife, expressed her appreciation of the good work she had done."

The host felt that a short speech of encouragement to the planters, all of whom had understandable misgivings about the future, was essential, but Mountbatten flatly refused on the grounds that it was an unofficial occasion and he might be reported in the press. Reassured that there were no reporters and the hall would be cleared of servants, Mountbatten still refused and continued to eat ("and no one enjoyed the meal more than the ex-Supremo himself! "). The host then appealed to Edwina, telling her how disappointed everyone would be. "Lady Mountbatten immediately got the point, and cupping her hands, leaned over to her husband and earnestly spoke to him." Mountbatten at once nodded and indicated that he would make a speech. And, of course, it was superbly done and had exactly the right tonic effect—"a clear case," noted the now satisfied host in a grave understatement, "that behind every successful man is a woman!"[12]

Mountbatten was always good at the diplomatic touch. A signals officer in the control tower at the landing field at Palam recalls how the viceregal Rolls-Royce, waiting in the shade, would speed out to meet the viceregal plane as it taxied in. The chiefs of staff, or their deputies, would line up.

"His Excellency would greet the representatives as though he was about to miss the last train, but before entering the Rolls, he never failed to stop, turn round, raise his hat and wave to our little group on the balcony. I never once saw him fail to do this, no matter how hot, tired or harassed he might be. How we loved him for his small courtesy!"[13]

Edwina's action in "saving" the tea planters' lunch was noted by all the wives. It says a great deal for the quality of mind and tolerance of the British women in India (contrary to common belief) that they accepted and admired Edwina's style as Vicereine, especially as she was widely known as a socialist and had—to say the least—a very liberal manner with the humblest servants. The fact that she had an affair with Nehru, and so many people knew or suspected it, in no way diminished her standing. Rather the reverse; and the relationship that developed between the beautiful forty-five-year-old Englishwoman of such notable wealth and aristocracy and the English-educated Hindu barrister from Allahabad, leader of the Congress Party and thirteen years older than Edwina, had the most profound effect on the negotiations for the transfer of power.

Gandhi, too, fell under Edwina's spell and was soon calling her "my dear friend." Gandhi was the first target of Mountbatten's "search for good will." With the Mahatma on his side, he would, as he defined it, "be halfway home."

"We didn't talk any business at all at our first meeting," said Mountbatten. "It was just a personal chat. He was fascinated when I told him about my efforts to bring about a meeting between him and the Prince of Wales when he was in prison in 1921. He talked about his early life, the development of his political beliefs and the nonviolent independence movement. We were together alone for two hours, and when we came out, the waiting reporters thought we must have been solving the difficulties of the transfer. Actually, we hadn't mentioned them!"

In fact, Gandhi now carried little weight politically, but it was of the utmost importance that Mountbatten should have a close understanding and friendship with India's beloved prophet, and this he succeeded in achieving. The other major politicians and statesmen in turn warmed to the aura of affection and good will and at the same time recognized Mountbatten's genuine love for their people.

But the one man who could drive home the bolt and secure the lock of a united India was Jinnah. "Jinnah *was* the Moslem League," said Mountbatten. "He held the future of India in his hands. I tried the same technique with him, but it was almost impossible to warm him. He had only one dream, and that was a separate Moslem state." Jinnah was cold ("My God, he was cold!"), arrogant, vain, inflexible—all the characteristics that make negotiation virtually impossible. He was as thin as a reed from the Ganges, narrow in face, his brown skin dry even in the hottest weather, his eyes bright and alert, missing nothing. He was a terrific dandy and appeared in a wide range of perfectly cut suits, with a monocle that completed the picture of some suntanned eccentric from a Michael Arlen novel.

At morning meetings of Mountbatten's staff ("the Dickie birds") the subject of Jinnah was more often on the agenda than anything else. In the end Mountbatten claimed to have thawed him. But everyone knew that the temperature change was that of one man's breath on a frosty dawn. Jinnah was seventy, in poor health, and destined to live little longer than a year. "It was Jinnah, and the Moslem riots and massacres that convinced me of two things soon after my arrival," Mountbatten said. "The first was that we had to be quick to find a solution. The second, that it was more important to be quick than to have an undivided India. Government was losing control. I decided that we had to be out not in fourteen months but in five months."

It was as if the sub-continent had been sown with politico-racial time-fused mines. As fast as Mountbatten and Edwina sped about the country defusing them, others were laid in their place. One of the worst problem areas was the North-West Frontier Province. On 28 April the Mountbattens flew to Peshawar. They were told that a number of Moslems, around 75,000, were about to march on Government House, and that their mood was violent. Mountbatten agreed to meet and show himself to the demonstrators. At the last minute Edwina insisted on joining him in the car. The sound of chanting, rising to crescendos, could be heard from a distance. The crowd was in a large park and its surrounding fields, stretching far into the distance. They were crying "Pakistan *zindabad!*" (Long live Pakistan!) over and over again, waving the illegal green flags of Pakistan. Their imminent march was also illegal and certain to lead to violence.

The Mountbattens climbed up onto a railway embankment, both of them looking informal in khaki bush shirts, and waved to the nearest people in the crowd. The word of their presence spread like a tidal wave. Children were held up to see them, and the cries soon changed to "Mountbatten *zindabad!*" No speech was possible. But their presence was enough. For nearly half an hour they exchanged waves and smiles before leaving for lunch with the Governor. They learned later that all of the demonstrators had dispersed peacefully and were returning to their homes.

Edwina later made a journey alone to the Punjab, where communal rioting was bloodiest and thousands had already met deaths almost as horrible as those in the Japanese camps two years earlier. It was a harrowing experience, emotionally as well as physically, with temperatures up to 114 degrees in the shade. She could do little to ease the misery directly. The indirect influence of her dangerous and exhausting work was profound, however. As soon as she returned, grieved and distraught by what she had seen, Mountbatten sent her to recount her experiences to Nehru.

Together, the leader of the Congress Party and the most powerful man in India and the exhausted Vicereine grieved for Mother India. Then Mountbatten himself worked on Nehru, socialist Viceroy and admiral and socialist barrister and politician, friends with so much in common, and no jealousy whatever on Mountbatten's side of Nehru's relationship with Edwina. On the contrary, he was proud of her role.

With every show of reluctance, Nehru agreed that the only way to communal peace and freedom for his country was to divide it. Whatever other conclusions can be reached about this stage in Indian history, whether or not a solution could eventually have been found without partition, however the figures of the massacred before and after the transfer of power are read, there can be no denying that if freedom for India was to be granted in months and not years, and partition was in any case inevitable, then the Mountbattens, between them, did a marvellous job in putting together the new dual structure of power.

Never in Mountbatten's career had Edwina's influence been more openly evident. Only Mountbatten himself fully appreciated the extent of her support through a quarter century of marriage, guiding him through the tricky channels of those early days in the Mediterranean, from healing the injured pride of fellow officers to charming captains and c.-in-c.s; supporting him in those months at Combined Ops, dealing first with the affronted Keyes, the eccentric specialists and wild men that this H.Q. attracted and the hard men of the services who disapproved of Mountbatten and all his works; above all impressing Churchill with the depth and glitter of her mind so that the war leader always saw Mountbatten as one half of a unique team.

Nehru capitulated. A great deal of choppy water lay ahead, but they had clawed their way off the lee shore of catastrophe. "So there we were," said Mountbatten. "We had all had dreams of a united India, handing over to a single government. Within weeks they were shattered, and we had to make do with second best. But that was better," he claimed, "than what I knew to be the alternative." By 3 June all seemed clear sailing. There had been last-minute hell from Jinnah and other problems. But now the Mountbatten Plan had been accepted; and on the same day that the leaders met, Attlee announced to the House of Commons what he claimed to be a complete success.

Four months earlier to the day, commenting on Mountbatten's appointment, the *Times* of London predicted that if he brought with him no new initiative, no solution, it "may reinforce the determination of the Congress Party and the Moslem League to make no concessions to each other." And then, under the threat of complete breakdown, there would be a decision "in favour of the claims of one side or the other." And now it had worked out exactly like that. India was to be partitioned and Jinnah had his Pakistan.

Hindu India formed the great central area of the sub-continent, and because of the approximate lines of religious population distribution, Pakistan was divided, East and West, without any linking corridor— the one concession Jinnah was forced to make. This was the broad outline, but there were many ragged ends, such as the provinces of Punjab and Bengal, and Kashmir. The legislative assemblies would deal with their future. The representatives of the Moslem districts and the others would vote separately in favour of partition or against it, a simple majority being decisive. If the vote favoured partition, then a boundary commission would set up the border line. The North-West Frontier, Sind and British Baluchistan would have a referendum on whether or not to join the Constituent Assembly or form their own.

This was the essence of the Mountbatten Plan. For all but a handful of veteran authorities on Indian politics, races, religions, frontiers, hates and loves, the complexity of the whole business precluded facile objections. That and the speed and decisiveness with which agreement had been reached were its chief strength. Its weaknesses were to manifest themselves over decades and generations to come.

But, at first, there were few dissenting voices. Not only Attlee proclaimed it a success. Millions of Hindus and Moslems regarded it as a triumph, and outside India some informed opinion and nearly all uninformed opinion considered it "a good thing." But of necessity, because of the self-imposed time factor, the surgeon had no opportunity to sharpen his knife, and the incisions of partition were coarse, leaving millions on the wrong side of boundary lines, and leaving the nawabs and rajahs, khans and maharajahs, many ruling vast areas in what Mountbatten truthfully described as "a pathetic situation."

They still had to be dealt with. "I knew some of them well, had played polo with them, and they were my friends," said Mountbatten. "But these were only a few out of five hundred, some of them rulers of only a small town or a few square miles, others of vast wealth controlling huge and rich areas.

"I saw some of them separately, and then summoned a full-scale meeting of the Chamber of Princes and told them they had until fifteen

August to make up their minds whether they would remain independent or throw in their lot with one or the other of the two new states."
Some Mountbatten bullied; with others he used more subtle methods.
"He could," commented one observer, "not only talk the hind leg off a
donkey but also the throne from under a prince."

A tremendous amount of other work remained to be done. Mountbatten had a much-photographed calendar in his office with a circle
around 15 August, and every day a date would be deleted to underline
the urgency. Friday, 15 August, 1947, was the most memorable day in
Indian history, and one of the most significant in the mid-twentieth
century. The world's greatest imperial power was handing over, volun-
tarily and (with some exceptions) gladly, a great sub-continent, which
would now control its own destiny. All over Pakistan and the new
India, speeches rang out and the new flags were unfurled. If anyone
questioned the good will that accompanied the exercise, an Indian or a
Briton could point to the figure of the first Governor-General, for
Mountbatten had been asked to stay on in this role in free India, and
had agreed, though for a few months only. (He had hoped to be Governor-General of Pakistan, too, but Jinnah, who had been granted almost everything for which he had worked, would not have that.)

The installation of Mountbatten as Governor-General was as elaborate and stately as his installation as Viceroy barely five months earlier.
Messages of good will from the world's rulers were read out, Mountbatten made a speech of friendship and gratitude, followed by one from
Dr. Rajendra Prasad, in Hindi and then in English: "Let us gratefully
acknowledge, while our achievement is in no small measure due to our
own sufferings and sacrifices, it is also the result of world forces and
events, and last though not least it is the consummation and fulfilment
of the historic tradition and democratic ideals of the British race." That
seemed to say it all.

Many more ceremonies and celebrations remained, and nothing, it
seemed, could tarnish the glitter and douse the happiness of that day—
only perhaps the thought that "at this moment the man who had done
more than all of them put together to win India her freedom" felt no
call to rejoice, rather to mourn. "It was true that the country was free.
But more important, it was also torn asunder and bleeding. For Mahatma Gandhi, there was only one place to be at this moment—in a
noisome slum where he could bring a little peace and comfort, where

he could fast for his people's sins, and where he could mourn the India, united as well as free, for which he had worked and prayed and schemed and dreamed."[14]

"No power in history," ran one Indian newspaper comment on these stirring days, "but Great Britain would have conceded independence with such grace, and no power but India would have so gracefully acknowledged the debt." But there were other debts to be paid—the anguish and sufferings of 12 million people forced to uproot themselves for fear of the future. Communal strife and frenzy on a scale never known before even in this great suffering land. No one has calculated accurately the number who were shot, burned, hacked, battered and tortured to death—perhaps one million, perhaps two million died in the months following partition—certainly many more than British and imperial (including Indian) troops killed in the First World War.

With fear and death, there inevitably came famine. Edwina set up a United Council for Relief and Welfare. At one time, with the hysteria of mass murder now sweeping into Delhi itself, many of her Muslim staff were murdered, and Edwina was seen, a mask over her face, helping to move the corpses to the mortuary and then touring the hospitals, tending the wounded and attempting to allay their fears. Delhi resembled a city of the dead, with no transport entering or leaving. Somehow, Gandhi appeared on the scene of horror, a frail little spindle-legged saint whom Churchill had once called a seditious Middle Temple lawyer now posing as a half-naked fakir.

In a few days it was his seventy-eighth birthday. "Send me only condolences," he said. "There is nothing but anguish in my heart. I cannot live while hatred and killing mar the atmosphere." He spoke, too, of the sufferings of the refugees. "I have heard that a convoy of Hindus and Sikhs fifty-seven miles long is pouring into the Indian Union from West Punjab. It makes my brain reel to think how this can be. Such a happening is unparalleled in the history of the world and it makes me hang my head in shame."[15]

In the midst of these scenes of anarchy and death across the sub-continent, with Edwina working as desperately and effectively as she had during the liberation of South-East Asia, Mountbatten insisted that they should both go home.

.   .   .

Nine months earlier, on 25 January 1947, the Mountbattens had given a dinner party at Chester Street for the royal family, a farewell celebration before their departure on a tour of South Africa. It was also in the nature of a pre-engagement party for Princess Elizabeth and Prince Philip. The King and Queen had finally given their approval of the marriage of their elder daughter to her cousin. The couple were clearly in love, and everybody was delighted. The official engagement announcement would not be made until July. Until then, the news remained highly confidential. But now their health was drunk in champagne in the house still used by the Mountbattens as their London base, a comfortable enough residence, but a far cry from the marble ostentation of Brook House in the old days.

Among the subjects they discussed was Prince Philip's name, and the business of naturalization—a mere formality. He would just come up in some list in the near future, along with a lot of others, probably mostly German-Jewish refugees. The name, of course, would be Mountbatten. He would have a surname for the first time. But Prince Philip's uncle, and the King and Queen and his future wife, were all anxious that none of the dirt of the Beaverbrook vendetta would brush off against Mountbatten's nephew with the taking of this name, let alone against the heir to the throne, whom he was shortly to marry. This was especially important because the campaign would intensify as Mountbatten took over as Viceroy, and he would inevitably be attacked more fiercely than ever by Beaverbrook's pro-imperial newspapers for being a traitor to his country and giving away the Empire.

"I told the King and Queen that I would talk to the Beaverbrook chairman on the subject," said Mountbatten. "When they asked if that wasn't putting my head in the lion's mouth, I said I thought I would survive. So I telephoned the chairman of Beaverbrook newspapers, not Max, and asked him if he would come along with his editors Arthur Christiansen of the *Daily Express* and John Gordon of the *Sunday Express* for a drink. He was very surprised and obviously couldn't imagine what it was all about, but said they would come.

"Prince Philip was there when they turned up, but after the introductions he kept out of the picture and didn't say anything. I said, 'I've asked you along because I would value your advice. Prince Philip is applying for naturalization, and if he is successful, he will assume the family name Mountbatten. You must know as much as anyone in the country about public opinion, and how the public will react to this. What do you think?'

"They all agreed in turn that they thought that it was an excellent idea—difficult to say anything else with him there—and that the British public would warmly approve. So I said, 'That's awfully reassuring and very good of you to come along and let me ask you frankly like this,' and so on. 'Have another drink?' Of course, when Max heard how three such hard men of the world had been outmanoeuvred, he was amazed, and when the official announcement was made, they were forced to say, What a wonderful thing."

Shortly after this the London *Gazette* published the names of 817 newly naturalized citizens. Under *M* was "Mountbatten, Philip; Greece; serving officer in His Majesty's forces; 16 Chester Street, London, S.W.1. 28 February 1947." This new Englishman would, it added, be known as Lieutenant Philip Mountbatten, R.N.

The wedding was to be on November 20. In the postwar era of gloom and austerity, it would be the greatest, most glittering royal occasion since the coronation of 1937. For Mountbatten it was a great deal more. The sealing of ties between the British monarchy and his own family was at once a triumph and the natural culmination (as he saw it) of his family's ascent from the dynastic depression into which it had fallen when his great-grandfather had married a commoner and the *Almanac de Gotha* had gone so far as to derate the Battenbergs.

Prince Louis's enthusiasm for the Royal Navy, his naturalization, his promotion in the service, Queen Victoria's affection and admiration for him, his young brother's marriage to the Queen's last daughter, the growing family ties with the royal family, Mountbatten's father's position at the very top of the Royal Navy, the birth of his sister's son Philip in the year of his father's death were all like the passing on of some great seal of office. And now with this boy's marriage to the future Queen the stage-by-stage progression seemed to have a sublime inevitability to it, which warmed Mountbatten's heart as no other family event could. If only his father could have been there to see it! How he would have approved. (His mother approved, too, but was being predictably matter-of-fact about the business.)

The November royal wedding had been in Mountbatten's mind when he cut the period allowed for the transfer of power, already far too short in the eyes of Indian Government officials, the Indian Civil Service, the Indian Army, the India Office and the Foreign Office in London as well as numerous senior politicians, all of whom conceded that self-government was eventually inevitable. A second consideration was his urgent wish to get back to the Navy.

By mid-August it looked as if he would be able to conform to his own compressed timetable. And then came the riots, on a scale and of a degree of horror no one had predicted. And there was no sign of any improvement in the situation throughout the whole sub-continent. Could he and Edwina leave for the wedding under these circumstances, with his office working day and night, with Edwina racing from a scene of riot to a hospital to a refugee camp, day after day, with military and civil decisions of a most crucial and life-and-death nature to be made daily?

If there was any struggle of conscience, it was a brief one. Edwina was deeply concerned about leaving her work and the unfortunate interpretation that would be put upon their departure; and for the captain of the *Kelly* who had not gone down with his destroyer, talk of rats and sinking ships was considered in the worst taste. Mountbatten's public relations officer loyally reassured Edwina that of course she must go. To cancel now would only add to the sense of crisis in the public mind. Mountbatten, independently, told the same officer that he was far from happy about leaving, right up to the last moment, and was similarly reassured, as he knew he would be.

They set off for their brief return home early on Sunday morning, 9 November, following their usual breathless schedule, and landed at Northolt. The arrival was in character, too, both Mountbattens throwing themselves into a whirlwind of telephoning, letter-writing, parties and arrangements. Edwina sped to Broadlands, lovely in its autumn colours, in such sharp contrast to Delhi. Here she completed arrangements for the honeymoon stay of the royal couple, a parallel of their own twenty-five years earlier. Mountbatten reported to Attlee, and got a warmer reception than Wavell. Then on to lunch with the King, then to unveil a portrait of Nehru at India House and back to Buckingham Palace for dinner. Then the christening of their first grandchild, Norton Louis Philip Knatchbull, by the Archbishop of Canterbury. An eve-of-wedding cocktail party, with Edwina as hostess and Mountbatten rushing off to Prince Philip's bachelor party. And so to the Abbey on the twentieth . . .

The Mountbattens were in India again a week later. Edwina went straight back to her relief work. Over and above the deaths by violence, thousands were dying from exposure in the November winds in refugee camps in the Punjab. Two events followed in swift succession, each marking symbolically the extremes under which the masses in India suffered. The first was the Silver Jubilee of the Maharajah of Jaipur, as grand and glitteringly ostentatious and extravagant an affair as ever occurred in the days of the British raj. In this land of extremes, the scene in Jaipur contrasted grotesquely with those of riot, pillage, rape and murder that stalked the nation.

In one more desperate attempt to stem the flow of violence and bloodshed, in the New Year, Gandhi began a fast, a fast unto death, and was soon so weak that he had to be carried to prayer meetings. Mountbatten visited him anxiously. Mahatma was just able to whisper. Roguishly, he said, "It takes a fast to bring the mountain to Mahomet."

Then, on the afternoon of 30 January 1948, Mountbatten returned to Delhi from a visit to Madras. He arrived to receive first the grave news that in a crowd being addressed by Nehru, two men had been found with grenades which were certainly intended for the Prime Minister. A few minutes later, the news came over the car's radio that shots had been fired at Gandhi, and that he had been hit three times. Before a doctor could arrive, Mahatma had died, muttering, *"Hey Rama!"*—Oh God!

"To say that I was appalled conveys nothing," said Mountbatten. "I was numbed and utterly terrified. His little pinched face looked serene in death when I went to his house, where a great crowd had already gathered. Someone in the crowd shouted, 'It was a Moslem that did it!' I immediately shouted back, 'You're a fool. You know nothing. It was a Hindu.' I had no idea, of course. How could I? But if it had been a Moslem, then civil war was inevitable and the carnage terrible. Luckily I was right. It was a Hindu fanatic."

Four months later, the term of Mountbatten's office expired, and he and his family prepared to leave India. It was a parting of friends, and warm were the words, glittering the ceremonies, generous the gifts on both sides. Edwina in particular had forged a deeply loving relationship with the people to whom she had given so much of her time and energy and compassion. Mountbatten was seen in the simple terms of a great and royal figure who had given them their freedom. Their love for him endured for his life. In Britain, when Mountbatten was murdered thirty-two years later, there was a day of mourning. In India, mourning was ordered for two weeks, and the feeling ran even deeper among all classes, including those who had grown up since the last days of the British raj.

Many judgements representing all shades of political opinion have been passed on Mountbatten's mission of 1947. To one extreme, which included Churchill, numerous pro-imperial politicians and Lord Beaverbrook, it was an act of criminal folly. To the extreme left, it came too late to avoid the massacres. Today, statesman hold widely divergent views on the transfer of power. "Whatever one thought of the instructions he was given as Viceroy, he was only doing his duty as a public servant in carrying them out. His judgement over Kashmir may have been good or bad," says Lord Hailsham. "I am in no position to say. But I think the Conservative Party treated him ungenerously considering that he was only carrying out his instructions. Certainly he was a very good selection as Viceroy, and it was a great strength for him to have the royal connection."[16]

Sir Harold Wilson says that his party was surprised at the bad reception Mountbatten got on the completion of his Viceroyalty. "I think everyone in the party agreed with what he had done," he said, "except perhaps a few diehards . . ."[17]

Lord Butler, who really knew the Indian scene, thought that Mountbatten's great mistake was in underestimating Jinnah, "an inflexible, tough and ruthless man, a terrifying chap." Butler thought that "we all underestimated the strength of Jinnah's jealousy of Mountbatten's relations with Gandhi and Nehru. Edwina was dynamic with Gandhi and Nehru, especially Nehru, but she was not dynamic with Jinnah. All the same, partition could not have been avoided even though the Cripps Mission had got so close to agreeing on a formula which would have avoided it. By 1947 and with Jinnah so jealous, it was too late. It was also inevitable that Jinnah would become Governor-General of Pakistan, in spite of all Mountbatten's efforts to become super-Governor-

General of both countries." Butler thought that Mountbatten deserved but actually escaped the full impact of the odium for the massacres.

Mountbatten's public relations officer described the acceptance by all parties of the plan as Mountbatten's "moment of personal triumph."[18] It was no such thing, alas. Given the time that the British government had calculated was needed, the Mountbatten mission might have pulled off what Sir Stafford Cripps had come within an ace of doing a year earlier. Wavell, given time, might have pulled it off, for, however hard he played the part of "the strong, silent man," he was greatly respected by everyone for his honesty and truthfulness. Even Jinnah respected him, and he was the key figure always. And Wavell had been sturdily neutral.

But the destroyer captain rang down "Full Speed Ahead" from the moment he put to sea on Operation Transfer, and Nehru and Congress were battered into accepting partition with the gunfire still echoing in their ears. No one really had time to think, except Jinnah, who got 90 percent of what he wanted. He certainly did not think that he owed any thanks. This old, sick, prickly Muslim had indeed seen Edwina being "dynamic" with Nehru, seen the warmth of Mountbatten's relations with Nehru too. Nothing in Jinnah's mind called for gratitude. Mountbatten himself knew, as always, that he had done the right thing, and in this case, the only thing. But even he did not regard it as the triumph claimed for him by his public relations chief.

It is the easiest defence in the world to claim that speed was essential. It can never be disproved. No one can ever prove that more, or fewer, lives would have been lost if there had been a greater show of patience and less need to finish the job in a rush, and then go tearing off to his nephew's wedding, and return for the assassination of Gandhi.

Three months after Mountbatten's death, on the day that the statue to Lord Attlee was unveiled in the House of Commons, the political commentator Alan Watkins wrote in the London *Daily Telegraph*:

> India independence, we can now see, was inevitable. But under Attlee a lot of people—the precise number is still disputed—were massacred. Perhaps the carnage would have been even greater if independence had not come at the time and in the way it did. We do not know. But it seems excessive, to say the least, to hail an act which directly led to the sanguinary deaths of millions of people as one of prudent and enlightened statesmanship.[19]

Attlee's self-defined "inspiration" in selecting Mountbatten stemmed from his recognition that India, as a deep barb in the new Labour government's flesh when there were so many other massive solutions to be sought and resolved, had to be extracted quickly, the flow of blood staunched.

The choice of Mountbatten was anything but an inspiration. But given that the transfer of power had to be accomplished swiftly and with the least possible regard for the long-term consequences for India and every regard for the short-term benefits for a harassed and near-bankrupt nation committed to an unparalleled volume of legislation, there was *no one* but Mountbatten available who could do the job, even without Edwina.

The job needed youthful energy, a lust for speed, authority, charm and ruthlessness. Edwina was the bonus, and the most subtle and percipient minister could never have predicted the unusual role that she would play. Attlee knew from wartime experience that Mountbatten possessed a sense of duty "deeper than did ever plummet sound," and also an urgent need to resume his career. Wavell would go on patiently negotiating, seeking justice for all, for years. But that was not good enough for Attlee. And so the soldier who had saved Egypt and defeated an army five times the weight of his own at a time when the British stood alone and with nothing else to cheer or hope for, was thrown out.

Wavell did not rule out partition as the final solution, but he never wavered in his belief that the transfer could be made to a united India. There must, as he told Attlee at their last unhappy parting in March 1947, be "detailed arrangements so as to avoid confusion when we leave." Alas, no such detailed arrangements were ever made. There was no time. Churchill's prediction that "a fourteen-month time interval is fatal to an orderly transference of power" was proved tragically true. In the Delhi files was a contingency paper written by Lieutenant-General Sir Francis Tuker, head of Eastern Command in India in March 1946, detailing the preparations that should be made if it should come to the division of India. Partition was inevitable, this soldier judged, if the negotiations for the transfer were rushed. Mountbatten never saw it, and of course no such contingency planning was made in the period of Mountbatten's Viceroyalty. There was no time; a decision in favour of partition was made within fourteen days of his arrival.

The result was the worst horror India had ever known, and inter-racial outrages on a terrible scale. Attlee believed, for the comfort of his conscience, that it could have been worse, that India would remain divided only temporarily, and he persuaded Mountbatten that this would be the case. Instead, more than thirty years later, the sub-continent, after several years and the threat of wars, remains as divided as ever, with incalculable consequences for both nations and for the defence of the world against revolutionary Marxism.

When Mountbatten's mother deplored his acceptance of the thankless task, she believed that whatever happened, he could not win. If he became involved in politics, some of the dirt was bound to rub off. When Noël Coward called the job "hopeless," he did not mean that Mountbatten was incapable of accomplishing it. He meant much the same thing. Whatever the outcome, he would be vilified. Both were right. Mountbatten should never have been given the job, which for reasons of duty he inevitably accepted. His German mind and naval upbringing made him constitutionally ill equipped for the slow, patient negotiations with the Oriental mind, navigating amid the intricacies of political and inter-religious, inter-racial shoals and currents.

Having completed the task, he should have tempered his judgement on the results of his mission with a touch of modesty. In view of the terrible suffering that followed independence and partition, he should not have looked upon Independence Day "with completely undiluted pleasure," as he described it.[20] A touch of humility and even shame was perhaps called for and, over the subsequent years, less readiness to recall with pride and vainglory his regal, busy days as "The Last Viceroy." So much of what he accomplished in his life he could be justly proud of. But not of those months in India. Churchill's word "scuttle" for the transfer of power was journalese and an exaggeration. But not much of an exaggeration.

10

FIRST SEA LORD: THE SUMMIT

*W*ith appealing self-perception, Mountbatten once said, "One of the reasons I was so keen to get back to sea and rattled that I had been frustrated was that I was sure I was becoming a megalomaniac. I had seen it happen to Winston, I saw it happen to Roosevelt, and I knew I was getting the disease, too.

"At the beginning you think it is going to be O.K., that you won't fall for this self-obsession. Then you begin to think you're doing the right thing, and you turn out right. Then everybody says you're right, and you begin to think how right they are to think you're always right. You get very pleased with yourself. I was getting very pleased with myself and I knew this was very bad for me. It means one can't do one's job properly.

"All this was a very important reason for getting back to sea, where you can never afford to get too pleased with yourself. And it was another reason why I wanted to get back to my proper substantive rank, and why I was so furious when they wouldn't let me."

On the Mountbattens' return to England in June 1948, after elaborate celebrations and an emotional farewell (compounded for Edwina by having to put down her beloved twelve-year-old dog, who she feared would not survive six months of quarantine), there was wide speculation on Mountbatten's future. Most ex-Viceroys were so old that they were put out to pasture with a load of honours and decorations. Mountbatten had just about every decoration, and the idea of his retiring at forty-eight was ludicrous. Nor did anyone not privy to Attlee's bargain believe that he could return to the Royal Navy, where he would have to serve under senior admirals who had recently been subordinate to him.

"A lot of posts were offered to me at around this time," Mountbatten recalled. "The Duke of Gloucester had already offered to hand over his governor-generalship of Australia, and I had politely turned it down. He was rather put out when I went to India instead. I was also offered the governorship of Malta, and, rather rudely in this case, turned it down, pointing out that there are more towns and villages in India than there are people on Malta.

"At a government dinner just after we got back, I found myself talking to dear old Ernie Bevin [Foreign Secretary in the Attlee government] and he said, 'You ought to be our man in Russia. If you were offered the post of ambassador, 'ow would you feel about it?' I said, 'I don't think I would be very popular there, even though I'm supposed to be a socialist.' ' 'Ow's that?' he asked. And I said, 'Well, the Bolsheviks murdered my father's first cousin, two of my aunts on my mother's side, and five of my first cousins.'

"Bevin looked shocked and puzzled. 'Who were *they*?' he asked. So I said, 'The Tsar and Tsarina, their five children and the Grand Duchess Serge.' I don't think he actually said 'Gaw blimey!' but it was something like that."

Not long after this, in 1949, Lord Jowett flew out to Malta to invite Mountbatten to become Minister of Defence. There were numerous other offers, political and diplomatic, including ambassador in Washington. "But everyone was wasting his time," said Mountbatten. "I was going to the Mediterranean again, and I was going to command the First Cruiser Squadron, and that was that."

Before leaving for the Mediterranean, there were official and domestic duties to attend to. They had never been at Broadlands, which had been in Edwina's possession for some ten years, for more than a few weeks at a time. There was much to be done here, as at Classiebawn Castle, where they spent a few days with Pamela and Patricia and her family, and where the lobsters were better than ever. Classiebawn became for Mountbatten's grandchildren the summer holiday centre, the rendezvous for the families, just as Heiligenberg had once been for Mountbatten.

A few more days in Canada to open the Canadian National Exhibition in Toronto, and then to the south of France to see a retired family retainer, and the Duke and Duchess of Windsor ("he was looking marvellous, and they had both thrived on the war"), but not Winston Churchill: he had refused to speak to Mountbatten since his "sellout" of India.

A last visit to Broadlands, this time with a surprise guest. Nehru had arrived in England for the Dominion Conference, and Edwina insisted that he come and spend a night at Broadlands, where she taught him to play Racing Demon. He remained a close family friend, and they met whenever they could. He outlived her by four years.

It was more than ten years since Mountbatten had served in the Mediterranean and Edwina had been a service wife in Malta. "It was an odd experience to go back again," said Mountbatten. "So much was the same and so much was different. I had seen once before Britain's defences run down, and now it was happening again. We still had quite a strong surface fleet, we had battleships still serving in the Navy, and my cruiser squadron was still powerful by the standards of that time. I found myself slotting back into the old life, and enjoying it." Asked if there was any problem about his rank, he answered brusquely, "Certainly not."

Casa Medina had somehow survived the holocaust but was now converted into flats. The wounds of the George Cross Island were to be seen everywhere, and Edwina and Pamela wondered how anyone had survived the years of bombing. They stayed at a hotel while Edwina searched for a house and at length (for there was a severe shortage) discovered a ruin.

The ex-Vicereine who had managed two hundred servants moved excitedly into one room and bullied workmen to prepare the rest of the house for occupation. The Villa Guardamangia made a modest but comfortable home for the Mountbattens, and they began entertaining again as in the old days, but—like everything else—on a diminished scale. In October 1949 Prince Philip arrived on the island to take up his appointment as first lieutenant in the destroyer H.M.S. *Chequers*. This was the happiest and most fulfilled period for uncle and nephew. What more could they ask for? They were serving on Britain's premier station, loved their work and their off-duty recreations—polo especially, and a new discovery for Mountbatten, aqualung skin-diving, a hobby he enjoyed for years. Princess Elizabeth joined them, and for a while the party was complete, enjoying the most relaxed and carefree time in their lives, sunbathing, swimming and playing games in privacy and with few of the weighty responsibilities they were soon to bear.

In 1950 Mountbatten was recalled to the Admiralty and appointed Fourth Sea Lord. It was a rung on the ladder, if a modest one. He was a vice-admiral now—a real, substantive one, and with only one ring less than seven years earlier. The anomaly of his position was easier to manage at sea than in a shore appointment. Senior admirals were inclined either to "pull" their rank or act in an ingratiating manner towards him. Sir John Lang, who had joined the Admiralty only days after Prince Louis had resigned as First Sea Lord, was Secretary of the Admiralty at this time and remembers a subdued Mountbatten, anxious not to appear to be throwing his weight around.

"He was relatively piano as Fourth Sea Lord," Lang recalls. "Dealing with the nuts and bolts, stores, victualling, seeing about oil supplies, transport, that sort of thing. He didn't attempt to interfere with anything outside his own department. He just got up and spoke his part on his subject and no more."[1]

But after a time he could not resist giving his opinion on other subjects, and began to show some of his irrepressible spirit. As First Lord of the Admiralty, Lord Longford found that the other members of the Board could find Mountbatten a handful. Admiral of the Fleet Bruce Fraser, a great war hero, was First Sea Lord, and successor to Somerville in the Far East when Mountbatten finally managed to succeed in having the latter removed. Not so long ago, therefore, Mountbatten had been his superior.

Lord Longford recalls a brief exchange, typical of many at meetings of the Board. Mountbatten had intervened again outside his department. "You leave me, young fellow me lad, to run my department, and I'll leave you to run yours."

Mountbatten responded at once in proper quarterdeck manner, "Well, sir, if that's how you put it, I must bow to your superior stripes."

Fraser, much chastened, replied, "No, no, my dear boy. We are all equal on the Board of Admiralty."

It was not a very comfortable time.

.   .   .

Mountbatten's first period on the Board coincided with a severe family loss. "My mother decided that she wouldn't die until she saw me safely back in the Royal Navy and on my way to the top. She never doubted for a minute that I should get there. She didn't care twopence about me being Viceroy, in fact she hated it. All she wanted was for me to be First Sea Lord, and that was because she understood how I felt.

"She was taken ill in the early autumn of 1950. She was at Broadlands at the time. When I went to see her she said, 'I must get back to London, Dickie. It's much better to die at home. I shan't be coming back here.'

"There was no point in arguing with her on something like this, though I argued with her about almost everything under the sun."

The doctor called at Kensington Palace. "He was a very nice chap," Mountbatten recalled, "and he came in and said, 'Your heart's giving out, but I think we can pull you round, though you're in a very bad way.' And my mother replied at once, 'Oh, that's good because I want to go quickly. I don't want you to interfere with this. I am eighty-seven and have decided that the time has come for me to die. Thank you so much for all you have done. Good-bye and please don't call again.' Next day he did call, and my mother said, 'What are you doing here? I told you I didn't want to see you again. Can't you let me die quietly?' Then she turned to me when he had gone and asked, 'Why do doctors always think they've got some sort of ghastly duty to keep one alive? I've come to the end of my useful life and that's that.'

"She wouldn't have any nurses either, but she allowed some nuns to come and help."

However, the Dowager Marchioness of Milford Haven did not die as quickly as she wished. She would wake up very cross. "Why am I still here?" she would demand. Her grandchildren had to come and see her to say good-bye twice, and this was contrary to her sense of order and tidiness. She was even more furious when she heard that Prince Philip and Princess Elizabeth had put off an important engagement on her behalf.

This very remarkable old woman died at last, without pain, on 24 September 1950. When the present Queen was a young girl, she saw little of her, but when she was eighteen, Victoria came to stay at Windsor Castle with the King and Queen to rest from the flying-bomb attacks on London, which were wearing even her down.

"She was dressed and shaped very much as old ladies were at that time," the Queen recalls. "She always wore large black hats, she said grey depressed her. Her voice was very loud and rather guttural, and she seemed masculine in many ways—she use to walk with heavy masculine strides.

"I don't think she liked children very much, and she thought we were rather a nuisance. But she talked *all* the time, coughing and smoking, with our instruction in mind. I remember her as having a man's mind, and she was very formidable and rather frightening. We certainly never teased her, any more than I would have teased my grandmother. We used to take her for walks to help look after her. Formidable, frightening, with a brilliant man's brain, that's how I would sum her up. A quite extraordinary woman."[2]

Queen Elizabeth the Queen Mother also spoke of Victoria Milford Haven's "practical man's mind," and recalled her long memory and her fund of stories going back to the German and Russian royal families. "What a great reader she was! She would read everything she could lay her hands on, and especially history. She was a very concise person, and she knew exactly what she wanted to say without any hesitation," she said. "She always got on well with the King, who enjoyed her company."[3]

Princess Alice, the Countess of Athlone, also a granddaughter of Queen Victoria, remembers her today as "a very fascinating person." This princess, now ninety-seven, can remember her as quite a young woman with a growing family, and ascribes her deep sense of responsibility to the early death of her mother. "Everyone who knew her liked her very much," she said, "but she was not the kind of person you loved greatly. She always used to say that Prince Philip had a better.brain than Dickie, and that is saying a lot."[4]

Prince Philip, for his part, remembers his grandmother's "remarkable mind."[5] And there is no doubt that this astute, analytical, incisive mind, which was Mountbatten's as well, also had a tremendous influence upon his development. To have a mother of the calibre of Victoria Milford Haven for fifty years of your life, a wife of the calibre of Edwina for thirty-eight years, with a nimble brain yourself, and the privileges of wealth and royal birth, is bounty for any man.

With the loss of his mother, who had taught him from his earliest years and had always been so close, emotionally and cerebrally, a gap, wider than that caused by the death of his father, made itself felt to Mountbatten. "I missed her terribly," he said, "and would have loved her to know for certain that I would be First Sea Lord. Perhaps she did in her heart."

If she did, she showed brave confidence in her son, for many obstructions still lay between Mountbatten as Fourth Sea Lord and his ultimate ambition. First, at his own request, he went to sea again, his last active seagoing command, the one to which his father had aspired. In May 1952 he was appointed C.-in-C. Mediterranean, his old Brook House model cabin reality at last.

It was a very different fleet, in its strength and the nature of its matériel, from the Mediterranean Fleet of 1907 when Prince Louis was second-in-command. By no stretch of statistics could Britannia be said to rule the waves. The United States Navy was immeasurably more powerful, and the Soviet navy was growing fast, too—so fast and so threateningly that a North Atlantic Treaty Organization had been set up to deter any further excesses of Russian aggrandizement. In the 1870s Prince Louis had taken part in the naval moves in the Mediterranean to contain Russian expansionism. Now, in 1952, Mountbatten was appointed NATO Supreme Commander Allied Forces, Mediterranean. Once again, father and son strode through the ever-repeating cycle of history, separated by no more than a few steps.

"By now I had had some experience of dealing with a multinational force, some of whom had been our enemies, some our friends, others neutral in the last war," said Mountbatten. "Of them all, the only one with whom I had much difficulty were the French. They remember for a long time, and many of them still had not forgiven us for destroying their fleet at Oran.

"I made use of the same formula I had always believed in—I made friends with the commanders and persuaded them to work together. It wasn't easy at first, but we slowly thrashed it out, and then we began training—just as we had in SEAC back in 1943-44."

This was, without a doubt, Mountbatten at his best: at sea, but with great responsibilities that could be sustained only by his special qualities of firmness and charm. At the lower level, he was loved and admired by almost everyone he came across, just as he had been in the little *P. 31* thirty-five years earlier. "He attended to the everyday affairs of the ship as if his promotion depended on it," wrote the chaplain of his flagship. "Also he was on the easiest of terms with the sailors and never failed to jump up on a bollard and address the ship's company about a forthcoming cruise or exercise. The closeness to every man in the cruiser [H.M.S. *Glasgow*] showed that the man had not changed. He had the rare virtue of being able to communicate with all from top to bottom."[6]

That he had succeeded with the top, too, was demonstrated at the end of his tour of duty in December 1954 when six admirals, representing the Allied commanders-in-chief under him, formed a crew and rowed him—all grinning broadly—to his flagship. No one could have devised a nicer and more symbolically appropriate conclusion to his last service at sea.

Shortly before he left the Mediterranean Fleet for the last time, there took place what seemed at the time to be a rapprochement with Churchill. Late in 1954 Churchill celebrated his eightieth birthday. He was still Prime Minister, the Conservatives having returned to power in 1951, but long past his best and long due for retirement. He was staying in Beaverbrook's villa at Cap d'Ail when Mountbatten's despatch vessel, H.M.S. *Surprise*, which the Mountbatten family used as a sort of glorified yacht, anchored at Villefranche. "A message arrived," Mountbatten said, "inviting us for dinner. So Edwina and I went and Clemmie was there, but no one else. We had a very good dinner, and when Winston and I were alone with some good brandy and cigars, he said (and there were tears in his eyes), 'Dickie, I have always loved you, and I am glad we are friends again. I can even forgive you for the terrible things you did in India.'

"So the next day I invited him on board the *Surprise* and he said he'd like to see a submarine, so I fixed that. He was very interested in everything, and there were flashes of the old Winston, but he was very doddery. A few nights later the Préfet of the Alpes Maritimes gave us both a dinner. He made a long, flowery speech full of *entente cordiale*, and I replied, and Edwina and Clemmie bullied Winston into making one, too, all in his usual terrible accent."

So it seemed that the two men were friends again after the years of silence, and that when the vacancy for First Sea Lord came up in 1955, Churchill would give his full support to Mountbatten's appointment, just as he had to his father forty-three years earlier.

Within the Admiralty, there was a lot of opposition to Mountbatten's appointment. "There were many brilliant men who had made great names for themselves in the war," Lieutenant-Commander Kemp recalled, "men who had mostly followed the classic path upwards, with a big staff appointment, then a sea appointment, and another staff appointment, and so on up the ladder the traditional way. These were the people who were the candidates for First Sea Lord, and there was very strong prejudice against Mountbatten by hard-core professionals like Bruce Fraser." It was all a long way from the admiring fraternity of the NATO admirals.[7]

Another opponent, long since retired but as an Admiral of the Fleet and wise old bird certain to be canvassed was "A.B.C.," Admiral Lord Cunningham of Hyndhope, who had succeeded Dudley Pound in 1943. "A.B.C." had, in Mountbatten's eyes, been the first culprit in depriving him of ships for his last big operations in SEAC in 1945. And a senior officer at the Admiralty at the time recalls how Cunningham, after receiving a further request for carriers, declared firmly, "I don't give a damn, I'm not going to send any more ships to that bugger Mountbatten."[8]

Relations between the two admirals had been cool ever since, and when Mountbatten's candidature for First Sea Lord came up and Cunningham was asked for his opinion, he gave an emphatic "No." But Cunningham was always prepared to listen, and to change his mind if he was convinced he was wrong: it was one of his great qualities. It happened that Mountbatten's chief of staff in the Mediterranean was Rear-Admiral Sir Manley Power, who had formed a very high opinion of his c.-in-c. and at a suitable opportunity he passed this opinion on to Cunningham. Mountbatten was, said Power, exactly the right man for the job of First Sea Lord. Cunningham accepted Power's judgement and passed his reversal of view on Mountbatten through Admiral Sir Rhoderick McGrigor, the retiring First Sea Lord, the First Lord, J. P. L. Thomas (later 1st Viscount Cilcennin) and thence to the Prime Minister, Churchill. And there it stuck.

Vice-Admiral Sir Arthur Pedder says today that "Winston wouldn't have him because he 'had given away the British Empire.' "[9] Mountbatten himself believed that Churchill struck his name out because he had lost all belief in the Navy in the context of the nation's future defences ("a few fast gun vessels and submarines—that's all") and wanted to run it down in favour of the RAF. "He made a long speech in Cabinet," said Mountbatten, "three quarters of an hour long and full of the most brilliant invective. Sir Norman Brooke, the Secretary, economically recorded it thus: 'The Prime Minister then passed a few observations concerning the Navy.' But with *me* in the Admiralty he knew he wouldn't get away with it," said Mountbatten.

Undiscouraged and as determined as ever, Mountbatten continued to lobby through his friends. A particularly useful ally at this time happened to be passing through the Mediterranean, the Emperor of Abyssinia, Haile Selassie. Mountbatten entertained him on board his flagship at Malta on 7 October 1954 and asked him, when a suitable moment arrived, to work on Churchill on his behalf.

Mountbatten's luck was in. Soon after his arrival in England, Haile Selassie was a guest at a reception in his honour in the long picture gallery at Buckingham Palace. The aged Emperor cornered the aged Premier and told him through an interpreter of Mountbatten's hospitality. "He will no doubt be the next First Sea Lord," said the Emperor as if it were a *fait accompli*. By further happy chance, Prince Philip was nearby, and his ears pricked up at the subject of the conversation. No doubt Churchill knew that he must finally bow to the inevitable, that Mountbatten's cause must prevail. What better time than now to concede defeat and make it appear a victory and please the royal family all at once, something he always enjoyed?

Turning to Prince Philip, Churchill said, "Sir, I want you to be the first to know that your uncle is to be the new First Sea Lord." "What excellent news! I'm delighted," replied the Prince.

To Mountbatten's amusement, one of the first to congratulate him on his appointment was Churchill himself. "He had done everything to stop it, and now this," said Mountbatten. "He really could be a very naughty boy."

It was some days before the Admiralty was informed. Perhaps Churchill forgot his decision (he was by now forgetting a great deal), and only remembered later. To many of those in the Admiralty hierarchy, the news came as a rude and unwelcome shock. Others had seen the writing on the wall for some time, including the wise old Sir John Lang, who believed that "Winston may well have reflected on the repetition in history and been guided by it."[10] Or it may have been the intervention of an aged Emperor.

On 18 April 1955 Mountbatten entered the First Sea Lord's office at the Admiralty for the first time as professional head of the service to which he had committed his life. He was in his mid-fifties, still extremely spritely, his hair only just beginning to turn grey in places. His father, at fifty-eight, had appeared a great deal older. For Mountbatten, it was a highly emotional day, charged with memories. As always on momentous occasions, the scene had long since been set with care. He had arranged to use his father's old office, his father's old desk, with a portrait of his father behind him above the fireplace and a bust of his father standing on a pedestal outside the door.

Suggestions from his staff that he might prefer the present First Sea Lord's office because the old one had been empty for so many years and was considered unusable were brushed aside. Mountbatten would have Admiral Prince Louis of Battenberg's old office, no matter that the magnificent view across the sweep of Horse Guards' Parade had been cut off with the war and replaced by a solid concrete blockhouse wall at a distance of a few feet. A further irritation was the frustration of his order that a colour portrait of himself should be placed in every office. He was told, with every show of regret, that the Treasury provided no funds for this sort of thing.

In 1955 the Royal Navy was still a force of great strength, the most powerful navy in the world after the American navy, with foreign stations almost as world-wide as they had been in 1912, although not so numerous or so powerful. There had been a massive cutback, as there had been after World War I, but it had been applied to ships and matériel rather than to personnel and committees. The Navy was top-heavy, slack and with only indifferent morale. With the acceptance of the need for an independent nuclear deterrent, defence costs had gone sky-high, not at all parallel with the growth of the economy. If Mountbatten was to save the service from the fate Churchill had decreed for it, there would have to be urgent and drastic pruning.

Lord Cilcennin was still First Lord, and Mountbatten said that he went straight to his office and gave him a friendly speech. "I have come in to reorganize the Admiralty prior to reorganizing the services," he said. "The Admiralty is an absolute mess because it never streamlined itself after the war. It requires a proper committee to investigate it. I suggest that it should consist of myself in the chair, the Sea Lords as deputies, with junior ministers in attendance, and of course John Lang. But not you," he continued firmly. "With you it would make it the Board of Admiralty. Ours will be a sub-board, with members making up working parties, thinking up reforms, doing all the briefing.

"When the sub-board passes a resolution, then everything will come before the Board of Admiralty, with you in the chair, and you will pass our proposals. They will be Board decisions, and the whole thing will be done in ten minutes.

"Jim [Cilcennin] said he'd think about it, and I said, 'No, don't do that. Now is the time for decision. You can either go down in history as the First Lord under whom the Admiralty stagnated, or you can go down in history as the First Lord under whose wise direction the Admiralty entirely reformed itself.' "

Cilcennin said he would back Mountbatten, and the work began in earnest. "My 'Way Ahead' committee, as I called it, succeeded in cutting seven thousand uniformed personnel and twenty-three thousand civilians in short order," said Mountbatten, "and we were saving fifteen million a year without losing a single ship from the seagoing fleet."

Sir John Lang, while not allowing himself to be bullied, observed a new Mountbatten from the admiral who had been Fourth Sea Lord in 1951. "We all recognized that this was a new era of a very emphatic person," Lang recalled, "although he was never overpowering with me. Mountbatten's term of office was a period of fundamental difficulty for the Admiralty. Duncan Sandys [Minister of Defence] had no time for the Navy, and like Churchill, would have done away with it altogether if he had had his way, but Mountbatten withstood the onslaught very well. He recognized areas in which cuts could be made and entered into economies in a spirit of willingness. The 'Way Ahead' committee worked well, and Mountbatten sought economies in less hurtful areas, while keeping our strength of defence where it most mattered."

But Lang's judgement on Mountbatten was not without criticism. "He expected everything to be crisp, but Dickie himself was very verbose. He didn't seem able to stop talking and bubbling over. My impression is that he became more verbose the higher up the ladder he climbed. Unlike Edwina, he had no sense of time. If he had ten minutes to inspect something, he would get caught up with someone and become completely involved. When he wanted to know something, it had to be everything. Now, Edwina had an inbuilt clock. If she was inspecting a hospital, it was ten minutes here, five minutes there. She never had to look at her watch or needed anyone to remind her. This was quite unlike Dickie."[11]

The Mountbattens had a town house in the Regency style in Wilton Crescent now. Broadlands was back to its old perfection, with the additional benefit of modernization. As in the last years before the war, they went there for weekends from London, and for entertaining and shooting.

They had both been deeply affected by the death of George VI and moved by the Proclamation of Queen Elizabeth II on 8 February 1952. "The King had great strength," said Mountbatten, "and a great sense of duty and determination. He saved the monarchy by taking over, reluctantly, from his brother and did a marvellous, unrewarding job. I knew him well, and we had a tremendous amount in common, especially the Navy, of course. He always loved to talk about the Navy and took a great interest in it. But I felt even closer to our new Queen and her family. I had known her since she was a baby, and she and Princess Margaret were great friends with Patricia and Pammie. I became her personal A.D.C. the following year and always adored being with her. She is a marvellous person."

The Mountbatten family grew at a great rate in the late 1950s and early 1960s. A third grandchild was born in the year Mountbatten bacame First Sea Lord, and Patricia had four more children. Pamela had married an interior decorator and designer, David Hicks, in 1960, and they had three children. The pilgrimage to Classiebawn Castle in August became a ritual that was rarely broken.

At Classiebawn, Mountbatten's children and grandchildren saw a completely new figure, far from the responsibilities of office, recharging his giant batteries for another year of swift endeavour. He set about being on holiday with the same practical purposefulness he applied to everything he did in life. He rode, climbed, fished, swam, spearfished with his aqualung, played games, ate his usual huge meals (his capacity almost equalled his father's) and played tirelessly with the children. Classiebawn was synonymous with peace, family relaxation and the happiness of children, right up to the fatal summer of 1979.

Mountbatten would have made a good primary-school teacher. He treated children completely naturally, talked to them as if they were adults, listened to them with a patience that would have amazed his staff at the admiralty, told them funny stories, played with them, swam with them, took them for walks, holding their hands and chatting away. His own enjoyment in their company was transmitted to them, and they loved him for it.

A special relationship developed with Prince Charles, whom he saw as frequently as his own grandchildren. Throughout his boyhood, and later at Cambridge and in the Navy, Prince Charles found a marvellously relaxed and amusing alternative at Wilton Crescent and Broadlands to the predictable rituals of Buckingham Palace, Windsor, Sandringham and Balmoral. The age gap meant nothing to either of them, from the time when Mountbatten used to bathe him as a small boy until the end. If, during his naval instruction, he was on a course at Portsmouth, he would drive over to Broadlands for dinner and the night. Prince Charles could remember when Uncle Dickie used to play polo and took up the game himself, instructed all the way by Mountbatten as well as by his father.

Nothing showed more clearly that age meant as little to Mountbatten as creed and colour than to be with him, first, when he was with his nephew, then on another occasion with his great-nephew. As always the generations melted away, whether they were arguing about some fine point in a polo match, a technical matter connected with some new device of Mountbatten's (and there seemed to be no end to these) or recounting the details of some journey, whom they had met, what had been said.

Two elements were invariable: as in Mountbatten's boyhood with his family or his clever nonstop-talking German relatives, there was always argument. It would be certain to break out at some point, and it would often be heated. After a long tour of remote Easter Island in the Pacific to study the unique archaeology, once they were back on the royal yacht the argument on the likely origins of the statues was long and ardent. But not content with that predictable subject, when this was exhausted an argument broke out concerning the number and breed of wild horses on the island. It was prolonged and acrimonious—full of fascinating information.

The second certainty was that any discussion, any argument, almost invariably (as in this case) ended in laughter, the deep rumble of Mountbatten's laughter matching that of Prince Philip with its higher pitch.

The evident enjoyment of all three men—thirty-one, fifty-eight and seventy-nine years old at the end—in one another's company, the matching minds and opinions, the speed of thought, the repartee (Mountbatten's much the swiftest and funniest), together with the intermittent but frequent breaks into laughter, made a marvellous impression of mutual compatibility and happiness. But of the three, the eldest and youngest were closest, sharing a deep emotional bond.

In Whitehall, in 1955, Mountbatten continued to make many allies and many enemies, and many reforms. "The Royal Navy loves rows," Harold Macmillan commented on Mountbatten's period at the Admiralty. "They always have done." And Mountbatten himself spoke of the spikeyness of many naval officers. "It's quite unlike the Army," he said. "In the Navy you've got perhaps only a few fellows locked up in a small ship for weeks on end. There are bound to be rows and clashes of temperament. There always have been. It's better in bigger ships, but not much better."[12]

"Jackie" Fisher, the arch-reformer of the Navy at the turn of the century, had been ruthless and made numerous enemies; in fact, he prided himself on his "three Rs"; on being "ruthless, relentless and remorseless." Mountbatten's reforms, and his methods of bringing them about, made enemies, too. He claimed to have worked well with his First Lords, but only because (like Cilcennin) he tamed them. Given the smallest lead, he would launch himself into a series of stories to prove this point. There was the First Lord who after a mere ten days in office went off for the weekend, at a highly critical period, without informing anyone. ("I thought that was a bit offside!") Mountbatten claimed to have called up Scotland Yard and had him brought back by the police. "I had no more trouble with him."

According to Mountbatten's stories, First Lords who tried to interfere with appointments were, in the cricket expression, "hit for six." "The First Lords amounted to nothing in my time. None of them knew

Christmas from Easter," Mountbatten boasted. "When they fought me, I defeated them quickly, and when they didn't fight me they had to go along with me. Churchill in his time appeared to run the Admiralty, but he didn't."

Why did Mountbatten have to open fire with a full broadside every time the relationship between the civil and professional branches of the Admiralty was mentioned? Why all this bombast? His father and Churchill had worked in admirable harmony and did great things together, but when the necessity arose, it was Churchill who told him he had to go. Churchill was in command, finally. From all accounts, the same applied to Mountbatten, and he worked in good harness with his First Lords under the Ministry of Defence, and great things were accomplished.

What is even more curious is that these stories were either grossly inaccurate as to date and the people involved (one of them was about Lord Longford, who had been briefly First Lord over four years before Mountbatten became First Sea Lord) or complete fabrications and could very easily have been proved false. Nor could they be accounted for as the wanderings of an aging mind because these stories were being recounted many years earlier. Moreover, no one was a greater stickler for accuracy, and Mountbatten's memory was normally marvellously reliable. Only the irresistible need for self-glorification can account for this astonishing contradiction. But why did a man so glorified by the nation and loved by his family have to brag so much and so often?

There are a number of reasons, but the most important was the same old insecurity, which led to the overreaction and overcompetitiveness that hounded him all thorough life. Speaking of Mountbatten's seeming arrogance, Lord Butler said, "I had a funny feeling about Mountbatten. One was a little defensive with him. He so liked an argument, and then it all came back in your face. I think he felt that he had missed something important in life, that it had been one-sided, that whatever else he had achieved, he had missed the academic and intellectual side. He felt he had been left out of that world, and he resented it."[13] Lord Longford also referred to Mountbatten's intellectual insecurity, and remembers him saying once, "You know I am much more intelligent than you think."

Sir Harold Wilson believes that his insecurity stemmed from his being uncertain of what he was, royal or nonroyal. He also told the same story as Lord Butler, both of whom had been appointed Knight of the Garter, the highest of all honours. Before the service in the Royal Chapel, one goes to be robed in a special room. There one meets old friends, a handful only, for it is also a very rare honour. But Mountbatten was absent, and people were asking, "Where is Dickie?" "Dickie's not here." And of course he always attended, as he loved the pomp and ceremony of it all. And then at last he emerged, but from the entrance reserved for the sovereign and members of the royal family, the royal entrance, with an expression of great solemnity upon his face. "He was only a half royal," added Sir Harold, "but he made up for it by becoming the shop steward of European royalty."[14]

"Why did he never speak in the House of Lords?" asked Lord Longford. "You would think he would have done so often. But he never did. Was it that he feared people might think he was not really royal?"[15]

In fact, he very nearly did once, at a critical time when he was trying to save the Navy. He refrained at the last moment, out of deference to the royal family, he said. In view of their special relations with the Royal Navy one would have thought they would have been delighted.

Lord Hailsham confirmed again that he had excellent relations with Mountbatten, even though "he was highly emotional about Suez."[16]

This is no overstatement. In June 1956, fourteen months after Mountbatten took office as First Sea Lord, Colonel Nasser came to power in Egypt. After the breakdown of negotiations, Nasser nationalized the Suez Canal. The Israelis invaded Sinai, and on 5 November, French and British forces attacked Port Said, instigating a world crisis.

Mountbatten disapproved of the operation at every level—humanitarian, diplomatic, moral and military. "A complete disaster" was his summing-up, although he always defended the performance of the three services once the operation got going. "It was the reverse of everything I had tried to do in South-East Asia and India immediately after the war, so of course I hated it."

Anthony Eden had succeeded to the premiership a few days before Mountbatten became First Sea Lord; and as inevitable hostilities approached, his attitude towards Mountbatten was half patronizing and half censorious. His remark to Edwina at a 10 Downing Street party about a week before the operation reflected his feelings towards his First Sea Lord. "Dickie is being splendid," he said. "He disapproves of everything I am doing but is taking every step to get the Navy ready."

"The only one who showed any guts was Eden," said Mountbatten, "and he was completely and utterly wrong in everything he did. [Minister Delegate Walter] Monckton had one outburst and then disappeared and wouldn't resign. He seemed to think that he could control the ministers better by staying in the Cabinet. Then Hailsham took over from Cilcennin, and that made more sense. But Eden, you'll notice, doesn't mention him by name, or me, in his account, which was kind of him and I told him so later, because if he had said anything, he could only have blasted me.

"I had told Eden from the beginning that Nasser would be certain to block the canal as a countermeasure, and it would take three months to clear it. As night follows day, when the fiasco was all over, Macmillan—who had taken over from Eden, who was ill—approached me at a diplomatic party at Buckingham Palace. The Queen was putting a brave face on the whole terrible thing, and that was more then Macmillan could do when I answered his question 'How long will it take to clear the canal?'

"I said, 'All steps have been taken to mobilize salvage vessels and experts, and I can assure you it will take no longer than three months.' Macmillan was horrified. 'Three months! The country'll be bankrupt in that time with the long haul round the Cape . . . It must be quicker.' I told him, 'I said from the beginning it would take three months. I have spoken out clearly all along, so don't complain now because the Navy can't get you out of your mess.' Then I turned on my heel and walked off.

"But it is a great credit to Macmillan that he loved me enough not to sack me when he became P.M. I thought he would."

No man was to have a greater influence on Mountbatten's last professional years than Macmillan. He had been Minister of Defence for seven months immediately prior to Mountbatten's arrival at the Admiralty, and had at that time attempted to bring about a reform of the services.

"The Norwegian campaign in 1940 was the first lesson in the need for combining the services," Macmillan says today. "The top men simply didn't know what was going on. This led to the creation by the Chiefs of Staff of Dickie Mountbatten's own Combined Operations. Then, ten years after the end, came Suez, and that showed again the need for unifying the services at the top.

"I tried to do something about this when I was at Defence but the opposition was too strong. The Prime Minister [Churchill] was not interested, and diehards like Boyle [Marshal of the RAF Sir Dermot Boyle, Chief of Air Staff 1956–59] would have none of it."[17]

Under the premiership of Macmillan, and with Duncan Sandys as Minister of Defence, the economies and streamlining of administration completed, Mountbatten set about reshaping the Navy for the future—in spite of Sandys' doubts and initial lack of support. It was a very different service, fined down, fast and twice as professional, when Mountbatten's term of office expired in 1958, with nuclear power, missiles, computers and commando carriers all in use or on order. The age of technology was firmly established, space programmes were all the rage, battleships were for museums, the Americans were already launching nuclear-powered aircraft carriers and nuclear-powered ballistic missile submarines. Mountbatten revelled in it and loved to quote the comedian who had satirized him saying, "Actually, I invented technology."

Far from the fascinating fields of technology, Mountbatten in 1957 was able to perform an important service for justice and an old friend. Admiral Sir Dudley North, Mountbatten had always believed, was made the scapegoat for the Dakar fiasco in 1940 when Vichy French cruisers had escaped through the Strait of Gibraltar and caused the failure of an expedition to capture the French African base.

The ties between North and Mountbatten had always been close in the service. North had served alongside Mountbatten's brother Georgie in the *New Zealand* in World War I, and had been with Mountbatten as an Extra Equerry to the Prince of Wales afterwards on the world tours. They had met frequently between the wars, when North served in the Admiralty and was Flag Officer Royal Yachts. He was an able, amiable, not outstandingly gifted officer, who did not deserve the rough charge of neglect of duty thrown at him by Dudley Pound and Churchill. He had, ever since, unsuccessfully pressed for a court-martial. There had been a number of abortive attempts to clear his name, but always politicians, and most notably Churchill, had brushed them aside. A sensational book defending North reopened the affair and there was talk about another Dreyfus case.

"I knew that this time something had to be done, not only for Dudley but also for the good reputation of the Navy," said Mountbatten. "So I went along and saw Macmillan and told him so. He completely agreed but said there couldn't be a court of enquiry or court-martial. 'But we have a number of Admirals of the Fleet,' he said. 'They're all on the active list. Why not get them together to thrash the thing out?'

"Macmillan was always a fast mover, and he sent messages and cars, and all these old boys got together—all except Chatfield, who was ill. The upshot was that they all said Winston had behaved disgracefully and the Admiralty had behaved disgracefully. So we drafted a statement exonerating Dudley but not actually accusing Winston, who was still just alive."

This signed statement gave Dudley North great satisfaction and relief. Macmillan provides a postscript to this *cause célèbre* today. "All those old admirals who had been First Sea Lord at some time were against any action beyond this statement, and those who hadn't, like old Lord Cork and Orrery, were dead set on doing more."

In no area was Mountbatten's sense of justice more aroused than towards individuals who had been harshly treated while in search of freedom. Gandhi's incarceration when Mountbatten was in India with the Prince of Wales outraged him as much as that of Makarios at the height of the Cyprus crisis many years later. "I remember a staff meeting at the time of his banishment to the Seychelles, and a Colonial Office official came in and asked me if they could have a frigate to take him there. I said, 'Certainly. But would you be good enough to ask the Colonial Secretary how long the frigate would be needed?' The official replied that it could leave again at once. So I replied, 'I think we'll keep her at the Seychelles to save fuel.' 'How do you mean, sir?' 'Presumably you want to keep the negotiations going, and as they can't move one inch without Makarios, the frigate had better be ready to bring him back again.'

"This didn't go down very well with everybody. Afterwards General Templer said, 'I hate you, Dickie, you're anti-British—you're just yellow!' So you see how I was always getting into trouble."

Lieutenant-Commander Peter Kemp, who was still at the Admiralty in the spring of 1958 and remembered Mountbatten in the early days in the Mediterranean, recalls a lunch he gave at the United Services

Club. "We were talking about Mountbatten, and I made the rash prediction, 'Well, he's obviously going on now, and will be our new Chief of Defence Staff.' I remember everyone threw up his hands and said, 'Not in a thousand years,' or 'Never a hope.' To me it was as certain as night following day."

It was to Mountbatten, too. He never had the slightest doubt that he was next in line for the highest defence post. Moreover, he always claimed he knew exactly and precisely what he was going to do in his term of office, which began in July 1958. He was going to reorganize the whole defence structure of the country and integrate the three services into one. "I really started this on a small scale with Combined Operations Command, then developed it further in SEAC, and later in peacetime when I headed NATO in the Mediterranean."

In fact, Mountbatten knew that Macmillan as Minister of Defence had conceived the shape of the new integrated defence structure and attempted to bring it to life. "Dickie always claimed the credit for it, of course, but I didn't care twopence," Macmillan recalls. "That was all right. Dickie was a great extrovert. My only care was that it should come off."

Suez had shown the need more than ever for this reorganization, and it was much more difficult for the earlier opponents to sustain their case. "I could have done it without Dickie, of course," says Macmillan. "But he was a great help, and he did his part very well. Surprisingly enough, he was quiet and restrained about it, and of course very loyal. He was especially good at handling the difficult people. He always somehow made the opposition feel small."[19]

There are plenty of people today, including Macmillan's son-in-law, Julian Amery, who think it was all a mistake. "I am one of those who believe the English operate best in small units, like public school houses, clubs, and so on. I was therefore against combining the three services. With the services combined, the sense of corporate loyalty disappears. It's a typical German conception and reduces opportunities of access. For anyone to get to the minister now, it is a long and difficult process. Peter Carrington, Hugh Fraser and I fought against it but were defeated."[20]

"This hostility had almost gone when I became Prime Minister in 1964," said Sir Harold Wilson, "and the job was almost complete. Certainly Mountbatten was happy with the outcome for the Royal

Navy, which had been so threatened. Mountbatten was the first Chief of Defence Staff in the strategic sense to recognize the impact and have an understanding of the importance of technology."

Sir Harold recalled Defence Committee meetings when he was in the chair. "If Mountbatten thought anything might go wrong, he always came to see me privately beforehand, and I always found him extremely stimulating. Solly was very useful then on the scientific side, and he used to report to Winston for old times' sake."[21] Solly Zuckerman had re-entered the Mountbatten orbit with his appointment as Scientific Adviser to the Ministry of Defence in 1959; and "Ronnie" Brockman, now a rear-admiral, was among those who rejoined the old Mountbatten team and made up the heart of it—the "brains," and what the staff often referred to as "the social chap."

"Solly was Mountbatten's brains," a senior member of Mountbatten's staff said. "The sheer speed of Solly's mind was amazing. They stimulated each other, although in brainpower, Solly was vastly superior." As for Brockman, this same officer was told by Mountbatten at his first interview, " 'Now, if you are ever in any doubt what goes on in my mind, go and see Ronnie Brockman.' The first time this arose, I quickly discovered that the one person who did not know what was going on in Mountbatten's mind was the admiral. But he was very charming, very nice, very good-looking and very ordinary—and absolutely terrified of Mountbatten."

The reaction of many young officers coming to the ministry for the first time was one of amazement that Mountbatten was there at all. It was nearly twenty years since the end of the war, and in most minds Mountbatten was connected with the war. "My first thought," said one officer, "was 'Is he still alive?' He was such a distant figure connected with the war. But one soon learned that he was alive, all right. I was amazed to find out what an enormous influence he was in Whitehall, dominating it completely. And inside, you suddenly found that when dealing with lieutenant-generals or air marshals, there was a gap a mile wide between them and the Mountbatten retinue. It was like the difference between the Duke and the dustman. I also soon learned that he loved the young and didn't like the old at all. Once he told me that everyone was finished when they had reached two stars.

"Another curious thing—when I was told I was joining his staff, some chaps said, 'Oh, you're going to be a spy—one of Mountbatten's spies.' And I laughed. But I soon found out that it was true. The first thing I found on my desk was a confidential office memorandum: 'Do you know, have you ever met, Chapman Pincher [chief defence correspondent of the Beaverbrook newspapers and a ruthless investigator]? Write me the answer please.'

"I answered this truthfully in the negative, and when I went to see Mountbatten, he said, 'Your job is to get into the Whitehall machine and find out what is going on and report to me.' And that's what it was all about, because he always had to be a jump ahead of everybody. The chaps he was two jumps ahead of were those who thought he was an old has-been. They failed to recognize the danger. The Foreign Office was crammed with these people, and Mountbatten always outmanoeuvred them."

It was not a restful life at the Ministry of Defence in those days. As Sir John Lang said of him at the Admiralty, "There was no question of a seven- or eight-hour day. You were lucky if you got a seven- or eight-hour night."[22] "He was always creating crises" was the comment of one of his staff. "It was as if he had this need for constant achievement, and terror of showing that he might not be wanted."

Mountbatten by now had his own Comet jetliner fitted out with every conceivable gadget and comfort, a bevy of the most beautiful Wrens, and, often, his current black Labrador, who refused to walk on and had to be carried. The dictation started before takeoff. "Memoranda, papers, etc., copies to Washington, copies to everybody. And sometimes, at the end of it all, I realized that we actually hadn't done a bloody thing!"

One of his Wren secretaries described a flight out to the Far East, quoting from her diary: "January 23rd 1964. Chris Warren [the other Wren] woke me at 5 A.M. After breakfast went to Wilton Crescent. Mountbatten had loads of luggage. Took off for Bahrein 0800. The Army polo team came with us, and Lady Brabourne and the Brockmans . . ." Then it was dictating briefs and letters and papers nonstop; and on the tour: "I had to go down to C.D.S. in the middle of breakfast. He was having a massage. Most embarrassing. He often dictated while getting ready for an official function . . . I sat outside the bathroom door while he splashed and shouted reports at me . . ."[23]

To those in his entourage, from Wren secretaries to his senior staff, the pace seemed unremitting. And then, at the end of a particularly heavy day, he might come into the office of one of his hard-pressed secretaries before leaving for some function, sit on the edge of the desk for a few minutes, deplore how hard he worked his women and fish out a box of chocolates as a reward. They loved it and so did he; and he would probably have one or two chocolates before he strode out of the room. The little touches were frequent, well-timed and always appreciated. One of his pilots recalled how he would always have a chat before takeoff ("Good morning, how delighted I am to see you again . . ."*), then he would enter the Comet briskly, stretch out on his special seat, which was more like a chaise-lounge, and instantly begin dictating "thank you" letters for a recent reception or hospitality, however trivial.

A glimpse at a typical working day at the height of his period as Chief of Defence Staff reveals several aspects of his personality and working methods. There is a staff meeting in the afternoon, and from the beginning the day revolves around this. His secret is briefing and preparation. Everything is worked out at preliminary meetings with his staff, what So-and-so is going to say about this item, what Admiral X will say he is going to do about that. The morning is employed in a full-dress rehearsal of the afternoon's meeting. This leads to great speed and efficiency at the main event, and hardly ever a surprise. At the end of the morning meeting he says—not for the first time—"I want to finish off on some high strategic note, some really statesmanlike 'above-it-all' remark." Then he turns to one of his staff: "Let me have something, will you?"

At one minute to three he comes straight out of the lift after lunch (probably at the Palace), walks in, feet wide-splayed, sits down and looks around the table. "Well, gentlemen, the first item is . . . I gather Admiral X has some views on this . . ." With a bored expression on his face, his eyes cast around the table, stopping at the admiral. He knows exactly what he is going to say, and what the next speaker is going to say, and what the decision will be on every item on the long agenda.

---

*This pilot, Wing-Commander G.P.B. Bailey, RAF (Retd.), remembers how amused he and his fellow pilots were with Mountbatten, who had the sailor's preoccupation with the winds. "When he flew he was always more concerned with the 'winds' than any other problem an airman would be concerned with: i.e., cloud, fog, icing, diversions. 'What are the *winds* like?' would be his invariable question before takeoff." Perhaps he feared delay and disruption of his ever-tight schedule.

Tea is brought in; his eyes light up until he wills the waitress with the best plate of biscuits to put them in front of him. She does, and he takes a handful and eats them all before his tea and before anyone else has started. The meeting lasts until just after six. Mountbatten is due for a glass of sherry with a visiting potentate at Wilton Crescent, then a dinner party which will keep him from bed until two o'clock. He has left behind an immense amount of work for everyone. But before he leaves, he looks in at one or two of the offices. "Is everything all right? Did that meeting go well? Yes? Good." He is the only person any of the staff and their minions have known to work them so hard *and* do this, and the difference it makes—like the wave to the airfield control-tower balcony—is immeasurable.

A mid-rank young officer on his staff at this time who had known Field-Marshals Alexander, Montgomery and Templer claims that "to work with Mountbatten was the most exhilarating experience I've ever had. I've never known his like. He really was a most outstanding man, and marvellous to work with, not least because you never knew where you stood. He was an enormous man, in the Alexander the Great class, who, in a different age and setting, could have conquered the world."

But with the higher echelons he was less popular, and with many highly unpopular as well as feared. When angry or in low spirits, he was often heard to say, "They all hate me, you know." But the young were like the women in his life: he loved them all for what they were and because they presented him with no competition. Not everyone was as tolerant of his boasting as was Harold Macmillan. Julian Amery found his name-dropping and assumption of social superiority distasteful. So did many others. "He was grand in his position, and grand in his conceit of himself," said Amery, who was at the War Office in 1957-58. Nor did Amery care for his social manners at times, particularly at receptions, when Mountbatten would suddenly break off in the middle of a conversation "as if you had had your apportionment."

Amery also recounted how Mountbatten once told him that George VI had " 'expressed the view to me that he hoped that one day I would continue in the parallel ranks I was given during the war. I am now an Admiral of the Fleet,' he continued, as if the world did not know it, 'and I would also like to be a Marshal of the Royal Air Force and a field-marshal.' " Amery expressed the view that he did not think that this was a good idea, but he would follow it up for Mountbatten. But before he could do anything about it, he was asked to come to Mount-batten's office with John Profumo (who was Secretary of State for War for three years from July 1960) in order to press the matter again. They said, "We will discuss it, but frankly, it would be better if you did not press the matter because we may get a negative answer." Fearing this above anything, Mountbatten nodded, and no more was heard of the matter.

Julian Amery, who knew Mountbatten so well, did give him one great credit mark, besides his coaching of Prince Philip. This was his usefulness in remaining politically neutral yet royal. "During the cata-strophic period when the middle Labour Party was destroying all our institutions, Mountbatten as always continued to be acceptable to them and was a firm hand on the reins. For example—and to his eternal credit—at one weekend at Chequers, when the independent British nuclear deterrent was at risk at the hands of Denis Healey, Mountbat-ten talked him into keeping it. And his court connections, knowing people of importance socially, his rapport with Macmillan, all gave him an edge on anyone else."[24]

There was, then, a very mixed judgement on Mountbatten as defence chief in the early 1960s. Harold Wilson, who saw him through his last months as CDS, is full of praise for his performance. "While having confidence in those serving under him, he was also a long way ahead in his job, and in technology," he said. Among Americans, there were almost no reservations about him. Mountbatten described with relish a visit he made to Washington when he was Chairman of the Military Committee of NATO, and met President Kennedy.

"The first meeting of the committee wasn't much use. That was in Paris. Then we went to the U.S.A. for the next one, and we made it much smaller and easier-running, with no records kept except just one copy. Kennedy came with Lemnitzer [General Lyman L. Lemnitzer, Chairman of the Joint Chiefs of Staff], and afterwards I was asked to call at the White House as a NATO official. The meeting was supposed to last fifteen minutes, but it ran to fifty, and we went through the whole world situation. "I hadn't been very pro-Kennedy before, but I was now. I found him very intelligent, with clear views, well briefed and with a fresh approach. He knew about every subject we raised except Berlin, and at that time the NATO allies were not in step.

"Kennedy said that we must be firm and strong with the Russians, and Lemnitzer said that General Norstad's plans were complete on Berlin. These consisted of a small probe, followed by a battalion, and finally a divisional force, if there was any further trouble. I told the President that I thought this made no military sense at all. What would happen to a battalion on the autobahn? The Russians would blow up a bridge in front, a bridge behind, and then sell seats for people to come and laugh. And if that was a farce, a division would be a tragedy. It would require a front of thirty miles to keep moving—fifteen miles on each side of the autobahn, and it would be seen as an invasion of East Germany, and that would lead to all-out war.

"Lemnitzer disagreed, and Kennedy listened and believed me when I said that another airlift would be the only answer. If we went down the autobahn with a battalion or a division, we would be the aggressors. If we used planes again, they would have to shoot them down, and the Russians would be the aggressors. Kennedy smiled and said, 'I'll look into that.'

"Then I said to him, 'It's the same old story, we British are being accused of being yellow and against military operations. All we are doing is giving military advice. If we invade with a division, then it would certainly be war. If we supplied Berlin and kept the city alive by air as before, kept alert, militarily ready, and making it clear we would go to war if there was interference, then we are in a stronger, not weaker, position. I said, 'It is brave, not yellow, to show you are ready to go to war. And this is a time of great danger.' "

The degree of danger to the free world was emphasized by Mountbatten in the speeches he made around the world during his last years as Chief of Defence Staff. He would speak about "The Fast-Changing World," with science advancing at an exponential rate, with weapons systems developing so fast and at such costs that the aphorism "If it works it's obsolete" was a reality. He saw NATO as a stabilizing force; he recognized the continuous need to reassess defence philosophy, and the need to keep defence spending down.

In these speeches he constantly made the point that Russia had no intention of risking a nuclear war, that the damage caused by a nuclear war would be irreparable, that very soon we should have reached a point of nuclear sufficiency. He believed that the United States monopoly had long since gone and could never be recovered, and that the First Strike Option which had been open to the United States no longer applied.

The real danger, he would say, lay in the technical accident which might escalate into a general nuclear war. As for Britain's part, in 1965 he believed that Britain still had a significant part to play in "holding the flanks," in dealing with the unforeseen, and in providing an important maritime airborne strategy, with a powerful transport command and the means to charter aircraft at short notice for troop transportation.

The speeches were delivered with all the verve and inspiration of his speeches during the war, and those who had considered him a has-been when he came to the ministry seven years earlier were forced to change their minds.

The deaths of two of the most important people in Mountbatten's life occurred while he was at the Ministry of Defence, and within four years of each other: his wife; and Churchill, the man who had helped to make and break his father and who had been his own sparring partner, sentimental friend and implacable enemy, guide and mentor, admirer and critical observer, Nestor to Mountbatten's Achilles.

Edwina Mountbatten, after the flighty, fun-loving years of her youth and early married life, had steadied on her course in the late 1930s when, like so many of her contemporaries, she came face to face with the evil of fascism. From an Agatha Runcible in Evelyn Waugh's novel *Vile Bodies*, restlessly searching for new and ever more outrageous distractions, she became converted to the faith of good works. The relief of suffering began to absorb her and claim her time and passionate attention. She worked quite as hard as her husband all through the war. Just as she and Mountbatten had been identified together in the noisy vanguard of the bright young things in the 1920s and '30s, so the two of them were recognized as a pair, still colourful, still glamorous, but in the context of South-East Asia and India and their suffering millions instead of Mayfair and night clubs, royal occasions and chukkers of polo.

It was a remarkable metamorphosis for both of them, but especially for Edwina, whose only work until shortly before the war had been the running of large houses and organizing of large parties. When the St. John Ambulance claimed her, she generously gave them all her talents, charm, influence and organizing abilities. It is, for once, no exaggeration to say that she did the work of ten. Her charitable work became first a way of life, then a drug. She seemed unable to stop herself, any more than once she could restrain herself from wandering dangerously in faraway places. Long after the war, when the need had greatly diminished, she continued to work and travel as Superintendent-in-Chief of the St. John Ambulance Brigade.

Edwina Mountbatten overstrained herself year after year, like a fine-tuned engine racing at high revs. She was only fifty-eight when she left on one more whirlwind tour of the Far East on behalf of her charities. A few months earlier, one of her grandchildren had contracted chicken pox, and Edwina picked it up from her in a particularly virulent form—or perhaps it seemed so only because she was in such poor physical shape. She had had some angina pain recently, too, and she was not sleeping and was taking barbiturates.

It was February, Pamela had just married, and Edwina, in spite of the poor state of her health, had been especially radiant and admired at the wedding. No one could have suspected how near to breaking point she was. Her timetable was typical: utterly demanding and only just capable of fulfilment, if she went flat out.

"She was in Borneo," said Mountbatten of one of the great tragedies in his life. "I found out later that she had done a tremendous day's work and had to attend an official party in the evening. She had to be half carried to it, but once there, she pushed aside her supporters and put on her usual show, sparkling, charming and talking to everyone. After it she went to bed and never woke up. We had never been happier together, and I felt utterly pole-axed when the telephone rang at three o'clock in the morning with the news."

Her heart had ceased beating while she was asleep. She had expressed a wish to be buried at sea, and after her funeral at Romsey Abbey, where six weeks earlier her younger daughter had been married, her body was taken on board a frigate. She was "committed to the deep" off Portsmouth, within a few miles of Adsdean, where they had lived for so many years when they were the toast of "the bright young things."

.   .   .

The last years of Winston Churchill could not have been in stronger contrast, and filled Mountbatten with a dread of drug-supported old age. The relationship between these two remarkable men was compounded of passion, and mutual admiration, suspicion and mutual understanding, a canny, unspoken comprehension of the other's strengths and weaknesses. The relationship was like that between a famous, talented, jealous and proud uncle keen to show off his clever nephew, so long as the limelight is not too bright—and, alas, it often was.

Churchill, who all his life worried about money, envied "the golden boy's" wealth. And Churchill the deep-dyed aristocrat with insatiable ambition envied Mountbatten's easy access to the royal family and the palaces of Europe. He adored Edwina and loved to flirt with her and to please her. Together with his own Clemmie, they made a marvellous foursome of wit and mischief and wisdom.

Churchill also enjoyed teasing Mountbatten, but there could be a schoolboy's sharp edge of jocular provocation to it. This was a one-sided game. Mountbatten teased only women, the young and those who were no threat in the never-ending competition that was his propellant charge. There is a true story of lunch at Hyde Park Gate soon after Churchill's belated resignation as Prime Minister in 1955. Mountbatten, Julian Amery, Harold Macmillan and two or three others were present. Mountbatten had recently become First Sea Lord, to Churchill's chagrin. Churchill was grumpy throughout the meal, and they were all trying to cheer him up.

Towards the end, Mountbatten rose to leave early. The dining room at Hyde Park Gate was curiously constructed, with stairs leading up to a half landing below the door. On this landing Mountbatten paused and turned to address his audience below. "I'm so sorry," he announced, "but I have to go to a Chiefs of Staff meeting." This completed Churchill's cure, and when Mountbatten had gone he was grinning as he asked the others, "Who is that man? Ought I to know him?"[25]

Churchill felt great admiration for Mountbatten, and great regard for his abilities and his power to attract the affection and loyalty of the common man. It was for this reason that he made him Supreme Commander in SEAC. Only a genius of Churchill's calibre could have recognized in the young naval captain the ability to convert the morale and fighting spirit of a distant jungle army. But there was not much love there. Churchill found faintly distasteful what he regarded as Mountbatten's German characteristics, his preoccupation with his lineage, his medals and decorations, his seeming pomposity on parade, his name-dropping and stories proving how clever he was.

For his part, Mountbatten's admiration for Churchill was boundless, even though he never trusted him and often thought he behaved "a bit naughtily." Mountbatten once said, "Winston did a lot of naughty and a lot of silly things in the Second World War. But none of this detracts from the fact that if it had not been for him, we should have lost the war. It's as simple as that. He had this quality of leadership, this vision, this drive, and the courage. These are what his reputation rests on. Not on individual acts, many of which were appallingly stupid, like Dakar and his disgraceful behaviour over Dudley North, and his idiotic behaviour over the *Repulse* and the *Prince of Wales*.

"We could see Winston behaving disgracefully. But history will say that he saved us from defeat single-handed and won the war. And that's enough."

On the day before Churchill's funeral in January 1965, Mountbatten told one of his staff, "When Winston goes tomorrow, I'll be the only one of his original pallbearers on parade. I am the only one left. You'll see all sorts of admirals and air marshals and so on, but I am the only original. Winston laid it down in 1940 who was to carry his body, and I was included."

A few minutes later he was studying the seat-placing for the funeral, his keen eyes scanning the board like an admiral before a Royal Fleet Review. There was a sudden, indignant shout. "Where are the Poles?" He turned around and called out to the world at large, as if exposing some national scandal. "You haven't made any provision for the Poles at Winston's funeral. This is terrible."

It was exactly the small omitted detail of protocol and justice that he was sure to spot. Not only did he see to it that a contingent of Poles, the first to fight the Germans on their own soil, were provided for in the seating, but he made sure that they were seated in the front—and then left it to others to dig them out in twelve hours, some of them chefs in remote restaurants, and see to it that they came.

After the funeral—and there was not to be another like it until Mountbatten's—the whole world watched as a special steam train took Churchill's body to the little village of Bladon close to Blenheim Palace, where he was to be buried. Tens of thousands of people flocked to walk past the grave. A police officer helping to control the crowd observed a bare-headed figure, without overcoat, standing watching the slow-moving line. The policeman had last seen Mountbatten in a jungle clearing standing on a box addressing members of the 25th Indian Division on the Arakan front. He recognized him at once and noticed that he could not see the grave from where he was standing and was making no attempt to break into the queue.

The officer said, "I know you, my lord; would you care to come to see the grave?" The ex-Supremo and the ex-soldier did so, standing silently beside the policeman, who then led him back to his car, telling him that he had once served under him. "In 'The Ace of Spades,' sir." "Ah, the 25th Indian Division." They talked as old friends, of the war and of the greatness of the man just buried. "Then he shook my hand warmly and thanked me."[26]

The great statesman had come into Mountbatten's life during his first months in the Royal Navy as a cadet. Six months after Churchill's funeral, Mountbatten finally retired as Chief of the Defence Staff, all that he had sought to accomplish now fulfilled.

11

RETIREMENT

*I*n many ways, Mountbatten faced the same problems as any widowed sixty-five-year-old man in retirement. The Military Order of Merit and other decorations, his appointment as Colonel of the Life Guards, Life Commandant of the Royal Marines, Governor of the Isle of Wight, were retirement gifts, just as a retiring company director might be presented with a gold fountain pen.

"I suppose you can say I became an odd-job man," he said. "A Mr. Fix-it. I had two thousand acres to farm at Broadlands, and I had already formed an estate committee to help with this. I had also founded the National Electronics Research Council a year earlier, and in 1966 I became president of the British Computer Society."

In the mid-1960s Mountbatten was associated, often as president or chairman, with no fewer than two hundred organizations, ranging from the Variety Club of Great Britain and the Inner Magic Circle to the Swedish Naval Society. He headed an Immigration Mission for Prime Minister Harold Wilson and volunteered to lead an enquiry into prison security. He loved anything to do with the *Kelly* Reunion Association, of which he was very proud, the British Commonwealth ex-Services League, King George's Fund for Sailors, and of course the Burma Star Association.

Under the inspiration of Kurt Hahn, the founder of Salem and Gordonstoun schools, an Atlantic College was set up in South Wales to promote international education. Mountbatten became the first president and did his utmost to spread the principle and reality of United

World Colleges. For years this responsibility took up the greater part of his time.

Mountbatten espoused dozens of causes a year, small ones that grew in size, like United World Colleges, to individual acts of assistance or the correction of an injustice. For example, in 1970 the former commander of the Sierra Leone Army, Brigadier David Lansana, was sentenced to death for alleged treason and overthrowing the state. Lansana had known Mountbatten when he was Chief of Defence Staff, and when his case came to Mountbatten's notice, he wrote letters, spoke to people of influence, appealed personally to the High Commissioner and to the President of Sierra Leone. He at last got the conviction quashed. When the authorities went back on their word, hanged the brigadier and publicly displayed his body, Mountbatten was heartbroken.[1]

This was a rare example of defeat. He usually completed his odd jobs successfully, although the outcome of the prison-security investigations and recommendations was also unsatisfactory in his eyes.

Mountbatten always became uneasy with time on his hands for reflection, especially after the death of Edwina, whom he continued to miss painfully. Like most members of the royal family, he read very little. He either skimmed printed matter swiftly, acquiring the essence, or slowly, his lips moving with the words, even with a finger following them across the page.

His uneasiness was one reason he took on so much. Other motives were kindness and a sense of duty. Both the first and last of these reasons were behind his agreement to meet the newspaper magnate Cecil King at his London house in May 1968. The nation was in the depths of depression and anxiety about the future. In Cecil King's judgement Prime Minister Harold Wilson was destroying the country, which faced anarchy and civil war. King envisaged the temporary end of parliamentary democracy, and believed that the country would be forced to turn to "somebody like Lord Mountbatten as the titular head of a new administration, somebody renowned as a leader of men who would be capable of restoring public confidence . . ."

Hugh Cudlipp, a friend of Mountbatten's, brought about a meeting and was himself present. Mountbatten telephoned earlier in the day to indicate that Solly (now Lord) Zuckerman, would also be there. Cecil King said his piece about civil disorder and machine guns on street corners and ended by asking Mountbatten if he would head a new

administration. Mountbatten remained silent. Then turned to Zuckerman, who said firmly that it was rank treachery, and he would have
nothing to do with it, adding "nor should you, Dickie."[2]

And that was that. But what would have been the outcome if Mountbatten had not had his adviser at his side? Would the British people, at
their lowest ebb, have welcomed this royal neo-dictator? The answers
are less important than the fact that Mountbatten had insisted on
bringing Zuckerman and unhesitatingly followed his lead. Zuckerman
has written that "it did not take more than a few minutes for Dickie to
realize the madness of the idea." Those minutes (or seconds) were filled
with Zuckerman's advice.

As First Sea Lord, Mountbatten was the strongest proponent of the
nuclear deterrent and was more responsible than anyone for the con-
struction of the nuclear-powered Polaris submarines with their immense destructive ability. But as an old man in retirement, Mountbatten believed that he had been quite wrong, that Britain was "rushing
headlong towards a precipice" with its nuclear weapons. In one of his
last speeches, to the Stockholm International Peace Research Institute
in 1979, Mountbatten spoke about his sadness at the little that had
been achieved in the way of disarmament between the great powers,
especially nuclear disarmament.

Disarmament became the leading cause of the last years of his life.
Lord Zuckerman had for a long time proclaimed against the production of more nuclear weapons, and their proliferation, and repeatedly
stated that the Soviet military threat was greatly exaggerated. Soon
after the Cuban missile crisis and his visit to Kennedy, Mountbatten
softened to Khrushchev's thaw and wanted to send a naval good-will
mission to Russia. All thought of his likely "unpopularity" in Russia,
which he had expressed to Ernie Bevin, had now quite disappeared,
and when Prime Minister Kosygin invited him to the celebrations for
the thirtieth anniversary of the defeat of Germany, Mountbatten accepted eagerly. He made nostalgic tours of the palaces in Moscow and
Leningrad, delighting his hosts with accounts of grand banquets, visits
to the opera, and games with his beautiful young cousins.

Long before this visit in 1975, Mountbatten had turned against the
concept that nuclear war was an acceptable consideration.

One of Churchill's great attributes was that he was always prepared
to listen to advice. He was also very selective and wise in the choice of

his advisers. Mountbatten ranged more widely, especially when he was old and retired. One to whom he listened more than most was his son-in-law Lord Brabourne. According to Mountbatten, it was Lord Brabourne who persuaded him to embark upon an enormously long and profitable television series called *The Life and Times of Lord Mountbatten* soon after his retirement. It took three years to make and provided Mountbatten with a great deal of satisfaction. It certainly left out very little to his credit in a long and eventful life.

The growth of Mountbatten's vanity was something to which many people contributed, if only because it was such an easy way to please him. To some, especially the hard core of the upper echelons of the Royal Navy, Mountbatten's vanity and egocentricity were irritating and in poor taste. Churchill treated Mountbatten's vanity indulgently and with humour, which was sometimes acid-tinged. The royal family was always indulgent about it and never took it seriously.

When a title was being sought for a book about his mother and father, and there were difficulties about getting it right, Mountbatten turned to the Queen and Prince Philip for suggestions. "Why not just call it *Lord Mountbatten's Parents?*" Prince Philip suggested, with a show of innocence. The redeeming factor is that Mountbatten joined in the laughter.

He had a stock letter in answer to pleas from publishers and authors to write forewords and introductions, which claimed that it was his invariable practice to refuse, but under the very exceptional circumstances (which applied to the majority of enquiries), he would make a special point of doing so. The author or publisher was expected to draft out the "copy," which Mountbatten then sometimes changed by a word or two, approved and signed.

In this way, his name was given prominence on the jackets of so many books that it became something of a joke in the trade.

His private secretary, during Mountbatten's last years, always had the greatest difficulty in persuading Mountbatten to forgo some of the numerous invitations to speak at ceremonies, many of them of a very minor nature. His delight at being guest of honour knew no bounds and was a pleasure to behold.

Without the slightest trace of self-consciousness, Mountbatten allowed his private secretary, who wrote the text of the picture biography he prepared before his death, to describe him as "still handsome in spite of his years," and much more equally ridiculous flattery.

Although he had once been fearful of becoming a megalomaniac, Mountbatten's vanity went largely unchecked. The closest members of his family might have tried to tame it (his mother actually did, with no success) if they had not been able to laugh at it to his face. His sense of humour, as always, was his salvation.

His pride in his twelve-part autobiographical television series knew no bounds, and he could quote the number of times it had been shown in various countries throughout the world. He also took great satisfaction in dubbing his own dialogue in the German and French versions. It was while he was in Paris preparing the French script in 1972 that the Duke of Windsor telephoned and invited him to dinner.

The Duke's health was already failing, and he had recently undergone debilitating treatment for a tumour in his throat. Mountbatten remained blithely unaware of any coolness towards him by his old friend, but the Duke was determined to discover the reason why Mountbatten had not attended his wedding all those years ago. The Duchess fretted at all the nostalgic talk about old times as shipmates, and the goings on on board the *Renown* fifty years earlier. Then, when the women withdrew, the Duke posed the question. Mountbatten answered that it was because he had never been asked, although he had offered to be best man. The Duke was at first disbelieving, then contrite and forgiving and full of promises to make amends. The friendship that Mountbatten had never known had been broken was spliced. They saw each other the following day, but never again.

After a harrowing visit from the Queen when he was already dying, the Duke of Windsor died of throat cancer on 28 May 1972—almost certainly the fourth English king to die from smoking in this century. "He was my best friend all my life," Mountbatten said on BBC radio at the time of his funeral.

When the Duke of Windsor died, Harold Wilson was Prime Minister. His admiration for Mountbatten has already been mentioned. The four preceding Prime Ministers, Churchill, Eden, Macmillan and Home, all admired him, too, though not without reservations. Churchill claimed from time to time that he loved him, but it was really only the intermittent outpourings of shame-tinged sentiment. Only one of these men loved him and did not mind his vanity. "He was such a sweet man," Harold Macmillan told this writer. "He was slightly childish, with a sort of simple mind. He boasted a lot. But that didn't matter. That wasn't important. What did matter was that he was a charming character."[3]

The old story about always driving to naval dockyards, when living ashore, in a large, expensive car, compounding the sin by having a special emblem on the bonnet, was often cited by his fellow officers as proof of his vanity and bad taste. The emblem was of a signal rating with his arms positioned at the alphabetical sign, the right arm straight up with the flag in hand and the left arm horizontal from the shoulder.

To the lower deck, on the other hand, this was proof that he identified with them. One of them wrote on the day of Mountbatten's murder—"the saddest day of '79"—that "he gave loyalty and received loyalty in return" and that the bonnet emblem "was accepted as an honour to the Signalmen ratings who served under him."[4]

Mountbatten's vanity had many origins, but the most important was certainly his need to excel. When he did not win, or when he was crossed, he was not pleasant company. His voice suddenly became harsh, peremptory and arrogant. But he was not rancorous, and like most great men, he rarely harboured grudges. He was nowhere more competitive than on the polo field. He could not bear to be beaten, and his language was as bad as any player's—which is to say, in polo, very bad. In a vital finals in the inter-Regimental Tournament with the 12th Lancers on 11 July 1936, his Royal Naval Polo Team was beaten 6-4. It was hard to take.

"We were leading three goals to one at the end of the fourth chukker," he said in excuse, "and to save a certain goal the Twelfth Lancers committed a serious foul and knocked over our Number One's pony. The penalties awarded were, first, a free hit at goal, which I converted, making the score four to one, and, second, an opponent of higher handicap to retire unless our injured player was fit to continue. He elected to go on, although his left leg was broken, with the inevitable result that the Twelfth Lancers caught us up and eventually beat us."[5]

Thirty-seven years after the event, Mountbatten was still nursing this defeat like an old wound. At the time, the *Daily Telegraph*'s polo correspondent merely reported that "the Lancers showed themselves to be much the better side."

Mountbatten's tact, when needed, was boundless. He was also a very kind man. But it was possible for both qualities to be overcome by his self-esteem. An A.D.C. to the Governor of Bombay, who had been badly wounded in Burma, recalls Mountbatten's visit. "'43 or '44?" Mountbatten asked about the date of his action. The officer told him proudly that he had been fighting there since 1942.

Mountbatten then said, "One thing I have never understood. You had about the same number of troops we have now. Perhaps we have a little more in the air and a few West Africans. But you still couldn't do the job we're doing now."

The officer recalls today: "To hear such a grossly inaccurate and hurtful remark from a man in his position is almost unbelievable, but every word became indelibly imprinted on my mind. I returned and rejoined my fellow A.D.C.s, and caused consternation among them as apparently I had gone quite white."[6]

Another officer, commanding the Governor-General's Guard at Vice-Regal Lodge in New Delhi in October 1947, recalls the trouble he had in satisfying Mountbatten's demands for the daily ceremonial guard with pipes and drums. The guard consisted of a Gurkha officer and twenty men. Moutbatten had just returned with his host from visiting his princely estate where a far larger guard had received them. Mountbatten demanded the same size guard for the prince and himself. "The manpower was just not available," said the officer. "He was most annoyed about it and showed impatience at once."[7] Ceremonial equality was the last thing Mountbatten ever wanted to fail on, and rarely did.

Mountbatten's preoccupation with detail correctness bedevilled him all his life but increased with the years. He could spot a misplaced minor decoration at one hundred yards and would go to great trouble to establish whether, say, his guest was ex-RAF or ex-RAFVR in order to greet him wearing the right tie. One of his Staff at the Ministry of Defence said, "He'd go on for hours trying to work out how many guns ought to salute a CDS when there was a pile of work on his desk."

It is hard to believe that there were not more important things to be done on the night before Mountbatten left to take up command in South-East Asia than to draw phoenixes. But perfection was always the first priority; perfection for the satisfaction that it gave him, and perfection so that he could not be faulted.

This writer once suggested laughingly that his dog Kimberley was slightly overweight and received a very sharp denial: "Exactly right!" An old American friend who visited him a few weeks before his death told him that he had just learned that the reply to an invitation to a reception for a fellow historian and an authority on wartime resistance, M. R. D. Foot, had mistakenly been sent by Mountbatten's office to the Leader of the House of Commons, the Right Honourable Michael Foot.

"Dickie seems to have lost his sense of humour," said the American later, reporting Mountbatten's stony response to the "joke."

Failure and inefficiency on his part, and the Japanese, were the only subjects about which Mountbatten never laughed. But as a rule, his light touch, his quick repartee, the sheer certainty of pleasure, stimulus and laughter were always present. The spirit of liveliness, the knowledge that *he* was going to enjoy himself, was heady to experience. One could feel this even at a distance. It was one of his great qualities.

When Mountbatten was in his seventies, women continued to fall under his spell, and his charm was as powerful as it was in the 1920s. His need to have women around him was equally strong. Besides the women of the royal family, from Princess Anne to the aged but marvellously bright Princess Alice of Athlone (and of course the Queen herself, with whom he spent as much time as they could both spare), he made many new young friends, including Prince Charles's girlfriends, who often stayed at Broadlands, and whose numbers and variety made Mountbatten exclaim in mock dismay. Without exception, he made a great fuss over them.

He also kept up with older women friends, like Barbara Cartland, who knew him for fifty years, and very well for the last five. She said, "Wherever he was, in whatever company on whatever occasion, you at once felt his magnetism. He was the personification of leadership—everything was suddenly marvellous when he was there. He was so knowledgeable on every possible subject, so quick-minded, and—oh—so amusing! People forget his humour—and he was one of the most amusing men I ever knew. But never, never maliciously funny, because he was one of the kindest men alive."[8]

Mountbatten and Barbara Cartland usually met at least once a week, and during those last years she would stay at Broadlands and he at Camfield Place. They wrote a novel together in the last months, and she even succeeded in putting him on her vitamin diet. He claimed he felt marvellously improved in health by it, and he became one of her best proponents.

Mountbatten always preferred to be in control of things, in both the broadest and narrowest sense. He nearly always drove his own cars until the last ten years or so, often with his chauffeur at his side. He drove (and frequently dented) his cars before World War II, liked to be at the helm of his boats, even liked driving his trains.

"Placing his suitcase in a first-class carriage of the 6:04 P.M. train for Ashford," observed an amazed eyewitness, "he walked in front of me accompanied by a station official, went up to the engine driver, climbed into the cabin and remained there. When my train came alongside his near New Cross, I saw that Lord Mountbatten was driving the packed train, while the driver was just a bystander."[9]

The stories of Mountbatten's remarkable memory for faces are legion. It is a quality cultivated by many members of the royal family, but none of them has developed it to such a fine degree as Mountbatten. He said he ruined his memory by overwork during the war, and it is true that in the 1930s he needed only a week to learn the names of every member of a destroyer's company—about two hundred.

His powers of recognition remained almost uncanny. On the airfield at Habbaniyah in Iraq in 1943, when Mountbatten was on his way to take up his appointment as Supremo, ten pilots of the Communications Flight, with Air Vice-Marshal Champion de Crespigny, lined up to greet him. "The aircraft stopped," one of them recalled, "the door opened, and down stepped Lord Louis in naval uniform, followed by half a dozen of the most beautiful Wrens."[10] Twenty-two years later, in the spring of 1965, the same pilot was at Labuan when Mountbatten as Chief of Defence Staff made a tour of the service bases in Sarawak and Malaysia. On leaving, he was climbing up the boarding steps of his famous Comet when he turned and came down again. "Gathered dignitaries wondered what had gone awry—as I did. He walked twenty yards along the ranks to me and asked me where I had served in Burma . . ." He had recognized not only the Burma Star, but the man's face.

This power of recall certainly kept his subordinates on their toes. Mountbatten himself remembered an investiture in Assam during the Burma campaign. "A man of the First Burma rifles came forward for his Military Medal," he said. "I recognized him at once and turned to his colonel. 'This man received his M.M. [Military Medal] from the Viceroy at Imphal.' The colonel turned white and apologized. I asked him why he had been brought up again, and the colonel said that his regiment was not on parade last time. I told him, 'I don't mind him being brought up again, but I think I ought to have been told.' This went rocketing around the troops!"

Mountbatten's thrift was less widely known. At its worst (failure to pay a debt without considerable nagging) it was aggravating. It could also be counterproductive (to use one of the favourite words he learned from his elder son-in-law), and it was amusing to hear him on the long-distance telephone for many minutes seeking a modest discount on a modest product. Although he felt he always had to travel first class, he encouraged his family to travel economy, and they often did, nipping in to his more exclusive part of the cabin for a chat from time to time.

This care with money was instilled in him from his earliest days, mainly by his mother, not because his parents were poor—although they were not very rich—but because of the Victorian ethic of thrift and economy handed down directly from the Queen herself. At school and at Osborne, Mountbatten was always on the lowest scale of pocket money and was encouraged to take every care with his clothes.

A companion to Princess Beatrice, Queen Victoria's last daughter, who married Mountbatten's uncle, Prince Henry of Battenberg, re-counted to her niece how she helped keep the young Dickie's clothes in order. Once the boy asked her, "Please, can you make new collars for these shirts from the tails?" Which, she thought, revealed early signs of thrift and inventiveness.[11]

When Admiral Sir Arthur Pedder, who knew Mountbatten well, heard of his death, he exclaimed, "Good God, what was he doing placing himself at that risk with his family?" The world was soon to learn that he was protected by minimum security. It was the same through all the years when he was famous, as Chief of Combined Ops, as Supreme Commander, even as Viceroy when hundreds were being assassinated daily around him.

A retired major in the Intelligence Corps, G. P. Bartholomew, told of his horror on first arriving at Mountbatten's H.Q. at Kandy, to find "Supremo" living not in the well-protected military establishment but in the Queen's pavilion, protected by a two-feet-high brick wall and (during daylight hours only) a Royal Marines sentry at the door, playing the part of butler. This officer soon discovered that Mountbatten did not consider security, so he organized some NCOs to enter the pavilion at night and scatter cigarette tins marked "BOMB" around.

After this, Major Bartholomew was allowed to take some modest security action, without Mountbatten's knowledge, because it was well known by his staff that he detested it. At a reception Mountbatten approached the major and said, "I understand you want to improve the security here. Well, I'm not going to have sentries in army boots thumping around the place keeping everyone awake." He was assured that there was no question of that and was invited out onto the lawn, with its beautiful flowers and scattered shrubs. "There are the sentries, sir."

The major had placed sentries with dark-brown faces and jungle-green uniforms among these shrubs, each with a line of sight to his neighbour. Even at short range, Mountbatten could not identify them. "Well, if *that's* all you want to do," he said grudgingly, "go ahead. But do you really think the Japs would think me a worthwhile target?"

The major, it seems, was "not prepared for such a breath-takingly modest question."[12]

Was it really modesty—at Kandy, New Delhi, Singapore, Classiebawn Castle—that led Mountbatten to disregard security risks? It could also have been stupidity, arrogance, rashness or blind courage. It was probably not any of these alone, though nearest the last. It was a kind of lofty fatalism, a prince's belief that his destiny was laid down when another name—that of Francis Albert Victor Nicholas—was etched into that Hessian family tree with its roots in Charlemagne, and that no power on earth except God's could disturb its course.

Mountbatten—on his destroyer's bridge, racing blindly up fjords and over minefields, handling a machine gun against diving Stukas, striding up to the Arakan front or into a mob of frenzied zealots—was governed in his mind and conduct and in his physical stance by the tradition of timeless chivalry in which fear played no part. A prince with a bodyguard indeed!

It was all very splendid and very medieval. But it could be tragically wasteful of human life. When questioned about his personal security in Ireland, he is known to have asked, "Do you really think the I.R.A would think me a worthwhile target?"

As always, he took it for granted that his family and those who served him should show equal fearlessness, or fatalism, for to hint at safety measures was to hint at caution. So, whether it was marching into a rioting, hysterical mob with his wife and daughter at his side, or through a minefield with the lives of two hundred men at risk, or—as an obvious target for assassins—puttering about with his family in an old launch looking for lobsters, everyone had to be prepared to share the dangers. And that was that.

Speed—speed in reaching decisions, speed in all his activities, from polo to driving cars, destroyers and speedboats—was essential to his style of living. From the dreamy little boy with his white mice, who fell over things, who emanated charm but from whom little was expected in the way of achievement, there developed in adolescence this "swash-buckling dynamo," as he was once called.

The more Mountbatten loved being known for his fast pace in every-thing, the faster he became, with "Full Speed Ahead, both engines!" rung down to the engine room. His record time of 1 hour 14 minutes for driving from Brook House in London to the dockyard gates at Ports-mouth was widely known. It was a record he loved to quote, adding that it must be remembered that it was done in a car with rear-wheel brakes only on rough and narrow roads.

He could cite the speed of all his victories in *Shadow II*, and adored reading in the newspapers about his reputation for getting on with things.

> We all admire the energy and enterprise of Lord Louis Mountbatten, who has many of the buoyant qualities of the Prince of Wales. His polo players are situ-ated normally at Portsmouth. He is therefore buying an aeroplane to get them to and from the matches in time. Five fast cars are not swift enough. What his friends are wondering is whether he is going to have the ponies strapped on underneath, so that men and mounts can come together.[13]

That was in 1929. In India in 1947, and on a less light-hearted level, in negotiating the transfer of power his speed had not diminished one knot; nor had it in 1966 during his investigations into prison security and reform, when Lord Longford found him "too much in a hurry," with the result that "prison reform may have been put back twenty-five years."[14]

.   .   .

Mountbatten's love of speed, of his reputation for swift decision-making, his vanity and boasting, his preoccupation with the ceremonial and ritual and genealogy, even his practice of winning by any means, fair or almost foul—all these characteristics were judged as either vulgar, irritating or engagingly lovable. The better you knew him, the more tolerant you became of them. He was, as Harold Macmillan said, "a simple man" fundamentally.

But it is wrong and unjust to deny him his enormous positive qualities, his compassion and kindness, the fulness of his love so that he saw humanity as one. His obsession with detail in his professional life was open to criticism, but it also led to a concern in detail for the sufferings of others, so that some injury or loss of which he had heard would be remembered and enquired about months or years later.

If he was not widely known for his financial generosity, he was generous above what most of us have ever met in other ways. Many writers have been impressed by his willingness to give his time, and his concern that they should get everything right. He would read passages of manuscript, proofs, correct detail and give interviews, all with care. Elizabeth Longford recalled a long session with him when she was writing her book about the House of Windsor. The following day she was invited back, bringing a tape recorder this time, so as to be sure that she had got everything right.[15]

Ever since he helped Ray Murphy back in 1945 to gather material for the first Mountbatten biography, Mountbatten frequently gave help to other writers, historians and journalists who were writing biographies of books relating to certain periods in his life. Among many others, Professor Arthur J. Marder, Dr. Martin Gilbert, Arthur Swinson (whose excellent biography was published in 1971) and the present writer have all benefited from his delight at giving his views and speaking at length about himself and his achievements.

There was no need for Mountbatten to tell Churchill at Quebec that he had a congenital weakness for believing that he could do anything. Churchill knew that already. He had long ago seen in Mountbatten the qualities of his own younger days: courage, the possession of a radical and experimental mind, the absolute self-confidence that no obstacle was insurmountable, no convention unbreakable, and no one unpersuadable. He did not always win. Mahatma Ali Jinnah beat him, and so did the 12th Lancers. But victory over Mountbatten was a very rare event.

Mountbatten was not always sharply discriminating. He chose some lightweight advisers and sometimes took lightweight advice. But so great was his charm and attraction, his position and rank, that he also attracted some brilliant advisers; and Mountbatten had a canny instinct for taking their advice over really important decisions—for example, at the abdication crisis, at Suez and at Cecil King's suggestion that he should become a dictator. Only in India was he poorly advised, and this led to great tragedies and loss of life and to the major error of coming home for the royal wedding in the middle of it all.

Any historical judgement on Mountbatten will be bound to show that his inspiration to achievement was greater than his actual achievement. His power to lift spirits, to bring out the best in people, has been experienced by thousands and is undeniable. The aura of greatness around him never failed to inspire, and in his presence, one could physically feel the adrenaline rising when he became enthused or determined. His charm and humour, the speed and agility of his mind, were a revelation every time you met him.

The roll of tangible achievement is not so impressive, however. His detractors could make out a negative list. He did not win a victory at sea. The enemy frequently damaged his ships, and finally sank him. He is remembered as Chief of Combined Operations for the Dieppe raid rather than for laying the foundations for the successful invasion of Europe. Certainly, the Fourteenth Army cleared Burma of the enemy, but it was denied a great invasion and land victory, just as the admirals were denied a great Eastern sea victory, by the dropping of the atom bombs. The fates of war were not on his side: yet one more parallel with his father.

He encouraged the demand for independence of once-colonial or imperial nations at a speed that satisfied even the Americans, divided India and transferred power in some twenty weeks. Later he deprived the three British services of their independence and forced them to become one.

So much for the negative side, and it would be unjust to his memory to ignore it. Unfairly, it is more difficult to define convincingly his positive contributions to the winning of the war, and the creation of a freer and more compassionate society since. His energy and the quality of his mind made his contribution to the creation of the will to win second only to Churchill's. He deserved that tribute from the war leaders on D-Day. He deserved to be credited with the saving of India from the Japanese armies.

Mountbatten's love of America, and the Americans' love of him, was a monumental war-winning factor. Who else could have welded together such a disparate number of difficult nationalities into a great army? Roosevelt loved him, MacArthur admired him, even Stilwell judged him to be a limey who would actually fight.

Mountbatten's contribution to the British monarchy has also been immense, as the Queen has testified. She and Prince Philip loved him and relied upon his advice on a thousand occasions. His relations with Prince Charles were even closer and more affectionate, and the Prince is the first to underline the extent of his debt for advice, guidance and friendship.

Mountbatten was a passionate believer in the importance and value of the family unit, and through the years of the so-called generation gap he had no trouble bridging it with all his grandchildren, although he could be as fierce and firm with them as a ship's commander with a recalcitrant rating. His numerous and widespread family loved him in return. Only with the Queen Mother was there a small shadow of reserve, still traceable forty years later to Mountbatten's close friendship with the man whose failure to do his duty forced her own husband onto the throne, and caused him to die prematurely.

Like all his emotions, his grief at the death of his friends and relations was extraordinarily intense. He was distraught at the loss of his only brother, at the loss of his sister, the Queen of Sweden, in 1965, and of his eldest sister. Alice had spent her last years in a suite on an upper floor of Buckingham Palace, living very quietly after her sometimes tumultuous and tragic life. Unlike some women, the Queen loved having her mother-in-law living with her. "The Queen," said Mountbatten, "was the only person who could speak to her in her normal voice and make herself completely understood—every word. My sister was completely normal at the end. People simply couldn't believe it when they met her. During the war, Dolla [her daughter Theodora] had sent to her in Greece a diamond-and-sapphire cross worth about ten thousand pounds as she knew that her mother, living in a community of nursing sisters, was very poor. She took it straight to the church, hung it round the Virgin's neck and said, 'I give this to you.'

"But twenty years later at Buckingham Palace she had more influence on the Queen than anyone. The Queen adored her, and she adored the Queen. The Queen is fond of her mother, but she got on infinitely better with my sister."

When in London, and when both were free from the heavy burden of official duties, Mountbatten would always have afternoon tea with the Queen and Princess Alice at Buckingham Palace. On one of these occasions, as he recounted to this writer shortly after Alice's death, Mountbatten exclaimed indignantly at the tea, "I don't like China tea," I told the Queen. "I hate your tea, and you never serve Indian tea." My sister interjected, "Dickie doesn't like China tea, he always had Indian tea as a boy."

According to Mountbatten, the Queen, laughing and only mock-outraged, replied, "Are you telling me that Dickie always had a special pot of tea? That's entirely his upbringing. He's always been spoiled, and he's spoiled to this day. I suppose that's what his mother did to him—I can see that now."

Mountbatten was always prepared to accept that he had been indulged as a child. "My brother and sisters treated me as the baby and forgave me for everything. I'm afraid that I was the favorite. I was spoiled, and no one minded."

This story and these remarks were typical of his engaging and humorous frankness about his minor weaknesses. But his repertoire did not include anecdotes about any alleged failure in his achievements and his major claims to be recorded by posterity.

The doctors responsible for Mountbatten's autopsy judged him to have been a fit man for his years, and there is good reason to believe that he would have lived much longer. His private secretary, John Barratt, who knew him as well as anyone alive, predicted in 1972, "I think he will either live to a great age or go out suddenly." How soon? "Oh, in about eight years." He was off by less than a year.

Mountbatten complained only of vertigo in his last years. This would strike him briefly but sometimes at awkward public times. He was little affected by extremes of heat or cold, and did not seem to register the temperature of a room he entered. His houses, in London and in the country, tended to be chilly, and that is perhaps the reason why he suffered from frequent winter colds, which in no way affected the pace of his work or his general cheerfulness.

His appetite continued voracious into old age, but he did not put on weight after about forty-five, though he often complained that he was overweight. All his life he took exercise, but always mixed with some sport or recreation. In his mid-seventies he would still shoot all day with scarcely a rest, and though he had long before given up polo, at Broadlands he would ride for two hours every morning with guests, including the Queen when she came to stay, but more often with a young girl—the daughter of one of the servants from nearby Romsey with whom the flow of conversation was almost unbroken, for horses, and the young, were always two of his great loves.

Many people have suggested that the manner of Mountbatten's death was as he would have wished it. He dreaded senility and old age. He died, after all, in what his assassins claimed was a war; and no death could have been more spectacular or aroused a greater, world-wide sensation. The headlines could not have been bigger and blacker, and that would have amused and pleased him.

He also liked the coincidences and ironies of history. And it is a considerable coincidence and irony that Mountbatten, who liked most to be remembered for what he did in India, was assassinated by po-litico-religious fanatics in another divided, strife-torn land at almost exactly the same age as his old friend, Mahatma Gandhi. In their own way, they were both martyrs.

ACKNOWLEDGEMENTS

The author wishes to thank Their Majesties Queen Elizabeth II and Queen Elizabeth The Queen Mother, His Royal Highness The Prince Philip, Duke of Edinburgh and his sisters Princess Margarita of Hohenlohe-Langenburg and Princess George of Hanover, and Her Royal Highness Princess Alice, Countess of Athlone, for their reminiscences about Lord Mountbatten's parents and about Lord Mountbatten himself, when I was working on the family history and dual biography of the 1st Marquis and Marchioness of Milford Haven. Their contributions were so generous that much of what they told me appears here for the first time.

Other people, too many to list by name, have helped with reminiscences and, through their personal knowledge of Lord Mountbatten and their friendship with him, have also been able to check information. Hundreds more answered my public appeal for reminiscences, and I am grateful to everyone who responded with contributions ranging from important information and anecdotes, to small details which have helped me to form a more complete and accurate portrait of Lord Mountbatten.

I must, however, single out for my thanks the following who have been especially kind and forthcoming: Julian Amery, Sir Arthur Bryant, Lord Butler, Barbara Cartland, Lord Cudlipp, Dr. Martin Gilbert, Lord Hailsham, Vice-Admiral Sir Charles Hughes Hallett, Lieutenant-Commander Peter Kemp, Sir John Lang, the Earl and Countess of Longford, Harold Macmillan, Professor Arthur J. Marder, Vice-Admiral Sir Arthur Pedder, Tom Pocock, Lady Soames, Sir Herbert Thompson, Sir Harold Wilson and Captain A. V. S. Yates.

My thanks are offered also to the staff of the RUSI, Cirencester and London libraries, to Douglas Matthews, Librarian of the London Library, for the index, and to Jackie Gumpert for her swift and accurate typing.

CHAPTER NOTES

All unattributed quotations by Lord Mountbatten, and anecdotes recounted by him, originate in taped or noted conversations with the author at various dates between 1972 and 1978, and are not individually cited.

Conv. = conversation   Windsor = *A King's Story*   Corres. = correspondence

Chapter I The Boy Sailor

1. R. Hough, *The Mountbattens* (Dutton, 1975), p. 111.
2. Conv. Lady Pamela Hicks.
3. Royal Archives, Windsor.
4. Victoria Milford Haven (Princess Louis of Battenberg) to Miss Nona Kerr, 14 April 1903.
5. Hough, p. 219.
6. *Ibid.*, p. 218.
7. *Ibid.*, p. 220.
8. *Ibid.*, p. 220.
9. W.S. Churchill, *The World Crisis*, Vol. I (Butterworth and Scribner's, 1923), p. 212.
10. Hough, p. 279.
11. *Ibid.*, p. 300.
12. M. Gilbert, *Winston S. Churchill*, Vol. III (Heinemann and Houghton Mifflin, 1971), p. 149.
13. The Duke of Windsor, *A King's Story* (Cassell and Putnam, 1951), p. 108.
14. V.M.H. to Nona Kerr, 30 Oct. 1914.

Chapter 2 The Golden Couple

1. Hough, pp. 319-20.
2. *Ibid.*, p. 320.
3. V.M.H. to Nona Kerr, 7 June 1917.
4. Hough, p. 325.
5. *Ibid.*, p. 340.
6. Windsor, p. 106.
7. *Ibid.*, p. 152.
8. J. Terraine, *The Life and Times of Lord Mountbatten* (Hutchinson, 1968, and Holt, 1980), p. 35.
9. Windsor, p. 159.
10. Hough, p. 342.
11. *Ibid.*, p. 333.
12. Windsor, p. 164.
13. *Ibid.*, p. 171.
14. *Ibid.*, p. 178.
15. M. Masson, *Edwina Mountbatten* (Jarrolds, 1958), p. 66.

16. *Ibid.*, p. 76.
17. Hough, p. 344.
18. *Loc. cit.*

Chapter 3 Family Affairs

1. Conv. Vice-Admiral Sir Charles Hughes Hallett.
2. *Ibid.*
3. Conv. Princess Alice, Countess of Athlone.
4. Masson, p. 57.
5. Conv. Barbara Cartland.
6. Corres. Mountbatten to Captain Andrew Yates, 13 Oct. 1926.
7. Corres. Commander P. du Cane, 22 Feb. 1980.
8. A.J.P. Taylor, *Beaverbrook* (Hamish Hamilton and Simon & Schuster, 1972), p. 308.
9. Cited R. Murphy, *The Last Viceroy* (Jarrolds, 1948), p. 63.
10. Conv. Lt.-Commander P. K. Kemp.
11. Hough, p. 347.
12. Masson, p. 97.
13. Conv. Princess Alice.
14. Conv. Rt. Hon. Julian Amery.
15. Conv. Kemp.

Chapter 4 Signals of Danger

1. Terraine, p. 56.
2. Conv. Vice-Admiral H.T. Baillie-Grohman.

Chapter 5 The Kelly at War

1. Harold Nicolson, *Diaries & Letters 1939–45*, ed. N. Nicolson (Collins and Atheneum, 1967), pp. 47–8.
2. Churchill, I, p. 477.
3. C. de Wiart, *Happy Odyssey* (Cape, 1950), p. 174.
4. K. Poolman, *The Kelly* (Kimber, 1954), p. 133.

5. Corres. H. V. Rogers.
6. Corres. Lt. C. J. Jones.
7. Corres. Commander the Rt. Hon. Allan Noble.
8. Corres. P. Watson.

Chapter 6 Combined Operations

1. Conv. Lady Pamela Hicks.
2. B. Boothroyd, *Philip: An Informal Biography* (Longmans and McCall's, 1971), p. 39.
3. N. Coward, *Future Indefinite* (Heinemann and Doubleday, 1954), p. 208.
4. Taylor, p. 815.
5. Coward, p. 209.
6. *Ibid.*, p. 211.
7. Terraine, p. 83.
8. Conv. and corres. Dr. Martin Gilbert.
9. *Chips: the Diaries of Sir Henry Channon* (Weidenfeld, 1967), p. 328.
10. Hough, p. 379.
11. B. Fergusson, *The Watery Maze* (Cape, 1961), p. 89.
12. Conv. Hughes Hallett.
13. Churchill, IV, p. 178.
14. Conv. Hughes Hallett.
15. Conv. and corres. Kemp.
16. Corres. C. Trent Thomas.

Chapter 7 "Supremo" I

1. Churchill, V, p. 73.
2. R. Lewin, *Churchill as War Lord* (Batsford and Stein & Day, 1974), p. 214.
3. Churchill, V, p. 73.
4. By the official historian of the Royal Navy in World War II, Captain Stephen Roskill, *vide* his *Churchill and the Admirals* (Collins and Morrow, 1977).
5. Churchill, V, p. 82.

6. D. C. James, *The Years of MacArthur,* Vol. II (W. H. Allen and Houghton Mifflin, 1975), p. 362 (citing the *Ohio State Journal*).
7. Churchill, V, p. 269.
8. A. Eden, *The Reckoning* (Cassell and Houghton Mifflin, 1965), p. 404.
9. Corres. Edward Ivermee.
10. Corres. G. Francis.
11. B. Tuchman, *Stilwell and the American Experience in China 1911-45* (Macmillan, 1971), p. 471.
12. De Wiart, p. 251.
13. Conv. and corres. Major R. A. Cooper.
14. Churchill, V, p. 365.
15. *Loc. cit.*
16. *Ibid.*, p. 497.
17. Churchill, VI, p. 186.

Chapter 8 "Supremo" II

1. Corres. Major A.W.M. Dickie.
2. Churchill, VI, pp. 538-9.
3. Cited C. Thorne, *Allies of a Kind* (Oxford University Press, 1978), pp. 590-1.
4. *Ibid.*
5. *Ibid.*
6. F. Williams, *A Prime Minister Remembers* (Heinemann, 1961), p. 49.

Chapter 9 Viceroy

1. Corres. Captain R.C. Todhunter.
2. Conv. Rt. Hon. Lord Butler of Saffron Walden.
3. *Hansard*, March 1947.
4. Conv. Amery.
5. *Hansard*, March 1947.
6. Williams, p. 208.
7. *Ibid.*, p. 209.
8. A. Campbell-Johnson, *Mission with Mountbatten* (Jarrolds, 1951; Dutton, 1953), p. 68.

9. A. Wavell, *The Viceroy's Journal* (Oxford University Press, 1973), pp. 432-3.
10. *Ibid.*, p. 433.
11. *Ibid.*, p. 433.
12. Corres. R. Walker.
13. Corres. Arthur E. Gilbert.
14. L. Mosley, *The Last Days of the British Raj* (Weidenfeld, 1961; Harcourt, 1962), p. 63.
15. Masson, pp. 206-7.
16. Conv. Rt. Hon. Lord Hailsham of St. Marylebone.
17. Conv. Rt. Hon. Sir Harold Wilson.
18. Campbell-Johnson, p. 106.
19. *Daily Telegraph*, 12 Nov. 1979.
20. Terraine, p. 157.

Chapter 10 First Sea Lord: The Summit

1. Conv. and corres. Sir John Lang.
2. Conv. H.M. Queen Elizabeth.
3. Conv. Queen Elizabeth the Queen Mother.
4. Conv. Princess Alice.
5. Conv. Prince Philip.
6. Corres. Rev. H. I. Clutterbuck.
7. Conv. Kemp.
8. Corres. Vice-Admiral Sir Arthur Pedder.
9. *Ibid.*
10. Conv. Lang.
11. *Ibid.*
12. Conv. Rt. Hon. Harold Macmillan.
13. Conv. Butler.
14. Conv. Wilson.
15. Conv. Rt. Hon. The Earl of Longford.
16. Conv. Hailsham.
17. Conv. Macmillan.
18. Conv. Kemp.
19. Conv. Macmillan.
20. Conv. Amery.
21. Conv. Wilson.
22. Conv. Lang.

23. Corres. Mrs. A.F. Whitehead.
24. Conv. Amery.
25. Conv. Amery and corres. Gilbert.
26. Corres. T. Jeacock.

Chapter 11 Retirement

1. Corres. Desmond de Silva.
2. Corres. and conv. Lord Cudlipp, and his book *Walking on the Water* (Bodley Head, 1976).
3. Conv. Macmillan.
4. Corres. L.J. Lennocks.
5. Corres. W.R.M. Maxwell.
6. Corres. Mountbatten.
7. Corres. Lt.-Colonel J.A.I. Fillingham.
8. Conv. B. Cartland.
9. Corres. Mrs. Denise Silvester Carr.
10. Corres. Eric A.C. Berfoot.
11. Corres. Mrs. Margaret Wade.
12. Corres. Major G.P. Bartholomew.
13. *Daily Mirror*, 17 June 1929 (*Daily Telegraph* archives).
14. Conv. Lord Longford.
15. Conv. Countess of Longford.

INDEX

(Ranks and titles are generally the highest to be attained)

RICHARD HOUGH was born in 1922 and trained to fly for the RAF in California in 1941. A trilogy of novels based largely on his subsequent experiences as a fighter pilot has just been published. Hough was a publisher from 1946 to 1955. His first major success as a biographer and naval historian was *The Fleet That Had to Die*, which ran in *The New Yorker* in 1958. His history of the Mountbatten family and dual biography of Lord Mountbatten's parents was commissioned by the Admiral and published in 1975. Hough's most recently published historical work is *The Last Voyage of Captain James Cook*. He lives in Cotswold country in the West of England and is married with four children.